THE
JESUS
PRINCIPLE

⌘ WHAT PEOPLE ARE SAYING. . . .

"The Jesus Principle by Charles Wade is superb, practical book on the church and the Christian life. His scholarly background and his long pastoral experience qualify him to write this book which should be read widely and put into practice by pastors and laity."
-Dr. William Hendricks, Brite Divinity School, Texas Christian University

"In *The Jesus Principle,* Charles Wade shares with us the biblical and visionary approach to doing church that he has "fleshed out" during his pilgrimage. Being the Body of Christ and reflecting Jesus' character is the focus of his challenge to us. Every pastor and church member will profit from a careful reading of this book."
-Dr. Clyde Glazener, Pastor, Gambrell Street Baptist Church, Fort Worth, Tx
President, Baptist General Convention of Texas, 1999-2001

"Dr. Wade has condensed over 40 years of pastoral ministry in one volume of practical and helpful insight for pastors who want to center their lives, leadership, and ministry on the person and work of Jesus Christ. Wade describes trans-cultural Biblical principles of building New Testament churches, explains the functions of a local church, and provides excellent helps for Christ-centered ser-vant leadership. I wholeheartedly commend this book to pastors, laypersons, and ministry leaders who want to positively impact their communities for Christ."
-Dr. Albert Reyes, President, Hispanic Baptist Theological School

"The Jesus Principle has been an incredible supplementary teaching tool in our church. It has been taught in several adult Sunday school classes, but the way it was put to its best use was in a men's small group study, meeting weekly on Tuesday mornings. We studied this book for nine months! These men abso-lutely loved digging deeper into how to 'be and do' church."
-Larry Link, Associate Pastor, First Baptist Church, Arlington, Texas

"An inspiring book based upon the "Great Commandment" to love God devot-edly and to love your neighbor as yourself. It reveals how a church can be the presence of Jesus in its community and through caring ministries and faithful witness introduce people to the Savior. Charles Wade effectively communicates his philosophy of ministry and provides valuable insights for pastors and church leaders who wish to reach their local mission fields for Christ."
-Dick Maples, Former Associate Executive Director,
Baptist General Convention of Texas

"From the crucible of daily church life comes this volume which both informs and inspires. Experience, not mere theory, shapes the heart of the book. Based on the Bible, focused on Jesus, and infused with practical insight, here is a guide to help lift a church from the deadly doldrums of failed mediocrity to the heady heights of victorious ministry."

-Dr. Bill Pinson, Executive Director Emeritus,
Baptist General Convention of Texas

"Dr. Charles Wade shares a wealth of wisdom gained from forty years in the pastorate and from his sensitive denominational leadership. With great insight and spiritual maturity, he helps church staff ministers, lay leaders, college and seminary students and individual Christians focus on what it means to be the Body of Christ, courageously doing God's work in the world today. *The Jesus Principle* gets beyond rhetoric to what is real. It simply, yet eloquently, addresses the questions of what the church is and what the church should be doing to fulfill the great commission and the great commandment of our Lord. Among the many books on church growth in circulation, this one is not merely theoretical, but comes from a practitioner who has tested and lived out its proposals."

-Dr. Russell Dilday, Distinguished Professor of Homelitics
George W. Truett Theological Seminary, Baylor University

"The fact that this book stems from the experiences of one of the more effective pastors among us makes its contribution more significant. Heed this advice from one who has been there. *The Jesus Principle* is a genuine contribution to the literature on church leadership."

-Dr. Ebbie C. Smith, Former Professor of Ethics and Missions
Southwestern Baptist Theological Seminary

"Charles R. Wade has written a thorough account of how the church can ever more perfectly be made to reflect the character of Christ. I can say from personal experience as a former staff minister of his church that Charles Wade practices what he preaches. His life and his church make you want to cozy up close to learn. This book brings him and the church he served closer to us all. More important, it brings us closer to the Christ who is the sole authority for all churches."

-Dr. George Mason, Pastor, Wilshire Baptist Church, Dallas Texas

"This book is an easy to understand guide to the Christology of the New Testament church. Any pastor will benefit from its practical approach to church development. I highly recommend it to new church pastors as they seek to lead their churches to be all that our Lord expected His church to be."

-E. B. Brooks, Coordinator of Missions and Evangelism,
Baptist General Convention of Texas

"For kingdom's sake, read *The Jesus Principle*. Integrate its practical wisdom into your approach to leadership. Then live it!"
--Robert M. Parham, Executive Director of the Baptist Center for Ethics
Nashville, TN

"*The Jesus Principle* encourages us to understand church health is ultimately determined by the Great Physician, not by the patient. It helps us to see church health as a body of healthy believers, growing to be more like Jesus, becoming Jesus kind of people. Most unhealthy churches are not growing, healthy churches are growing, but not all growing churches are healthy. An emphasis on church health enables a congregation, regardless of size or location, to focus on its relationship with God, with one another as fellow members, and with its community and the world. This book reminds us that a church should not measure vitality simply by a net gain or loss in resident members, but in terms of growth in spiritual maturity, in biblical knowledge, in relational skills, and in fulfilling its mission. Whatever its present state, every church deserves an opportunity to assess its condition and to seek God's prescription for achieving and maintaining good health."
-Lynn Eckeberger, Ph.D., Coordinator, Church Health and Growth Section
Baptist General Convention of Texas

"The spirit and thrust of *The Jesus Principle* should run through every class and activity of church Bible study and discipleship, leading their members to become all that God wants them to be. The healthy and balanced church addresses all of the functions of the church and works to involve every member in developing his or her own meaningful ministry."
-Bernie Spooner, Former Director, Bible Study/Discipleship Division
Baptist General Convention of Texas

"In his book *The Jesus Principle*, Dr. Charles Wade does a marvelous job of creating for churches a dynamic blueprint by which they can make an authentic kingdom impact in the lives of their members and in their community. That blueprint is Jesus Christ! Churches that use this blueprint will be healthier and better able to reach out more effectively to a hurting and lost world. Lost people are looking for Jesus and they need to find him in our lives and in our churches!"
-Lorenzo G. Peña, Coordinator of Associational Ministries & Administration
Baptist General Convention of Texas

⌘

ABOUT THE AUTHORS

DR. CHARLES R. WADE has served as pastor of churches in Oklahoma and Texas for over forty years, including leadership of the First Baptist Church, Arlington, Texas for over twenty-three years, where his pastorate produced a healthy and dynamic church that gained national recognition for its innovative community ministries through Mission Arlington. In 1996-97 Dr. Wade served a two-year term of office as president of the Baptist General Convention of Texas and in 1999 was elected Executive Director of that body which is comprised of over 6,000 affiliated churches. Charles is a graduate of Oklahoma Baptist University and holds a doctorate in theology from Southwestern Baptist Theological Seminary.

LEE AND CAROL BOWMAN are active members and lay leaders in First Baptist Church, Arlington. Lee is a graduate of William Jewell College, with a theology degree from New Orleans Seminary and a masters degree in art from Vanderbilt University. A former editor of *The Student* magazine with Lifeway Christian Resources in Nashville, Lee teaches art at Dallas Baptist University as well as Dallas and Tarrant County Community Colleges. Carol is a graduate of Southwest Texas State University and holds a masters degree from the University of North Texas. After many years as a business consultant, she is currently the director of *Hope for Home,* a family ministry initiative with the Christian Life Commission of the Baptist General Convention of Texas. Together Lee and Carol write, edit and publish books on Christian health and growth.

THE
JESUS
PRINCIPLE

BUILDING CHURCHES
IN THE LIKENESS OF CHRIST

CHARLES R. WADE
LEE & CAROL BOWMAN

THE JESUS PRINCIPLE
BUILDING CHURCHES IN THE LIKENESS OF CHRIST

© 1998, 2002 by Charles R. Wade, Lee Bowman and Carol Bowman

Published by:

Clear Stream Inc.

P.O. Box 122128, Arlington, TX 76012
817-265-2766   817-861-0703 fax
   website: http://www.clear-stream.com
   email: info@clear-stream.com

Cover design by Lee Bowman
Leaded glass art on cover by C.E. (Cyrel) Allen

Printed in the United States of America

ISBN 0-9637741-3-1
Library of Congress Number 00-193339

Also available in Spanish:
LOS PRINCIPIOS DE JESÚS PARA EDIFICAR SU IGLESIA
ISBN 0-9637741-5-8

⌘
DEDICATION

*To my **wife, Rosemary**, who makes everything I do possible and satisfying.*

*To my **four children and their families** who are unfailing sources of joy to my life.*

*To my **Mother and Father** who lived and died with great faith in God and constant hope for their children.*

*To **First Baptist Church, Arlington**, who really is a Family of Faith, a living laboratory in which God is working out His purpose for His people.*

*To the **Baptists of Texas** for their willingness to allow me to work with them as together we put our arms around Texas and hug it up close to God.*

⌘
ACKNOWLEDGMENTS

*I am deeply grateful to **Lee and Carol Bowman** who took what I have said and written and patiently helped to organize it into a book. Their faith in this project, their unfailing encouragement to me, and their deep love for Jesus and His Church have blessed my life forever.*

*My thanks to **Barry Rock**, Associate Pastor of Music and Worship at First Baptist Church, Arlington, for his insights on worship, and to **Tillie Burgin**, Associate Pastor of Missions, who so faithfully models community ministry through Mission Arlington. **Susan Wolcott**, my secretary, patiently managed my schedule and assisted me in so many ways. And **Mary Margaret Basham** provided excellent suggestions and proofreading.*

*The **staff members at First Baptist Church, Arlington** were always an unceasing source of strength and encouragement to me. The completion of this book was largely due to their commitment to help me juggle the myriad responsibilities of our church.*

*My thanks to **Baptist General Convention of Texas staff** who work for Texas Baptists and are gifted individuals who truly care for the people and churches of Texas.*

*I am especially appreciative to those who had faith in and gave early support to this project: **Jim and Janeth Richardson, Keith and Cissie Cargill, Robert and Sally Walker, Doug and Ann Higgins, Richard and Ann Morris, Dan and Linda Dipert**, and **Lillian Miller**.*

Any errors in judgment or insight fall to my account.

⌘
PROLOGUE

If we had known how difficult it would be to write and publish this book, we probably would not have begun. However, much of life is like that. We begin worthy journeys in faith with little sense of what challenges, detours and surprises will greet us along the way. Praise be to God who often takes our hopeful but hazy beginnings and produces fruitful endings.

In truth, this book has taken over forty years to write. The lessons of pastoral ministry have been etched deeply in my heart. I have worked hard at knowing where I stand on issues, both theological and social. I have studied situations and people over the years to make godly sense out of what I see and experience. The two years I served as president of the Baptist General Convention of Texas while writing the first edition of this book in 1998 helped to mature and sharpen my thinking about the Church in many ways. Balancing pastoral responsibilities with the demands of denominational leadership made writing more difficult, but also lent depth and substance to the project. Now after a few years of serving as executive director of the Baptist General Convention of Texas, I have the privilege of sharing with pastors and churches in Texas, as Christians continue to be the presence of Christ in our communities, our state, our nation and our world. I thank God for the way He lets us adjust to His timing.

We place this book before you with prayerful hope that God will use it to strengthen His churches and to encourage church leaders, ministers and students everywhere. We have expressed what we trust is an authentic Biblical view of Christian leadership and Christ-centered church life, a *Christological ecclesiology*.

My prayer is that God will use this effort to help His congregations become churches who reflect Jesus. The only worthy future for any local church is to keep on growing to be like Jesus.

Blessings to us all!

CRW

CONTENTS

SECTION THREE

BUILDING JESUS KIND OF CHURCHES

⌘
INTRODUCTION

The health of a church does not depend on its size but on the degree to which its members are becoming more like Jesus. Church growth is not just a question of *"How many people have been added to the membership list?"* More importantly, it is *"Are the people more like Jesus now than they were when they first came to be a part of us? How much have the people grown to be like Jesus?"*

> **The health of a church does not depend on size, but on the degree to which its members are becoming more like Jesus.**

When individuals and churches are healthy, we grow in the way God intends. This book deals with *"Jesus Principles,"* biblical principles that teach us how to be a healthy, balanced, growing church (the Body of Christ) and to do God's will in the world.

"What is the church?"   "What is our task?"

As a pastor and denominational leader, I have spent the past forty-five years pondering those questions. I have grown to understand the church to be a baptized body of believers like you and me who are being transformed into the likeness of Jesus Christ. Our task is to be Jesus in our world, following His example in words and actions to fulfill His mission of bringing all creation into right relationship with God. I've also learned that we can't make ourselves grow. Only God by His Holy Spirit grows us as individuals and as churches. What we can do is to get close to God and to His purpose, to examine our lives in the light of Jesus' example, to listen carefully to His voice, to prayerfully nurture what He is doing in our lives and in our congregation, and to be fully available to become involved in building His kingdom on earth. When we do, we will grow.

This book is written for ministers, but *not just for people who call themselves ministers*. The principles laid out here are crucial for *every person* who takes seriously the privilege of being a Christian. The thoughts shared in this book are practical, not theoretical. They are a result of decades of hands-on church leadership experience, including mistakes, misunderstandings and misjudgments on my part in the ongoing journey of seeking His vision of being God's church in a community.

In essence, *The Jesus Principle* represents a battle plan for all who report for duty in Christ's church—pastors, staff members, deacons, elders, committee members, teachers, laity, and small group members. The ideas in this book can be helpful no matter what church you belong to, or even the denomination with which you affiliate. Wherever we serve as Christians, we must be about the Master's business—doing what Jesus Christ taught us by His perfect example.

> *"The Jesus Principle" represents a battle plan for all who report for duty in Christ's church.*

From experience, I do know that God fully equips His people to handle anything He calls us to do. He makes His way known and He gives us strength for the journey. As we seek Him, His Holy Spirit will help us to grow.

Just as the physical body needs a balance of good diet, physical exercise, intellectual stimulation and spiritual nurture, a healthy church will keep its functioning parts in balance to stay effective in building God's kingdom in the hearts of His people.

I have envisioned Jesus living His life in the shape of a cross, reaching up to God and outward to men and women. As Christians, God calls each of us to the journey—living those "Jesus Principles" of love of God and love of others that transform us into the likeness of Christ in our family, our church family and our community.

⌘

The writing of this book is from my heart, a pastor's heart. It is my "pot of stew" that has been continuously stirred over the fire of church leadership. After simmering for forty-five years, I now serve it up in written form for other church leaders to chew on. I hope you will enjoy a taste and perhaps long-lasting nourishment from this recipe of "Jesus Principles". The principles will no doubt seem familiar. Hopefully, the way I have presented them through the lens of my own experience will provide instruction and inspiration, encouraging new-found wisdom and renewed courage to take the next step in your own life and in your church's life.

SECTION ONE

THE CHARACTER OF JESUS
AND
THE NATURE OF THE CHURCH

⌘

THE CHARACTER OF JESUS

A church which succeeds in showing the face of Jesus to their community will be made up of people who are themselves growing to be like Jesus. If we are to have a Jesus kind of church, we must be Jesus kind of people.

How can we really know what that means? We can go to the New Testament Scriptures and find the character of Jesus shining through. Then we can hold our character up to that Light and ask Him to shine through us. Jesus was truly the Son of God, and He was also fully human. Many Christians have dismissed the idea that they are expected to be like Jesus by saying, "He was divine and you can't expect that of me!" But Jesus is accessible to us because He lived a life of flesh and blood just as we do. He was born of woman, grew to manhood, learned a trade, and made His way in the world. He worked and got tired and dirty. He experienced hunger and thirst. He enjoyed good times with family and friends and also endured frustrating times of trial. He experienced all the needs and temptations common to man. He was thoroughly human and as Christians we are called to grow up in His likeness.

In attempting to define the nature of Jesus, heretical teachings have developed through the centuries. Some taught that He was fully God, and only appeared to be in human form—an illusion of humanity. Others have taught that Jesus was fully human, a prophet and worthy example for us to follow—but certainly not God.

I affirm the witness of Holy Scripture. Jesus was the Son of God, fully divine and sharing in the mystery of the triune God: Father, Son and Holy Spirit. Yet the Jesus revealed to us in the New Testament in a very concrete way was the "Word made flesh" *(John 1:14)*. He was God incarnate. The Son of God was born into humanity and experienced everything that we as humans experience.

For we do not have a high priest who is unable to sympathize with our weaknesses, but we have one who has been tempted in every way, just as we are—yet was without sin.
(Hebrews 4:15)

As we look at the character of Jesus and see Him as the one we want to be like in every way, the most remarkable thing about Him was how He loved God. Jesus had a deep spiritual consciousness in His life that grew out of an awareness of who He was and to whom He belonged. It was His total purpose to do His Father's will.

Although Jesus was deeply focused on matters of the Spirit, He was not an ascetic, living in an unreal world isolated from others. He enjoyed those experiences of fellowship common to us all. He attended weddings and parties and visited with friends in their homes. He worshipped, taught in the synagogues and traveled about the countryside having conversations with those He met along the way.

Jesus knew who God was and yearned to make God known to others. As He taught, prayed and ministered, He modeled for us the possibility of living in personal relationship with the Heavenly Father. The people who heard Him speak about God thought He spoke for God as well. When asked what the greatest commandment was, Jesus got to the heart of the matter when He replied:

> *"Love the Lord your God with all your heart, and with all your soul, and with all your mind, and with all your strength."*   *(Matthew 22:37)*

But even Jesus couldn't answer the question in one sentence. He had to say that along with the first commandment, there is a

> *" second . . . like it: Love your neighbor as yourself."*
> *(Matthew 22:37)*

Thus, it is not surprising that Jesus had a deep love for people. He knew the best gift He could give others was to let them know of God's love and to encourage them to develop the good sense to do the will of God. Because He loved people, He was unwilling to let them hide behind their cultural biases and religious legalisms. He confronted people who thought they were worshipping God, but who had stopped short and were worshipping the idols of this world. He called people away from their false gods of religion, material success, and even family. He loved people and wanted them to know how much God loved them too. He didn't want anybody to miss the blessing. He came not to condemn, but to save the world *(John 3:17)*.

Reaching Up to God and Out to People

The character of Jesus is reflected in the double dimension of reaching up in love and obedience to God and reaching out in love and compassion to people. His very character took the shape of the cross. Christ's mission was to bring reconciliation between man and God. As Jesus lives in us and we live in Him, that mission of reconciling man to God becomes ours as well. Jesus taught that the Holy Spirit would come as a helper to act directly on the hearts of men and women.

> *"If you love me, you will obey what I command. And I will ask the Father, and he will give you another Counselor to be with you forever—the Spirit of truth."*   *(John 14:15-17)*

The Holy Spirit empowers us to hold in balance our love of God and love of others so that both are renewed and strengthened as we live in harmony with God and with each other.

Jesus taught that we cannot truly love God if we do not love our neighbor, and we cannot fully love our neighbor if we do not love God. It is in that double movement of our love that the unique character of the Christian is found—and that is the unique character of the Christian Church.

⌘

The word NEXUS comes from the Latin word *nectere*, meaning to bind together. It refers to a connection, tie, or link among individuals of a group. Nexus is a good description of the function Jesus performed as the Savior who was sent by God to bind all creation in restored relationship to Himself as Creator.

Jesus who died on the cross for our sins links us to God. He shows us how to live in reborn relationship with the Father. Jesus, the Nexus of our spiritual life, is represented by that point on the cross where the vertical beam, which reaches up to God, meets the horizontal arms, which extend out toward others.

In the first section of the book, that image of the cross will be our focus as we explore the character of Jesus Christ:

Chapter 1   JESUS LOVED GOD
Chapter 2   JESUS LOVED PEOPLE

- The vertical beam of the cross of Christ reaches upward with love toward God.

- The arms of the cross reach outward with love toward others.

- Jesus is the NEXUS, demonstrating for us how we are to love God with all our heart and love our neighbor as our self.

⌘

1

JESUS LOVED GOD

What is it that distinguishes the character of Jesus? Who was He? What motivated Him? How did He behave? What was it about Jesus Christ that set Him apart from others and made Him the model for all of us who call ourselves Christian?

Is viewing Christ as our "model" aspiring too high? Granted, we can never be all Jesus was. To model ourselves after Him is the never-achieved challenge, the ever-before-us calling. Do we need grace to seek to be like Jesus? Certainly! But this high calling forever prevents us from boasting. Some lesser goal might be achieved, but seeking after His likeness is worthy of our life's effort.

> *. . . until we all reach unity in the faith and in the knowledge of the Son of God and become mature, attaining to the whole measure of the fullness of Christ.* *(Ephesians 4:13)*

Failing to achieve the goal fully, we are still successful. For here it is true—the journey is the thing; the direction is the key. At the end, even after we fall short of fully mirroring Christ-likeness, He Himself will take us all the way to our heavenly home. We will have an eternity in which God will fashion us ever more to our Savior's likeness.

> **The journey is the thing; the direction is the key!**

> *Now we see but a poor reflection as in a mirror; then we shall see face to face. Now I know in part; then I shall know fully, even as I am fully known.* *(1 Corinthians 13:12)*

✝

JESUS LOVED GOD

THE UPWARD THRUST OF THE CROSS:
WAYS JESUS DEMONSTRATED HIS LOVE FOR GOD

In the following pages, we will examine how Jesus expressed His love for God in four areas and consider how we may learn from His example and express love for God in our lives:

✝ **Jesus cherished His relationship with God, His Father.**

✝ **Jesus rejoiced in perfectly obeying the will of His Father.**

✝ **Jesus gave Himself wholeheartedly to the establishment of God's Kingdom.**

✝ **Jesus relied on God to fulfill His mission.**

⌘

✝ JESUS CHERISHED HIS RELATIONSHIP WITH GOD, HIS FATHER

✝ Jesus:	⌘ By His example, we learn to:	📖 Scripture
✝ Worshipped God in praise and thanksgiving.	⌘ See ourself as God's creation. ⌘ Give praise to the Father, Lord of heaven and earth.	Matt. 11:25-27 Luke 6:12 Luke 10:21-22
✝ Spent time in prayer, seeking God's will.	⌘ Daily find a place and time to be alone in quiet meditation and prayer. ⌘ Pray with a humble spirit, seeking God's will.	Matthew 14:13 Matthew 14:23 Matthew 6:9-15 Luke 22:39-44 John 17
✝ Knew the Scriptures and understood God's hand in human history.	⌘ Grow toward Christian maturity through Bible study, practical education and application.	Matthew 4:4 Matthew 5:17 Matthew 13:14
✝ Fasted, prayed and observed worship rituals as spiritual discipline.	⌘ Participate in corporate worship. ⌘ Practice self-discipline as an act of spiritual devotion.	Matt. 6:16-18 Matt. 9:14-17

Jesus had a strong sense of who He was as the Son of God. This undoubtedly was a growing awareness since He entered the world as a human baby born of an earthly parent and was nurtured by Mary and Joseph as a child. The Scripture tells us, *"Jesus grew in wisdom and stature, and in favor with God and men" (Luke 2:52).*

We have very little information from the gospel writers about the development of Jesus as a youth. Luke tells only of anxious parents finding their missing twelve-year-old son happily engaged in conversation with the religious teachers in Jerusalem's temple. In response to his worried parents, He said, *"Why were you searching for me? Didn't you know I had to be in my Father's house?" (Luke 3:49).*

We have no New Testament accounts of Jesus as a teenager and young man, but we do know that the thirty years of preparation for His ministry included much study. Jesus was literate, well versed in Hebrew history and Scripture, and was clearly recognized to have the wisdom and authority of a rabbi. Throughout the gospels, those who met Jesus addressed Him as teacher, rabbi and prophet.

It perhaps was not until His baptism by John and His temptation in the wilderness that Jesus came into total awareness of His identity and purpose as the Messiah, the anointed one of God. John prophetically affirmed Him when He came to the Jordan to be baptized. At the baptism itself, God directly ordained Him when the heavens opened and the Holy Spirit descended on Him in the form of a dove.

> *And a voice came from heaven: "You are my Son, whom I love; with you I am well pleased."*   *(Luke 3:22)*

Jesus had a God-consciousness that focused on an ongoing personal relationship with His Father. He worshipped God in reverence and praise through prayer and study of the Scriptures. He revealed how powerfully sufficient the Holy Spirit is to those who allow God control of their lives.

As Jesus taught, He lived out His identity as the Son of God and patiently brought His followers to a realization of who He was. In that confident self-knowledge, He exhibited a powerful personal spirituality.

> *"I am the way and the truth and the life. No one comes to the Father except through me . . . Believe me when I say I am in the Father and the Father is in me; or at least believe on the evidence of the miracles themselves."*   *(John 14:6, 11)*

> *"Who do you say I am?" Simon Peter answered, "You are the Christ, the Son of the living God." Jesus replied, "Blessed are you Simon son of Jonah, for this was not revealed to you by man, but by my Father in heaven."*
> *(Matthew 16:15-17)*

> **Everything in our life depends on who we believe we are.**

As we strive to emulate the character of Jesus, we must remember that everything in our life depends on who we believe we are. The greatest blessing parents ever give to their children is to help them know they matter to God and that they have value as individuals. It doesn't cost parents anything to communicate to their children that the family has been wonderfully blessed because of them. When children feel they are making a contribution to the family and to the well-being of those who are the most significant people in their life, their self-esteem flourishes.

I was reminded of this one time when our children and their families were visiting us and we were getting ready Sunday morning to leave for church. One of our daughters was buttoning her young nephew's shirt and she commented to him, *"Taylor, you are a fine boy."* And Taylor responded to his aunt, *"My daddy tells me that all the time."* Then when they were ready to leave the house, I said to him, *"Taylor, I heard you say your daddy tells you that you're a fine boy."* And he smiled real big, pointed at me, and said, *"Yes, and I know who he learned it from."* I thought to myself, *"What we put into our children we get back in our grandchildren."*

When we come into a realization that Jesus Christ is our Savior, and that through Him we are restored to full relationship in the family of God, that knowledge resets the foundations of our own identity. We belong to Him. We have purpose and identity in life. Wherever we go in obedience to the will of God, we establish a spiritual foothold and the Kingdom of God expands in that very place.

⌘

✝ JESUS REJOICED IN PERFECTLY OBEYING THE WILL OF HIS FATHER

✝ Jesus:	⌘ By His example, we learn to:	📖 Scripture
✝ Resisted temptation by focusing on God's will.	⌘ Stand firm in God's Word to avoid falling into sin.	Matthew 4:1-11 Mark 1:12-13 Luke 4:1-13
✝ Lived by faith, obedient to God.	⌘ Walk daily in the example of Jesus and under the leadership and strength of the Holy Spirit.	Matthew 4:1 Mark 1:12 John 5:19-23
✝ Lived the spirit of God's law.	⌘ Look beyond religion and the law to seek the heart of God and live in the spirit of His will.	Matt. 12:1-13 Mark 2:23-28 Mark 3:1-4 John 7:23-24

Jesus resisted temptation by focusing on God's will.

The Jews expected a messiah who would lead in power like King David. But God's will, made clear at His baptism, was for Jesus to be a different kind of messiah.

> *"This is my Son, whom I love; with him I am well pleased."*   *(Matthew 3:17)*

Taken from Psalm 2:7 and Isaiah 42:1, the word Jesus heard was a call to be a royal son, a kingly presence—but to be so as a man of sorrows, acquainted with grief. Jesus knew, at least from His baptism forward, that the cross loomed ahead.

The devil sought to turn Jesus aside from obeying the will of God by tempting Him in three major ways. After Jesus had fasted for forty days, He was hungry. Then Satan lured Him to be a ***bread messiah*** by saying:

> *"If you are the Son of God, tell these stones to become bread."*   *(Matthew 4:3)*

In essence, the tempter was saying, "Feed the people and they will follow you. You don't have to die for them!" But Jesus replied:

"It is written, man does not live on bread alone, but on every word that comes from the mouth of God."
(Matthew 4:4)

In John 6:15, we find that the people wanted to make Jesus king after He fed the multitudes with the bread and fish. In His obedience to God's high calling, He rejected the offer of earthly glory.

Then Satan's ploy was to call Jesus to be a ***spectacular messiah***, to jump from the roof of the temple and be rescued by the angels. The Jews expected a messiah who would do miraculous things in the temple to demonstrate His power. The devil was saying, "Why go to the cross when you can win over the people by an amazing feat?" Jesus responded:

"Do not put the Lord your God to the test."
(Matthew 4:7)

Finally, the tempter took Jesus to a mountaintop to look out over the world. He purred:

"All this I will give you if you will bow down and worship me." *(Matthew 4:8)*

Satan was clever. "Be a ***smart messiah***. Just follow me instead of God and I will give you the world. You don't have to die for it." Jesus replied:

"Away from me Satan! For it is written: Worship the Lord your God, and serve him only." *(Matthew 4:10)*

Each time Jesus was tempted, He found God's Word powerful in providing strength and direction for His life. Finally in the garden, with His disciples asleep on the job, Jesus cried out for another option. Could there be some other way for the salvation of the world?

"Father, if you are willing, take this cup from me; yet not my will, but yours be done." *(Luke 22:42)*

When a Christian is able to pray this prayer of willing agreement with God, he or she is going to be more and more like Jesus. We seek God's will, not our own will. Remember how Jesus taught us to pray: *"Your Kingdom come, your will be done on earth as it is in heaven" (Matthew 6:10).*

Jesus lived by faith, obedient to God. We know Jesus loved God by the way He lived—obedient to His Father, not out of fear or duty, but out of reverence and honor. It wasn't by words but by deeds that Jesus demonstrated most convincingly His love for the Father. He responded to God by always putting His Father's will and purpose above His own. He focused His life on doing the Father's business.

> *". . . the world must learn that I love the Father and that I do exactly what my Father has commanded me."*
>
> *(John 14:30-31)*

Jesus lived the spirit of God's law. Jesus came to fulfill God's purpose, but not through strict legalism in interpreting the Law as the Jewish tradition had done. He continued to interpret the Law and refocus the understanding of those He taught, so that the spirit of the Law, rather than the letter, was primary.

> *Looking for a reason to accuse Jesus, they asked him, "Is it lawful to heal on the Sabbath?" He said to them, "If any of you has a sheep and it falls into a pit on the Sabbath, will you not take hold of it and lift it out? How much more valuable is a man than a sheep? Therefore it is lawful to do good on the Sabbath."*   *(Matthew 12:10-11)*

We also can easily make mistakes of worshipping our religious practices rather than God and of blindly obeying our codes of morality rather than Jesus. If we are to live the spirit of God's law, we must let the Spirit of Jesus Christ transform us at the deepest level and allow His character to give direction to our lives.

⌘

✝ JESUS GAVE HIMSELF WHOLEHEARTEDLY TO THE ESTABLISHMENT OF GOD'S KINGDOM

✝ Jesus:	⌘ By His example, we learn to:	📖 Scripture
✝ Served God - not things of this world.	⌘ Invest our life in God's. ⌘ Seek to do things on earth that have eternal value.	Matthew 5:20 Luke 12:33-34
✝ Trusted in God's wise provision.	⌘ Trust God to provide what is needed ⌘ Choose not to burden our self with worry.	Matt. 6:25-34 Luke 12:22-29
✝ Lived a simple, focused life.	⌘ Seek fulfillment through God's Kingdom rather than investing our self in the pursuit of wealth. ⌘ Keep desire for money from being an obstacle to faith.	Matt. 6:19-21 Luke 12:32-34 Luke 18:22
✝ Directed praise to God and not to Himself. ✝ Ministered unpretentiously.	⌘ Proclaim the reality of God's Kingdom. ⌘ Do good without thought of recognition. ⌘ Work to relieve oppression. ⌘ Befriend and give aid to the poor and disabled.	Matthew 6:1-4 Luke 4:16-19 Luke 14:12-13 John 7:16-18
✝ Put love of God above all else, including loyalty to family.	⌘ Love and respect family, not letting them become an idol or obstacle to following Christ. ⌘ Relate to those who live as the Body of Christ as our extended family.	Mark 3:31-35 Matt. 10:34-37 Luke 8:21

Jesus served God—not things of this world. Sometimes we love things and use people when we ought to be ready to love people and use things. If we are to love God with all our heart, soul, mind, and strength, then we are to have no other gods, persons, or ideologies above our devotion to Him. Jesus lived this out. He rejected all idolatry, exposing the temptations to place devotion to religious piety, family, power, and material wealth above our commitment to God. He didn't want people to miss the real God by pursuing superficial satisfactions offered by the world's false gods!

The problem with all idols is that they cannot carry the "God weight." When we lean hard on an idol as though it has the strength of God, it crumbles and fails. We build our idols out of wishful thinking and false hope. They are only fragile shells. Under pressure, they crack and fall and we tumble with them, bruised and betrayed by our own misplaced trust.

Jesus trusted in God's wise provision. We have no account in Scripture that Jesus owned a house or land or any other accumulated wealth. Although He had been trained as a carpenter, He did not put His faith in a house He could build with His hands. When responding to a young man who wished to follow Him, He said:

> *"Foxes have holes and birds of the air have nests, but the Son of Man has no place to lay his head."* *(Luke 9:58)*

When Jesus was crucified, His only possession of value was a robe over which the Roman soldiers gambled. Jesus trusted God to provide for His daily needs of food, clothing and shelter. And in a more profound sense, He trusted God with His entire purpose and mission in life.

Jesus lived a simple, focused life. Clearly, His focus was not on building wealth and security, but on establishing valuable relationships with God and with His fellow man. Jesus did not condemn wealth, but He wasn't impressed by it either. He emphasized how difficult it is for a rich man to quit trusting his money and follow God. In fact, it is so difficult as to be impossible if God does not make a way.

> *"I tell you, it is easier for a camel to go through the eye of a needle than for a rich man to enter the Kingdom of God. With man this is impossible, but with God all things are possible."* *(Matthew 19: 24, 26)*

> *"Life is more than food and the body more than clothes. Consider the ravens: they do not sow or reap, they have no storeroom or barn; yet God feeds them. And how much more valuable you are than birds!"* *(Luke 12:23-24)*

Jesus directed praise to God and not to Himself. It was not Jesus' intention to become politically powerful, or even popular among the masses. He did not build a following around Himself alone. Rather, He always pointed those who followed Him to God, who was the source of all that they saw in Him.

> *"My teaching is not my own, it comes from Him who sent me. If anyone chooses to do God's will, he will find out whether my teaching comes from God or whether I speak on my own."*   *(John 7:16-17)*

Jesus was particularly offended by self-righteousness. Because Jesus loved His Father so deeply and desired that God's love and justice would penetrate to the hearts of eve-

> **The constant temptation of the human heart is to pretend a righteousness we do not have.**

ryone, He was visibly impatient with religious self-righteous people. The constant temptation of the human heart is to pretend a righteousness we do not have. We play spiritual one-upmanship on others by comparing our religious practices to another's carelessness in religious matters. We make the mistake of believing that God pays a lot of attention to our religious activity. In our hearts we see our religious rituals as a contest in which God will reward the most pious with a prize.

When we try to establish our own righteousness, rather than depending on the grace of God, we as much as say to God that we don't need His grace—we are quite capable of working out our salvation on our own.

Jesus castigated pious hypocrisy as one of the greatest sins because it pretends a righteousness we do not have and a self-sufficiency that shuts God out of our lives.

> *"On the outside you appear to people as righteous but on the inside you are full of hypocrisy and wickedness."*
>   *(Matthew 23:28)*

> *"And when you pray, do not be like the hypocrites, for they love to pray standing in the synagogues and on the street corners to be seen by men . . . And when you pray, do not keep on babbling like pagans, for they think they will be heard because of their many words."*   *(Matthew 6:5, 7)*

Self-righteousness always seeks to be at the center of attention. True righteousness does not call attention to itself. Jesus understood the importance of letting one's light shine and being a good witness, but He always tied goodness to the principle that we deflect the glory and praise to God the Father and not to ourselves.

> *"You are the light of the world . . . Let your light shine before men, that they may see your good deeds and praise your Father in heaven."*   *(Matthew 5:14, 16)*

Jesus put love of God above all else, including loyalty to family. As important as Jesus' family was to Him, He did not put family loyalties in front of His calling by God. He asked this same commitment from His disciples. If the family was to be an obstacle to their obedient discipleship and work for the Kingdom, allegiance to Christ's mission must come first.

Every family deserves the nurture, attention, encouragement, and protection of a father and mother. The Christian gives a profound witness when he or she properly attends to family. But families do not need all our time. Family members need to see their family as a part of their ministry in the world, and thus they all become partners in service to God.

Grown children do not owe their parents their lives. They are expected to listen to God's call and provide as necessary for their parents, but be willing to go wherever they sense God wants them to live and serve.

Jesus warned His disciples of the perils that might lie ahead for them. He attempted to prepare them for the worst by showing them how important it was to focus on the love and provision of God over all earthly loyalties.

> *Pointing to his disciples, he said, "Here are my mother and my brothers. For whoever does the will of my Father in heaven is my brother and sister and mother."*
> *(Matthew 12:49)*
> *"Anyone who loves his father or mother more than me is not worthy of me; and anyone who does not take his cross and follow me is not worthy of me. Whoever finds his life will lose it, and whoever loses his life for my sake will find it."*
> *(Matthew 10:37-39)*

Relationships between husband and wife must be carefully evaluated when there is disagreement about how the will of God is to be done in one's life. The marriage relationship is designed by God to be permanent *(Matthew 19:4-9).* Most Christian teachers and counselors would advise, "God is able to make both of you aware of what He wants for you." But sometimes there is painful, even bitter, disagreement about how or where God is to be served. Sometimes there is a stubborn and rebellious heart in one or both partners. My suggestion in this matter is this:

- Pray for God to give agreement in both hearts.

- If after a reasonable time there is no agreement, counsel with trusted, mature, experienced Christian leaders to see if they can reveal any factors to help clarify what each party needs to do.

- Understand that God values persons and promises, and we never can turn away easily or carelessly from either.

- In extreme cases there may need to be a separation in which one person leaves to do God's will in another place, in another fashion. But this will never be a leaving that frees us to go to the arms of someone else, or allows us to abandon our responsibility to provide for the needs of those left behind.

⌘

† JESUS RELIED ON GOD TO FULFILL HIS MISSION

† Jesus:	⌘ By His example, we learn to:	📖 Scripture
† Looked to His Father to give Him strength to bear the burdens of mankind.	⌘ Find rest and comfort by giving our burdens to Jesus.	Matt. 11:28-30 John 17:1-5
† Humbly submitted to God's plan in order to be a servant leader.	⌘ Humble ourselves before God. ⌘ Assume the role of servant to others.	Matt. 20:26-28 Mark 10:43-44 Luke 22:26 John 13
† Obeyed the Father and never wavered.	⌘ Remain faithful to God no matter what circumstances may confront us.	Matt. 11:25-30 Matt. 16:21-26

Jesus looked to His Father for strength. Whenever Jesus faced a challenge, He turned to His Father in prayer to receive direction and strength. God gave Jesus authority over all things. It is through Jesus that we can know God and receive the strength we need to face the challenges of life.

"And now, Father, glorify me in your presence with the glory I had with you before the world began."   (John 17:5)

Jesus humbly submitted to God's plan in order to be a servant leader. True stature and reward in the eyes of God comes through our simple and humble obedience to His will. This requires a child-like transparency of spirit and humble dependence on the loving grace of the Father. If we are to be leaders in the Body of Christ on earth, we must first be humble servants.

"...whoever wants to become great among you must be your servant, and whoever wants to be first must be your slave—just as the Son of Man did not come to be served, but to serve, and to give His life as a ransom for many."
(Matthew 20:26-28)

Jesus obeyed His Father and never wavered. Jesus demonstrated a confidence that He was the Son of God and that God's word was being spoken through Him. His love of God resulted in profound obedience to His Father. He overcame temptations by His commitment to do the will of God.

> *"Come to me, all you who are weary and burdened, and I will give you rest. Take my yoke upon you and learn from me, for I am gentle and humble in heart, and you will find rest for your souls. For my yoke is easy and my burden is light."*   *(Matthew 11:28-30)*

> *Jesus began to explain to his disciples that he must go to Jerusalem and suffer many things at the hands of the elders, chief priests and teachers of the law, and that he must be killed and on the third day be raised to life. (Matthew 16:21)*

He faced his crucifixion with enough confidence in God to say:

> *"Father . . . not my will but yours be done."*   *(Luke 22:42)*

We are called, not to be successful in the eyes of the world, but to be faithful to God. This world may produce severe challenges and even persecution and death. It is our calling to be so confident in God our hearts rise up in courage to say, *"Your will be done!"*

⌘

What then does the character of Jesus teach us about how to show our love for God? As Christians, we cannot compartmentalize our lives, giving God a few hours of devotion each week and then living the way of the world the rest of the time. If indeed we are a "new creation" through Jesus Christ, we will acknowledge that He lives in us, and we in Him—all of the time. How can we do this? Let the following principles be a guide.

⌘

⌘

JESUS PRINCIPLES
FOR SHOWING OUR LOVE TO GOD

⌘ Gladly give praise to the Father, Lord of the universe because we are His creation. Regularly participate in corporate worship.

⌘ Find a place and time daily to be alone in quiet meditation and prayer. Pray with a humble spirit, seeking God's will.

⌘ Prepare for Christian maturity through Bible study and practical application of spiritual truths to life. Practice self-discipline as an act of spiritual devotion.

⌘ Enjoy people who love God and grow through fellowship with them.

⌘ Stand firm in God's word to avoid falling into sin.

⌘ Walk daily in the example of Jesus and under the leadership and strength of the Holy Spirit.

⌘ Look beyond religion and the "law" to seek the heart of God and live in the spirit of His will.

⌘ Live life as an investment in God's Kingdom. Seek to do things on earth that have eternal value.

⌘ Trust God to provide what is needed and don't become burdened with worry.

⌘ Seek fulfillment through God's Kingdom rather than the pursuit of wealth. Keep desire for money from being an obstacle to faith. Learn to use financial resources to bless other people.

⌘ Be a loyal citizen of the Kingdom of God. In the name of Jesus, work to relieve oppression. Encourage and give aid to the poor and disabled. Do good without thought of recognition.

⌘ Love, provide for, and respect family, but do not make them into idols or allow them to become obstacles to following Christ. Relate to those who live as the Body of Christ as extended family.

⌘ Find rest and comfort by giving burdens to Jesus.

⌘ Be humble before God and assume the role of servant to others.

⌘ Remain faithful to God in every situation of life.

DEAR HEAVENLY FATHER:

WE UNDERSTAND SO LITTLE ABOUT THE DEPTH AND BREADTH AND HEIGHT OF THE LOVE YOU HAVE SHOWN TO US. FORGIVE US FOR OUR SHALLOWNESS OF THOUGHT AND FEELING, FOR OUR SELFISHNESS AND PRIDE. WE THANK YOU FOR THE GIFT OF YOUR SON, JESUS CHRIST, WHO NOT ONLY SAVED US FROM OUR SINS, BUT PROVIDED A PURE EXAMPLE OF WHAT YOU CREATED EACH OF US TO BE.

LORD, LIFT US THROUGH YOUR HOLY SPIRIT TO A NEW LEVEL OF LOVE AND DEVOTION TOWARD YOU AND TOWARD OUR NEIGHBORS. AS WE SEEK TO LIVE IN JESUS, HELP US TO OVERCOME THOSE BARRIERS OF OUR SINFUL NATURE THAT BLOCK HIM FROM LIVING FULLY IN US.

NOT OUR WILL, BUT YOURS BE DONE. WE PRAISE YOUR HOLY NAME.

AMEN

Life Application

⌘

JESUS LOVED GOD

1. In your own words, write a definition of what you think it means to love God. Share your definition with others and discuss what such an expression of love would mean to all of our lives if faithfully lived out.

2. What do you think God's expectations are for us as His creation?
   ♦ List words that come to mind describing attitudes that are pleasing to God.
   ♦ List words that come to mind describing kinds of behaviors that are pleasing to God.

3. Identify an activity in your life that you have made a priority, but which is not contributing directly to God's purpose for you as a citizen of His Kingdom. Evaluate how that priority might be changed to more fully express your love toward God.

4. In what ways are you preparing yourself:
   ♦ To have a deeper knowledge, understanding, and appreciation of God and how He is at work in our world?
   ♦ To deepen your personal love relationship with God through Jesus Christ?

2

JESUS LOVED PEOPLE

We have seen in Chapter One, *Jesus Loved God,* how the vertical beam of the cross of Christ can symbolize reaching upward in love to God. It also reminds us of God's love that first reached down to us (*John 3:16-17; 1 John 4:10; Romans 5:8*).

✝

JESUS LOVED PEOPLE

THE OUTWARD STRETCH OF THE CROSS: WAYS JESUS DEMONSTRATED HIS LOVE FOR OTHERS

In this chapter, we will examine how the horizontal arms of the cross symbolize reaching outward in love toward others. We will look at four areas in which Jesus expressed His love for people and consider how we may learn from His example to express love for others in our lives:

✝ **Jesus came to seek out and to save those who were lost.**

✝ **Jesus chose to live for others and minister to their needs.**

✝ **Jesus held people accountable to the high calling of God.**

✝ **Jesus equipped people for citizenship and service in the Kingdom of God.**

⌘

✝ JESUS CAME TO SEEK OUT
AND TO SAVE THOSE WHO WERE LOST

✝ Jesus:	⌘ By His example, we learn to:	📖 Scripture
✝ Announced the good news of God.	⌘ Witness to others about the love of God, the good news of salvation through Jesus Christ, and God's Kingdom of righteousness.	Matthew 4:23 Matthew 5:1-12 Mark 1:21 Mark 4:1-2 Luke 4:16-30
✝ Associated with sinners.	⌘ Look beyond the sinful behavior of people to see their true worth through God's eyes.	Matt. 9:10-13 Mark 2:15-17
✝ Spoke harshly to the self-righteous, but did not judge or condemn people unjustly.	⌘ Withhold judgment of others, knowing that as we judge, so shall we be judged.	Matthew 7:1-5 Mark 4:24 Luke 6:37-38 John 8:10-11 John 8:15-18
✝ Welcomed all who chose to follow Him.	⌘ Be inclusive and supportive of anyone who becomes a fellow Christian, giving counsel to anyone who would learn about God.	Mark 9:38-41 Mark 2:2-4 Mark 3:7-9 Mark 6:56
✝ Loved, accepted, and blessed people without prejudice. ✝ Always treated others fairly.	⌘ View those who do God's will as our brothers and sisters in Christ, deserving of our love and blessing. ⌘ Live by the Golden Rule, treating others the way we want to be treated.	Matthew 5:1-10 Matthew 7:12 Mark 3:34-35 Luke 6:21
✝ Spent time making and nurturing friendships.	⌘ Cultivate friendships with people we meet. ⌘ Minister to all in Christ's name.	Matthew 11:19 Mark 1:29-30 John 12:1-3

Jesus announced the good news of the Kingdom of God.
Jesus' ministry can be characterized foremost as a teaching ministry. Whether He was interpreting the Old Testament Law and Prophets, applying truth to life through the telling of parables, or demonstrating the power and authority of God through performing miracles, He was a consummate teacher in all that He did.

From town to town, He taught in the synagogues. Wherever people gathered, in homes or on the hillsides, He taught them the good news of salvation and the coming of the Kingdom of God. For those who were hungry to understand, He patiently took the time to explain. He taught with the authority of God's eternal word.

Jesus went throughout Galilee, teaching in their syna-
gogues, preaching the good news of the Kingdom, and heal-
ing every disease and sickness among the people.
(Matthew 4:23)

The people were amazed at his teaching, because he
taught them as one who had authority, not as the teachers of
the law.   *(Mark 1:21)*

Jesus is God's answer to a bad reputation. People seem to gravitate to a doctrine of a God filled with power and judgment (upon
others, of course, not themselves). God in the Old Testament has
great moments of mercy and forgiveness, but the idea of grace was
lost in the popular theology of Jesus' day. In many minds, God had
become a God of legalism and fear, remote and judgmental. As
Jesus taught, He brought God close. He called God "Father." To be
sure, Jesus knew God to be the Judge and the Master of the servants, but the overwhelming new note in Jesus' song was of a God
who yearned for the return of His children.

Jesus associated with sinners. In the midst of a religious culture which taught that sinners were to be condemned and ostra-
cized, Jesus actually sought out those who were shunned by society and affirmed their true worth in the eyes of God. Like a shepherd going out to find lost sheep, Jesus reached out to seek and to
save those who were lost. His greatest concern was for those who
had the greatest need for God's salvation. This confounded the religious establishment, but it spoke well for a God who loved the
world so much that He sent His only Son to bring the good news of
eternal life.

. . . "Teacher, this woman was caught in the act of adul-
tery. In the Law, Moses commanded us to stone such women.
Now what do you say?" . . . He straightened up and said to
them, "If any of you is without sin, let him be the first to
throw a stone at her." At this, those who heard began to go
away one at a time . . . until only Jesus was left with the
woman standing there. Jesus straightened up and asked her,
"Woman, where are they? Has no one condemned you?"

"No one, sir" she said. "Then neither do I condemn you,"
Jesus declared. "Go now and leave your life of sin."
(John 8:3-11)

Note: Although this text is not found in some of the best of the early manuscripts, the account certainly is consistent with the character of Jesus.

Jesus did not condemn people unjustly. Jesus certainly had harsh criticism for those who were self-righteous and who, with hardened hearts, heaped burdens of religious legalism on others. However, Jesus never judged others spitefully or unfairly. He looked into the hearts of people to see their true motivations. He reached out compassionately to sinners and rejoiced in their repentance. His anger was reserved for those who were locked in their pride and self-righteousness.

"You hypocrite, first take the plank out of your eye, and then you will see clearly to remove the speck from your brother's eye."   *(Luke 6:42)*

Jesus welcomed all who would follow Him. Among Jesus' disciples and friends mentioned in the Scripture we see a broad spectrum of people and personalities. He specifically called into special training and ministry those twelve who were closest to Him, and we are told He sent out seventy disciples into the villages of Galilee to preach, heal and drive out demons. Wherever He went, He welcomed all to come and participate in God's Kingdom. He loved and nurtured everyone who responded—rich and poor, male and female, Jew and Samaritan.

One of the evidences of our salvation is that we genuinely love others. Our hearts will condemn us if we don't. For all our talk about loving God, it is really quite easy to tell if we do or don't by the way we treat other people.

> *For all our talk about loving God, it is really quite easy to tell if we do or we don't by the way we treat other people.*

"A new command I give you: Love one another. As I have loved you, so you must love one another. By this all men will know that you are my disciples, if you love one another."
(John 13:34-35)

Jesus loved, accepted, and blessed people without prejudice.
Conditions which caused most people to shun the sick and disabled
were no obstacle to the love of Christ. He had unlimited compassion, stopping to heal those suffering from leprosy, blindness, paralysis or demon possession. In a Jewish culture rampant with racial exclusiveness, Jesus kindly ministered to the Samaritan
woman at the well *(John 4:4-25)* and to the son of the Roman cen-
turion *(Matthew 8:5-13)*. He befriended known sinners and went to
dinner with hated tax collectors. In all His relationships, He set the
example of looking past the externals and into the heart of those
He met.

> *. . . Jesus went out and saw a tax collector by the name of
> Levi sitting at his tax booth. "Follow me," Jesus said to him,
> and Levi got up, left everything and followed him. Then Levi
> held a great banquet for Jesus at his house, and a large
> crowd of tax collectors and others were eating with them.
> But the Pharisees and the teachers of the law who belonged
> to their sect complained to his disciples, "Why do you eat
> and drink with tax collectors and sinners?" Jesus answered
> them, "It is not the healthy who need a doctor, but the sick. I
> have come not to call the righteous, but sinners to repen-
> tance."*   *(Luke 5:27-32)*

Jesus spent time making and nurturing friendships. As He
traveled and ministered, He befriended people. He visited in their
homes, shared meals, related to their families, and stayed in touch.
He encouraged His disciples and His friends to develop and nurture loving relationships with each other.

> *Jesus entered Jericho and was passing through. A man
> was there by the name of Zacchaeus; he was a chief tax col-
> lector and was wealthy. He wanted to see who Jesus was, but
> being a short man, he could not, because of the crowd. So he
> ran ahead and climbed a sycamore-fig tree to see him, since
> Jesus was coming that way. When Jesus reached the spot, he
> looked up and said to him "Zacchaeus, come down immedi-
> ately, I must stay at your house today." So he came down at
> once and welcomed him gladly.*   *(Luke 19:1-6)*

Nurturing friendships is at the heart of Christian witnessing, discipleship, and fellowship. We learn to cherish those people we come to know intimately. We value them and want the best for them. We make time to be with them, encourage them, and welcome them into the family of faith.

⌘

✝ JESUS CHOSE TO LIVE FOR OTHERS AND MINISTER TO THEIR NEEDS

✝ Jesus:	⌘ By His example, we learn to:	📖 Scripture:
✝ Showed compassion for people by responding to their personal needs.	⌘ Recognize legitimate needs in people around us and compassionately minister to them.	Mark 1:41 Mark 5:22-43 Mark 6:34 Mark 8:2
✝ Prayed to His Heavenly Father for the needs of others.	⌘ Intercede in prayer for others and for the needs of our world.	Matthew 7:7-11 Luke 11:9-13 John 17
✝ Forgave sins.	⌘ Pray for the salvation of unbelievers. ⌘ Announce forgiveness of sins in Jesus' name for those who are repentant. ⌘ Forgive those who have sinned against us.	Matthew 9:1-8 Matthew 16:19 Matt. 18:21-25 Mark 2:1-12 John 20:23
✝ Healed the sick.	⌘ In the name of Jesus, pray earnestly, in faithful anticipation, for the healing of the sick and disabled.	Matthew 4:23-25 Mark 1:30-31 Luke 5:12-16
✝ Fed the hungry.	⌘ Minister to the physical needs of others as well as their spiritual needs.	Matt. 14:13-21 Mark 8:1-3
✝ Delivered people from demons.	⌘ Understand the reality of demonic forces in the world and deal with evil through the power of Jesus' name. ⌘ Don't be intimidated or anxious in the face of evil, remembering that Jesus has overcome the darkness.	Matthew 8:28-32 Matthew 9:32-33 Matthew 16:19 Mark 1:23-27 Mark 3:11 Mark 5:2-3 Luke 4:31
✝ Identified with people in pain and grief.	⌘ Reach out to people in pain and grief to comfort and support them with love.	Luke 13:34

Jesus showed compassion for others. The word *compassion* literally means to join together *(com)* in another person's suffering *(passion)*. Jesus recognized and shared empathetically with people who were lost, exploited, poor, and suffering from diseases. Jesus took the time to listen to people and understand their needs. He patiently taught people what they needed to know about God. Jesus gave wise counsel, healed the sick, forgave the sins of repentant sinners, and restored hope to the hopeless. Ultimately, He offered Himself in total sacrifice for the sake of the world's salvation.

> *. . . He had compassion on them, because they were like sheep without a shepherd. So he began teaching them many things.*   *(Mark 6:34)*

A little compassion can go a long way. As pastor at First Baptist, Arlington, I watched so many of our church's volunteer workers make a life-changing discovery while becoming involved in the Mission Arlington community ministry, helping people in need. They learned that what people need the most is a sense that another person truly cares about them. Help with groceries, clothes, furniture, healthcare, utility bills or rent is important. But demonstrating genuine caring to a person is what penetrates the heart. A listening ear, comforting words, non-judgmental counsel, kind helpfulness and simple love are reflections of a God who cares. Those acts of compassion become invitations to renewed hope.

Jesus prayed to His Father for the needs of others. Jesus was in constant touch with His heavenly Father. We are told repeatedly in the gospels how He turned to prayer, not only for His own needs but to intercede for the needs of others. Just before His arrest and ultimate death on the cross, He prayed not only for His disciples, but for all those who would eventually respond to the gospel message through the teaching of the disciples.

> *"Holy Father, protect them by the power of your name—the name you gave me—so that they may be one as we are one."*   *(John 17:11)*

> *"My prayer is not for them alone. I pray also for those who will believe in me through their message, that all of them may be one, Father, just as you are in me and I am in you."*   *(John 17:20-21)*

Never underestimate the power of intercessory prayer. If we affirm that God is ruler over heaven and earth, should we not place ourselves in total submission to Him and trust that He will bring about what is best for each of us? If we do not ask, how can we expect to receive His blessing? We cannot always fathom the ways of God, but as Christians we can support and encourage each other, asking God to meet our needs and shield us with His protection.

Jesus forgave sins when people came to Him in faith and repentance. The religious establishment considered forgiveness of sins an act reserved for God alone. In their view, Jesus acted blasphemously when He forgave sin. Jesus demonstrated His God-given authority both by working miracles and forgiving sin. Jesus granted this authority to His disciples and the Body of Christ as we who are members of His Body do the work of Christ in the world.

"As the Father has sent me, I am sending you . . . Receive the Holy Spirit. If you forgive anyone his sins, they are forgiven; if you do not forgive them, they are not forgiven."
(John 20:21-23)

It has always been clear to me as I preach and counsel that in the announcing and affirming of forgiveness, people do experience forgiveness. When I can affirm during counseling my sense that God has forgiven them, and I express my own love and acceptance, people are in fact set free from the old hurts and failures that have dogged them. The announcement of forgiveness, as Jesus commanded, produces a real healing.

But what of that last phrase? *"If you do not forgive them, they are not forgiven."* In a very real way people may, in fact, have received forgiveness from God in answer to their earnest prayers, but remain in a spiritual desert because they do not feel forgiven and they do not experience forgiveness because Christian friends withhold grace and acceptance. Until somebody they know affirms, expresses and lives forgiveness and mercy toward them in the name of Jesus, they feel "unforgiven." They may not be able to forgive themselves. In the gracious forgiveness of a Christian, they can fully experience the forgiveness of God.

Jesus healed the sick. The New Testament is full of accounts of Jesus healing the sick, restoring sight to the blind, causing the lame to walk, and even raising people from the dead. The miraculous power to bring healing in the name of Jesus was imparted to

His disciples as they took up His ministry. Healing has been a part of the testimony within the Body of Christ through the centuries. We do not understand why God brings about healing in some circumstances and not in others, but we can still respond in wonder and praise to the miracles God continues to bring to pass through prayer in our day as well as in the time of the New Testament Church.

Jesus fed the hungry. When the multitudes followed Jesus for days across the hills of Galilee, hungry to hear Him preach the good news of the Kingdom of God, He was aware that their need for bodily nourishment was also an essential factor to their well-being. He had compassion on them. In ministering to the whole person, we cannot separate body from soul. Food, clothing and shelter are necessities of life. Hunger of the soul cannot be separated from the physical needs of the body.

> *"I have compassion for these people; they have already been with me three days and have nothing to eat. If I send them home hungry they will collapse on the way because some of them have come a long distance."*   *(Mark 8:2-3)*

Jesus delivered people from demons. The New Testament describes many instances in which Jesus and His disciples exercised the authority of God to deliver people from demons. The reality of demonic forces in our world is certain, and there are varying degrees in which their influence is expressed. Satan opposes the Kingdom of God and will attack any weakness that can be discovered.

> *Your enemy the devil prowls around like a roaring lion looking for someone to devour. Resist him, standing firm in the faith.*   *(1 Peter 5:8)*

In societies where superstition and fear abound, many people complain of demonic powers that control their lives. Where Christ's gospel has been preached thoroughly and over time, the phenomenon of demon possession is more rarely seen. No Christian should immediately assume that all aberrant behavior is demon-induced. We ought to seek other answers available to us through medical and psychiatric treatment. If no relief is to be found, consider the possibility of demonic possession.

People who have not been exposed to the gospel of Christ, who have dabbled in witchcraft and the occult, or who have given themselves over to gross immorality or mind-altering substance abuse make themselves more vulnerable to attack by Satan. Attack left unchecked by the authority of God can lead to possession. The gospel of God and the name of Jesus have power over all the demonic powers of hell. It is appropriate for us to pray for people to be delivered and expect that in the name of Jesus they will be delivered.

> *"I will give you keys to the Kingdom of heaven; whatever you bind on earth will be bound in heaven, and whatever you loose on earth will be loosed in heaven."* *(Matthew 16:19)*

The presence of Christ in one's life is the greatest defense against demonic attack. If we belong to Jesus, our security is sure and we can laugh at Satan's impotence. We should not fear demons as though they are lying in wait behind every bush. With the Holy Spirit and God's angels as our defenders, we are delivered from all demonic threats.

Jesus experienced grief. The prophet Isaiah said the Messiah was to be a man of sorrows, acquainted with grief *(Isaiah 53:4)*. The writer of Hebrews said Jesus was a man like us *(Hebrews 5:15)*. Jesus had to know about grief because He loved others so deeply.

> *When Mary reached the place where Jesus was and saw him, she fell at his feet and said, "Lord, if you had been here, my brother would not have died." When Jesus saw her weeping, and the Jews who had come along with her also weeping, he was deeply moved in spirit and troubled. "Where have you laid him?" he asked. "Come and see, Lord," they replied. Jesus wept. Then the Jews said, "See how he loved him!"* *(John 11:32-36)*

Jesus was clearly in grief. He wept personally for the death of His friend, Lazarus, and He shared in the grief of Lazarus' sisters.

Anyone who has ever been around a family grieving at the loss of a loved one knows that people can drive for miles to attend a funeral, appearing to be composed. Yet when they come into the presence of others who have loved this friend as they have, they dissolve into tears. If Jesus could cry at His friend's death, we certainly are free to weep in our times of grief. In fact, in our tears we are more like Jesus. The only people who have never grieved are people who have never loved.

> **The only people who have never grieved are people who have never loved.**

There is no missing the pathos and sorrow in Jesus' heart for those who would not hear the good news, who were so tied to their sense of order and so determined to hang on to the status quo that they would not respond.

"O Jerusalem, Jerusalem, you who kill the prophets and stone those sent to you, how often I have longed to gather your children together, as a hen gathers her chicks under her wings, but you were not willing!"   *(Luke 13:34)*

⌘

✝ JESUS HELD PEOPLE ACCOUNTABLE TO THE HIGH CALLING OF GOD

✝ Jesus:	⌘ By His example, we learn to:	📖 Scripture:
✝ Dealt with people according to their spiritual capacity.	⌘ Accept people where they are and patiently nurture them to greater spiritual maturity.	Matthew 7:7-23 Matt. 25:14-30 Mark 4:33 Mark 11:27-33
✝ Was honest and courageous about exposing sin and injustice.	⌘ Be courageous in confronting those who compromise with evil and injustice.	Matthew 23:1-37 Luke 20:45-47
✝ Was frustrated with people whose pride and hardened hearts kept them from repentance.	⌘ Expect the best from people and refuse to be content to let them continue in their sin and spiritual blindness.	Mark 3:5 Mark 8:11-12 Mark 8:17 Mark 9:19 Mark 11:15-17 Mark 12:38-40
✝ Opposed hypo-critical legalism (keeping laws exter-nally while breaking them internally).	⌘ Seek to live the spirit of what God asks rather than slavishly following rules that may violate God's principles of love and justice.	Matthew 5:19-20 Matthew 23:1-37 Mark 2:24-27 Mark 7:6-13
✝ Was not impressed with political power.	⌘Work within the political system but do not be enamored with the levers of power or ensnared by its promises or pretenses.	Matt. 22:15-22 Luke 13:31

Jesus dealt with people according to their spiritual capacity. He expected the very best in people, consistently nurturing others with a patient expectation for them to grow and mature into their best selves. He expected each person to be accountable for his or her attitudes and actions.

> *"Well done, good and faithful servant! You have been faithful with a few things; I will put you in charge of many things. Come and share your master's happiness."*
> *(Matthew 25:21)*

Jesus was honest and courageous about exposing sin and injustice. He was consistently sensitive to the injustices in society and did not shrink from calling attention to the needs of the least and the left out. He was persuasive and confrontational. Willing to interfere with His world when He saw evil, He named sin for what it was. He exposed hypocrisy, raising the fundamental question of why people treat others as they do.

Jesus did not retreat from His mission in the face of disapproval from His community, angry attack from His enemies, or the threat of bodily injury. He cherished fellowship but did not shrink from facing death alone.

> *"You snakes! You brood of vipers! How will you escape being condemned to hell? Therefore I am sending you prophets and wise men and teachers. Some of them you will kill and crucify; others you will flog in your synagogues and pursue from town to town."*   *(Matthew 23:33-34)*

Jesus was frustrated with people whose pride and hardened hearts kept them from repentance. When people think about the love of Christ, they oftentimes focus on the freedom that His love brings to people through encouragement, comfort and acceptance. However, included in the way Jesus loves is the way in which He courageously calls people to personal accountability. Jesus freely forgave repentant sinners, but He was not happy with those who were hard of heart.

> *"Woe to you, teachers of the law and Pharisees, you hypocrites! You give a tenth of your spices—mint, dill and cumin. But you have neglected the more important matters of the law—justice, mercy, and faithfulness. You should have practiced the latter, without neglecting the former. You blind guides! You strain out a gnat but swallow a camel."*
> *(Matthew 23:23-24)*

> *"Give to Caesar what is Caesar's and to God what is God's."*   *(Matthew 22:21)*

"Power corrupts" is a truism certainly proven in the political arenas of our day—both in secular politics and in the struggle for control within Christian churches and denominations. It seems that those who are out of power will do almost anything to gain power; and once they gain power, they will do almost anything to maintain power. We rarely find truth, love and justice reigning in the hearts of those who are in power and authority.

If we follow the example of Jesus, we should know that Christians are expected to behave differently. The Kingdom of God has not been established within any political party. The Kingdom of God can neither be legislated nor coerced through the pressure of religious tyranny. Surely we will not forget the lesson of the Pharisees.

The Kingdom of God exists within the hearts of individuals whose sole allegiance and soul authority belong to Jesus Christ. The kingdoms of

> *The Kingdom of God exists within the hearts of individuals whose sole allegiance and soul authority belong to Jesus Christ.*

this earth (whether as nations or as religious structures) will rise and fall, but the Kingdom of God reigns forever.

⌘

† JESUS EQUIPPED BELIEVERS FOR CITIZENSHIP AND SERVICE IN THE KINGDOM OF GOD

† Jesus:	⌘ By His example, we learn to:	📖 Scripture:
† Set the example as a servant leader.	⌘ Seek to serve others, not expecting to be served.	Matt. 20:20-26 Mark 10:43-45
† Gave voice to those who were disenfranchised - the poor, the sick, women and children.	⌘ Love and nurture everyone in the name of Christ, seeking to bring them into full participation in the family of faith.	Matt. 19:13-15 Mark 10:13-16 Luke 18:17
† Encouraged those who responded to Him with childlike faith.	⌘ Seek God with childlike purity, faith and openness. ⌘ Protect the lives and faith of the children.	Matthew18:1-6 Mark 9:36-37
† Gave His disciples supernatural power to preach the gospel, to heal the sick and to have authority over demons.	⌘ In the name of Jesus, claim the authority and depend on the Holy Spirit of God to preach the gospel, heal the sick, and deliver people from demonic influences.	Matthew 10:5-10 Mark 6:7 Luke 9:1-6 Luke 10:1-12
† Called out workers into His harvest field to take the gospel to the world.	⌘ Look around to see where God is at work in the lives of people and join Him in the building of His Kingdom.	Matthew 9:36-38 Matt. 28:18-20 Mark 3:13

Jesus set the example as a servant leader. He asked nothing of His disciples that He would not do Himself. He set the example in love, service and devotion. He taught that those who desired to be great must first become servants *(Matthew 20:26)*. As an example of personal humility, He even washed the feet of His disciples.

"Now that I, your Lord and Teacher, have washed your feet, you also should wash one another's feet. I have set you an example that you should do as I have done for you."
(John 13:14-15)

The washing of feet was the regular task of a servant in a first-century household. It was not a religious act performed to demonstrate spiritual humility. The parallel for Christians today is to do acts of service, even, and perhaps especially, menial service in order to be helpful to others.

Jesus identified with and gave voice to those who were disenfranchised. His incarnation meant He identified with humanity. However, He particularly identified with the disenfranchised, the least and the lost. He healed the sick, gave voice to the weak, stood with the poor and oppressed, cared for the unlovely and defended women and children *(Luke 4:17-19)*.

We find no record in the Gospel writings that Jesus ever said directly to a person, "I love you." Yet it is clear in His behavior that He loved everyone with whom He came into contact. Loving people is accomplished by what we do, not by what we say.

> *Loving people is accomplished by what we do, not by what we say.*

The disciples wanted the children to be sent away because Jesus was busy and had no time for them. But Jesus said, *"Let the children come to me" (Mark 10:13-16)*. The woman caught in adultery was accused by her enemies, and they wanted Jesus to join in their accusations. But He lovingly said to her, *"Go now and leave your life of sin" (John 8:11)*. The woman at the well was a Samaritan, an outcast in the mind of most Jews. She had known many men, but she had never met anyone who loved her as Jesus did. She knew He loved her because He really listened to her. He took her seriously, told her the truth about herself, and opened the way for her to live differently in the future *(John 4:4-29)*.

Jesus encouraged those who responded in childlike faith. The Kingdom of heaven is not like earthly kingdoms in which people are admired for their political power and strength. God requires humility and simple transparency of spirit in order to be great in His kingdom.

". . . unless you change and become like little children, you will never enter the Kingdom of heaven."(Matthew 18:3)

We can tell a lot about people and churches by how they treat children. Jesus expects us to protect and carefully nurture them.

> *"And whoever welcomes a little child like this in my name welcomes me. But if anyone causes one of these little ones who believe in me to sin, it would be better for him to have a large millstone hung around his neck and to be drowned in the depths of the sea."*   *(Matthew 18:5-6)*

Jesus gave His disciples supernatural power. It was Jesus' intention to build a fellowship in which His followers could do God's work in the world. To that end, Jesus equipped them to minister as He ministered. They were given authority in the name of Jesus to carry the gospel message with power and to see wonderful miracles accomplished even as Jesus had done. The charge Jesus gave the disciples then is ours today.

> *"I tell you the truth, anyone who has faith in me will do what I have been doing. He will do even greater things than these, because I am going to the Father. And I will do whatever you ask in my name, so that the Son may bring glory to the Father."*   *(John 14:12-13)*

This idea has been misused by many, beginning with Simon the sorcerer *(Acts 8:9-25)*, but that is no reason for us to ignore this empowering promise. Though we must flee from any attempts of self-aggrandizement and misrepresentation, we do have the power of God for healing and blessing in the prayers of the church. Who can measure the incredible power that is released upon people because the church gathers to pray? Healing and miracles happens when God's people pray! The hospital and home visits of the ministers and lay leaders of the church should not be perfunctory nor casual. They can be humorous and upbeat, but when we hold a hand in prayer and reach out to God in our hearts, we can ask and expect from God real and powerful answers to our prayers. A Christian is doing a significant and mighty thing when he or she prays for another in Jesus' name.

Jesus called out workers to take the gospel into all of the world. Anything worth doing well usually requires help. Jesus sent his first evangelists out two by two. Witnessing to others will often be done one on one as we meet others in the daily encounters of life. But it is good to have another person with us when we visit with those we are praying will come to faith in Christ. Partners in witnessing can provide prayer support for each other. They can confirm one another's witness and gain increased credibility with the one to whom they are speaking. Partners provide a broader range of life experiences from which to draw in witnessing. And partnering is also an opportunity for one who has more experience to train one who is less experienced in witnessing. Jesus depends on the church He established to be His partner in getting the gospel out to the world.

There is an old story about Jesus discussing with the angels His recent sojourn on the earth.

"What plan do you have for getting the story told so everyone can hear?" the angels asked.

"I've left some disciples who will tell the story and prepare those who believe to tell the story to still others. I call it a church," Jesus replied.

"And what if they fail to do their job?" the angels questioned. To which Jesus replied, *"I have no other plan. It is up to them!"*

"All authority in heaven and on earth has been given to me. Therefore go and make disciples of all nations, baptizing them in the name of the Father and of the Son and of the Holy Spirit, and teaching them to obey everything I have commanded you. And surely I am with you always, to the very end of the age." (Matthew 28:16-20)

God's divine plan is to do His work through us. As we go, He has promised to be with us and finally take us all the way home with Him. Praise God!

⌘

⌘
JESUS PRINCIPLES
OF EXPRESSING LOVE FOR PEOPLE

⌘ Speak informally to people about the love of God, the good news of salvation through Jesus Christ, and God's Kingdom of righteousness.

⌘ Look beyond the sinful behavior of people to see their true worth in God's eyes.

⌘ Withhold judgment of others.

⌘ Be inclusive and supportive of anyone who wants to learn about God.

⌘ View those who do God's will as brothers and sisters in Christ, deserving of our love and blessing.

⌘ Cultivate friendships with people around you. Minister to them in Christ's name.

⌘ Recognize legitimate needs in people and minister compassionately to them.

⌘ Intercede in prayer for the needs of others and for the needs of the world.

⌘ Pray for the salvation of unbelievers, announce forgiveness of sins in the name of Jesus for those who are repentant, and forgive those who have sinned against us.

⌘ Pray earnestly and expectantly for those who are sick and disabled.

⌘ Minister to the physical needs of others as well as their spiritual needs.

❡ Understand the reality of demonic forces in the world, but deal confidently and courageously with evil through the power of Jesus' name.

❡ Reach out to people in pain and grief and support them with love.

❡ Accept people where they are and nurture them to greater spiritual maturity.

❡ Be courageous in confronting those who compromise with evil and injustice.

❡ Expect the best from people and refuse to be content to let them continue in sin and spiritual blindness.

❡ Seek to live the spirit of what God asks rather than slavishly following rules that may violate God's principles of love and justice.

❡ Work within the political system but do not be enamored with the levers of power or ensnared by its promises or pretenses.

❡ Seek to serve others, not expecting to be served.

❡ Love and nurture everyone in the name of Christ, seeking to bring them into full participation in the family of faith.

❡ Seek God with a childlike purity, faith, and openness.

❡ In the name of Jesus Christ, claim the authority and depend on the Holy Spirit of God to preach the gospel, heal the sick, and deliver people from demonic influences.

❡ Look around to see where God is at work in the lives of people and join Him in the building of His Kingdom.

DEAR HEAVENLY FATHER:

WE CONFESS OUR DIFFICULTY IN BEING OPEN AND ACCEPTING OF THOSE PEOPLE WHO SEEM TO BE SO DIFFERENT FROM US—THOSE WHOSE SKIN COLOR, LANGUAGE, CUSTOMS, DRESS, LIFESTYLE, RELIGION, OR POLITICS INFRINGE UPON OUR COMFORT ZONES. YET WE KNOW YOU HAVE COMMANDED US TO LOVE OUR NEIGHBOR AS OUR SELF. FORGIVE US FOR RETREATING FROM THAT COMMANDMENT IN SELFISHNESS AND FEAR.

WE ASK THAT THE ROOTS OF OUR PREJUDICE BE DUG OUT WITH THE SHARP SWORD OF YOUR SPIRIT. CLEANSE US OF OUR SINFUL UNCONCERN, SUSPICION OF OTHERS AND HATE. TEACH US THROUGH YOUR HOLY SPIRIT TO LOVE OTHERS AS JESUS LOVED. OPEN OUR HEARTS THAT WE MAY REACH OUT IN GENUINE COMPASSION TO DRAW OTHERS INTO THE FELLOWSHIP AND CARE OF THE BODY OF CHRIST.

AMEN

Life Application

⌘

JESUS LOVED PEOPLE

1. Identify any class or type of people whom you have found difficult to love.

   ♦ What personal experiences have shaped your feelings?

   ♦ How do you think God feels toward these people?

   ♦ What does God expect of you regarding your attitude and behavior?

   ♦ Is it possible to love the sinner and hate the sin, to accept the person and reject the behavior?

2. What characteristics of Jesus would it benefit you to imitate? *(See the charts throughout Chapters 1 and 2.)* Focus on one or two characteristics that seem most relevant to you at this time. Discuss ways in which these characteristics could come to life in you to nurture personal Christian growth and improved relationships with others.

3. Make an opportunity to share with another person what you have read and learned in Chapters 1 and 2 in this book. Explain to them the symbol of the cross, stretching in love vertically between man and God, and horizontally reaching out in love toward one's neighbor.

THE CROSS OF CHRIST :

WHERE LOVE OF GOD INTERSECTS WITH LOVE OF PEOPLE

The wisdom of Christ becomes evident in that nexus point where the vertical thrust of the cross toward God meets the horizontal thrust outward toward others.

Jesus had the wisdom to know that He could not change every one or every thing. He often said, *"Those who have ears to hear, let them hear."* He recognized that many would continue to walk in hardness of heart. He wanted all the people to repent and walk in the light, but He knew that not everyone would. The cultural strongholds of society and the governments of this world would not immediately be transformed. Working to bring in God's Kingdom has always required patience and faithful endurance.

Wisdom, good judgment and integrity

In all that He did, Jesus acted with wisdom and integrity. He expects those same qualities in us as we attempt to follow Him as our Lord and Savior.

Wisdom supports integrity. Integrity supports wisdom. If a person is wise enough to make good decisions but does not have the integrity to stand up for the truth, then his own wisdom stands in stern judgment over his lack of courage. If a person cannot make good judgments, then having the integrity to stand by them is no positive value. Integrity without good judgment is merely stubbornness and can lead to destruction.

Jesus sets the example for us to follow in making good decisions based on the greater wisdom of God's truth.

- ♦ He taught that love of God must result in love of people.
- ♦ He tempered judgment and justice with love and forgiveness.
- ♦ He measured quality of life by fruits of the Spirit.
- ♦ He measured the value of life in terms of God's Kingdom and eternal life.

✝

THE NEXUS OF THE CROSS:
WAYS JESUS FULFILLED
THE TWO GREAT COMMANDMENTS -

⌘ **To love the Lord with all one's heart, soul and mind**
⌘ **To love one's neighbor as oneself**

✝ Jesus:	⌘By His example, we learn to:	📖 Scripture
✝ Personified the character of God.	⌘ Discover the attributes of our Father God through the image reflected in His Son, God incarnate. ⌘ Develop a personal relationship with God through Jesus Christ. ⌘ Release ourselves to Christ so He may live in us.	Luke 10:22-23 John 1:1-4 John 8:14-19 John 14:6-11 John 14:15-20 John 15:16-18 1 John 1:1-4
✝ Expressed the love of God through His humanity.	⌘ Love the Lord our God with all our heart, mind, soul and strength, and love our neighbors as ourselves.	Matt. 22:37-39 Luke 4:18-21 John 3:16 John 14:21 John 16:25-30
✝ Fulfilled the true purpose of human-ity.	⌘ Live a life that imitates Jesus - become fully human through rebirth in Christ and being filled with the Holy Spirit.	Matthew 5:17-20 John 20:21-23 Romans 6:20-23
✝ Befriended many sinners, as teacher, prophet, and priest.	⌘ Live in the world but not of the world. ⌘ Act as leaven in society to help the world be ready to hear the word of God and acknowledge the rule of God.	Matthew 11:19 Matthew 13:33 Luke 19:1-9
✝ Became the wounded healer, burden-bearer of our sins.	⌘ Minister to others, introducing salva-tion and healing through Jesus Christ. ⌘ Bear the burdens of others through our own suffering and in intercessory prayer.	Matt. 11:28-30 Matt. 23:37-39 Matt. 26:26-28 Mark 8:31-35
✝ Is the Son of God and Savior of all people - the One who has the power to reconcile sinners to Holy God.	⌘ Receive salvation through faith in Jesus Christ, and in grateful response to God's gift of grace, live as faithful citi-zens in God's Kingdom - teaching, training, and nurturing others toward reconciliation with God and growth in Christian discipleship.	Matt. 16:13-19 Matt. 28:18-20 Luke 2:29-32 Luke 15:11-32 John 20:21-23

Jesus personified the character of God. The Son of God, the Living Word, reflected who God is through His humanity.

> *The word became flesh and made his dwelling among us. We have seen his glory, the glory of the One and Only, who came from the Father, full of grace and truth. (John 1:14)*

He talked and touched and gave physical expression to the character of God. Through Jesus, we have testimony to the reality of the eternal Father, who is light, and in whom there is no darkness *(1 John 1:5)*. The early Church believed with radiant confidence that Jesus was the One.

> *That which was from the beginning, which we have heard, which we have seen with our eyes, which we have looked at and our hands have touched—this we proclaim concerning the word of life. The life appeared; we have seen it and testify to it, and we proclaim to you the eternal life, which was with the Father and has appeared to us. (1 John 1:1-2)*

> *For in Christ, all the fullness of the Deity lives in bodily form . . . (Colossians 2:9)*

We see attributes of God the Father reflected in the person of Jesus Christ the Son:

•Righteousness	•Justice	•Holiness	•Mercy
•Loving-kindness	•Wisdom	•Goodness	•Truth

Jesus experienced the love of God through His humanity. The very act of God becoming flesh to bring us into reconciliation is the ultimate expression of love. John, the apostle, says it best:

> *For God so loved the world that he gave his one and only Son, that whosoever believes in him shall not perish but have eternal life. For God did not send His Son into the world to condemn the world, but to save the world through Him.*

> *(John 3:16-17)*

This is how God showed his love among us: he sent his one and only Son into the world that we might live through him. This is love: not that we loved God, but that he loved us and sent his Son as an atoning sacrifice for our sins. Dear friends, since God so loved us, we also ought to love one another. No one has ever seen God; but if we love one another, God lives in us and his love is made complete in us.

(1 John 4:9-12)

Jesus fulfilled the true purpose of humanity. When God created Adam and Eve, He did not intend for them to choose rebellion and sin. *God saw all that he had made, and it was very good (Genesis 1:31).* We do God's creation a disservice when we excuse our evil ways by saying, "After all, we're only human." To say that is to have it backwards. To be human is to be pure and good as God intended us to be. To do evil is to be *inhuman.* In Jesus, we see a man who perfectly fulfilled what God intended His human creation to be. He lived a sinless life in perfect harmony with His Father. When we say Jesus lived a sinless life, we mean:

- ◆ He kept the Old Testament law perfectly because He fulfilled the *spirit* of God's commandments for His people.

- ◆ He obeyed the will of God perfectly. He was not rebellious against the Father. Unlike Adam, God's first creation, Jesus, who was the second Adam, did not yield to temptation *(1 Corinthians 15:45-49).*

Jesus befriended sinners as teacher, prophet and priest. In a day in which there was much distrust and animosity among people over race, social class, religious affiliation, and political ideology, Jesus cut through the barriers of prejudice and hate. He dealt with people in mercy and love. By befriending Zacchaeus who collected taxes for the hated Roman government, Jesus inspired him to repent of his greed and dishonesty *(Luke 10:1-9).*

When others condemned and threatened a woman caught in the act of adultery, Jesus rescued her from accusers and ministered to her with graceful acceptance *(John 8:1-11).* Jesus ate with those who were considered sinful, but by doing so he brought truth and light to their lives. His teaching and his ministry among sinners produced changed lives. In response to His critics Jesus said, "Wisdom is proved right by her actions" *(Matthew 11:19)*.

Christians always have been tempted to shun the sinner for fear of being contaminated by the sin. And there is wisdom in choosing one's associates wisely in order to surround oneself with the nurture of Christian friends. But the love of Christ also reaches out to rescue the lost. If Jesus lives in us, we must be ready to introduce Him to a sinful world.

Jesus became the wounded healer, burden-bearer of our sins. Jesus frees us by carrying in His body a punishment that belongs to us, not to Him. Jesus suffered, died on the cross, and was buried, taking the full weight of mankind's sin upon Himself. He conquered death by rising from the grave, providing salvation and eternal life for those who believe in Him as their Savior. This work of Jesus changes us:

- ◆ He convinces us that our sin can be and is forgiven *(Mark 2:9-12)*.
- ◆ He releases us from the spiritual and psychological bondage of our sin and guilt *(Mark 5:32-34)*.
- ◆ He encourages us, through His example and through the empowering presence of the Holy Spirit, to follow Him in glad obedience *(Mark 10:24-31)*.
- ◆ He promises eternal life, now and forever, to all who trust in Him *(Mark 8:34-37)*.

Jesus is the Son of God and Savior of all people. As Christ, the anointed one of God, Jesus became the perfect sacrifice to provide salvation from sin *(John 1:29; Matthew 20:28)*. He makes possible reconciliation with God, reconciliation with other persons, reconciliation with our own inner being, and even reconciliation between mankind and nature *(2 Corinthians 5:17-20; Romans 8:19-21)*. Receiving Jesus Christ as Savior means that the living Christ comes to live in us, and we live in Him *(Galatians 2:20)*. He leads us in the way everlasting by His thoughtful and willing obedience to the will of the Father *(Matthew 4:1-11; 26:39)*.

✝

LEARNING TO LOVE GOD AND PEOPLE

Jesus Christ's sacrificial death on the cross for us is the source of the power that allows us to reach up in love toward God and out in love toward others. Jesus Christ transforms individuals, enabling us to love beyond our own capacity to love. And He transforms the Church (those who corporately make up the Body of Christ), enabling the Church to love as Jesus loved.

How does this happen? One man, speaking of how he came to know God, said he first loved people and didn't much care about God. In loving people, he discovered God was their best defender and best hope to meet their real needs. As the man tried to meet the needs of people, he came to love God who was already at work in the lives of the people he loved.

A woman said that she had never loved people much. She found them rather boring and bothersome. But she loved God for all the mystery, power and holiness of the Almighty. As she loved and worshipped God, she became aware of how God loved His creation and kept pushing her toward people. She learned to love others because of her love for God.

It may be there are some of us who begin with more of a love for God than we have love for people, and others who begin more with a love of people than we have for God. But in the fullness of Christian faith, wherever we begin, we will end up loving both God and our neighbor if we are honestly seeking the mind of Christ. God will not let us pour all our heart into worshipping Him without sending us out to minister to our neighbors who are His beloved people.

⌘

⌘

Jesus Principles
for Loving God
and Loving our Neighbor

⌘ Seek a personal love relationship with God through Jesus Christ, releasing self to Christ so He may live in us and we in Him.

⌘ Love the Lord our God with all our heart, mind, soul and strength, and love our neighbor as ourselves.

⌘ Live a life that imitates Jesus. Fulfill the purpose of our humanity through rebirth in Christ and the indwelling of God's Holy Spirit.

⌘ Live in the world but not of the world. Act as leaven in society to help the world be ready to hear the word of God and acknowledge the rule of God.

⌘ Minister to others, introducing salvation and healing through Jesus Christ. Bear the burdens of others through intercessory prayer.

⌘ Respond to God's gift of grace through joyous living and commitment to work in the building of God's Kingdom.

3

WHAT IS THE CHURCH?
Descriptive Images from the New Testament

A church is a called-out Body of people who are following Jesus Christ. Church members belong to each other; but primarily they belong to Christ. Therefore, a church is not free to be or to do whatever it wants. It is called to be like Christ and to do what Jesus did. The nature of the church defines its function—and the nature of the church is inseparably linked to the nature and character of Jesus. We are Christ's church only as we individually and corporately do God's work in the world. That was the calling Jesus had and it is our call as well.

Joe E. Lewis, famous comedian of an earlier generation, said, *"You only get to live once, but if you work it right, once is enough."* Once is enough for Christians if we live one life focused on the will of God, doing the work of God, and looking forward with anticipation toward God's salvation and eternal life.

God created each of us for a purpose. God does not force His will on His children, yet we learn early on that we do indeed reap what we sow. If we sow rebellion, we reap separation and bitterness. If we respond in apathy and unconcern, we reap detachment and confusion. When we take on a servant attitude and faithfully seek to live the spirit of God's love and grace, each experience along the way becomes a moment of opportunity to live out God's purpose for creation and we reap the blessings He has for us.

> *And we know that in all things God works for the good of those who love him, who have been called according to his purpose.* *(Romans 8:28)*

This favorite Scripture for so many does not mean everything that happens to us is good, or even that everything is God's will. It does say God will work with us in the midst of everything that

---

happens, whether good or bad, to salvage every good thing possible. If we labor alongside God, watching for His efforts on our behalf, refusing to quit, and journeying forward, He will always help us work good out of evil. He will help us find joy on the other side of sorrow. In particular, the good thing He is determined to accomplish on our behalf is that we grow to be like Jesus.

> **God will always help us work good out of evil.**

For those God foreknew he also predestined to be conformed to the likeness of his Son, that he might be the firstborn among many brothers. *(Romans 8:29)*

When I was a pastor in Enid, Oklahoma, Jack Allison and his family were members of our church. They owned a junkyard. Actually, it was a salvage company. They kept it clean and attractive to the public and they made a lot of money. One afternoon I visited with Jack and we walked around his property. I had never seen such a collection of parts and pieces in all shapes and sizes. He could find anything you might want—a water pump for a '65 Chevrolet, a bumper for a '59 Ford Fairlane, a transmission for a '69 Cadillac—it was all there. Jack explained, "Sometimes we can take a car that has been wrecked, tear it apart, and sell all the parts for more money than the car was worth before the accident!"

Later, I thought what a great parallel there was between Jack's salvage yard and what God does every day in the world. He moves through our world, salvaging broken hearts and wounded spirits. When our lives appear to be trashed by sin, neglect, abuse, or through unfortunate accidents, God lovingly gets down with us in the midst of our hurt and begins to help salvage every good thing possible out of our loss and pain. When we work beside Him, patiently and faithfully following His lead, we can get more out of the loss than we had going in and we grow much more into the likeness of Christ.

Some people say that all they want to do is fully serve Christ. They want to be like their Lord. But when sorrow and disappointment come, they are disillusioned and feel distant from Christ. In response, I think I can hear the quiet voice of God saying, *"But I thought you said you wanted to be like Jesus. How can you be like Jesus if you never know suffering?"*

For those who live faithfully, God uses even the painful experiences of life to enrich us on our journey and give us more to share as Christians. A life focused on God

> **God uses even the painful experiences of life to enrich us on our journey.**

not only reaps His blessings, but builds our credibility with others. We gain respect as we persevere through trials. Our faithful service moves us, experience by experience, into deeper Christian maturity. God faithfully equips us to succeed as we continue to make ourselves useful in the building of His Kingdom.

A church is a body of people who are being conformed to the likeness of Christ. As members of the body seek God's will for their life together, they know that His purpose for them will be like His purpose for Jesus—to do the will of the Father.

⌘

IMAGES FROM THE NEW TESTAMENT

The New Testament is full of wonderful metaphors used to help us understand what God intends for the Church of Jesus Christ to be. Consider the following six images as they reflect the will of God for His Church in the building of His Kingdom:

- •PEOPLE OF GOD

- •TEMPLE OF GOD

- •ARMY OF GOD

- •BRIDE OF CHRIST

- •ARK OF GOD

- •BODY OF CHRIST

PEOPLE OF GOD

God's Chosen People - When God called the patriarch Abraham out of Mesopotamia on a journey of faith into a new land, His
covenant with Abraham was sealed with a promise that his descen-
dants would become a great nation. That promise was fulfilled as
the offspring of Abraham through Isaac and Jacob became the
twelve tribes of Israel *(Genesis 12-50)*.

The twelve tribes were God's chosen people, called to live in
covenant relationship with Him. By so doing, they would enjoy
God's protection and provision. They also were expected to be responsible to God to be a people of the Torah (the Law of God) and
a *"light to the nations" (Isaiah 60:3)*.

Thus was born the concept of the people of God. They lived under the Law of Moses. Circumcision was the outward sign of their
covenant. Later, a new covenant was made. Salvation came by
grace through faith in Jesus Christ and not through the law. Physical circumcision, an outward sign of an inward faith, was not necessary to salvation. True circumcision became a matter of the
heart, growing out of a relationship with Jesus Christ. The people
of God came to include not just those of Jewish blood who faithfully lived under the covenant of the law, but all those, Jew and
Gentile alike, who live by faith in God's new covenant through
Jesus Christ.

> *But you are a chosen people, a royal priesthood, a holy*
> *nation, **a people belonging to God**, that you may declare the*
> *praises of Him who called you out of darkness into His won-*
> *derful light. Once you were not a people, but now you are*
> ***the people of God**; once you had not received mercy, but*
> *now you have received mercy.*   *(1 Peter 2:9-10)*

Citizens of God's Kingdom - True followers of Christ share in
the inheritance of the Kingdom of God and become a part of God's
household. This gives us the image of Christians as citizens of the
Kingdom and members of the family of faith.

> *You are no longer foreigners and aliens, **but fellow citi-***
> *zens with God's people and **members of God's household**,*

built on the foundation of the apostles and prophets, with
Christ Jesus Himself as the chief cornerstone.

(Ephesians 2:19-20)

As Christians, we are citizens of two kingdoms—citizens of the
land in which we live and citizens of the Kingdom of God. We belong to that divine kingdom no matter where we live on earth.
Christians form a union of people who are freeborn citizens of
God's Kingdom.

A church is a kind of outpost of the Kingdom of God. All over
the earth, wherever a church gathers to worship and serve, the
Kingdom of God is present in that place. The outpost may not be
very impressive, or it may have signs of prestige and power, but
wherever God's people gather, a foothold is established for the
Kingdom of God. The church is a place to sing and bear witness, to
serve and convince people that God really does love and care for
them.

In lonely places, in dark and sinful places some people might
call "God-forsaken country," the church sets up its tent and hangs
out its shingle. The church enters into dialogue with the community and begins to give itself away. Right there, the presence of
God's people establishes a foothold—an outpost of the Kingdom.

God's Family of Faith - As we come into relationship with Jesus Christ and become the Church, we become children of God. As
we are growing in Him, Jesus is not ashamed to call us His brothers and sisters because we are brought into the inheritance of God
through our faith.

While Jesus was still talking to the crowd, his mother
and brothers stood outside, wanting to speak to him. Some-
one told him, "Your mother and brothers are standing out-
side, wanting to speak to you." He replied to him, "Who is
my mother, and who are my brothers?" Pointing to his dis-
ciples, he said, "Here are my mother and my brothers. For
whoever does the will of my Father in heaven is my brother
and sister and mother." *(Matthew 12:46-50)*

Another way of expressing these ideas is to say that those who identify with a church are members of "a family of faith." That is the biblical idea behind First Baptist Church, Arlington's slogan, **"A Family of Faith, Caring for You."** We got the idea for a two-part slogan from Jesus' two commands:

> *"Love the Lord your God with all your heart and with all your soul and with all your mind. This is the first and great-est commandment. And the second is like it: Love your neighbor as yourself."*   *(Matthew 22:37-40)*

As described in Chapters 1 and 2, we envision these two com-mandments in the shape of a cross. Our love of God is the vertical bar thrusting upward toward heaven. Our love for those around us is the horizontal bar, stretching out in ministry to a needy world.

⌘

TEMPLE OF GOD

Those who share life in Christ are members of God's family. The church, like a dwelling, is built on Christ, and its integral parts fit together to fulfill God's purpose.

> *As you come to him, the living Stone—rejected by men but chosen by God and precious to him—you also, like living stones, are being **built into a spiritual house** to be a holy priesthood, offering spiritual sacrifices acceptable to God through Jesus Christ.*   *(1 Peter 2:4-5)*

> *In him the whole building is joined together and rises to* ***become a holy temple in the Lord.*** *And in him you too are being built together to become a dwelling in which God lives by his Spirit.*   *(Ephesians 2:19-22)*

Christians de-emphasize the building in which the church meets by saying, "The church is the people, not the building." That's true, of course. However, congregations of believers need a meet-ing place like a family needs a house in which to put their home. This text helps us to treasure, but not worship, the building.

I heard about a church several years ago that built a new building and chose to use bricks that were secondhand or irregular rejects. They built the pastor's study of these bricks as a reminder that the church is made up of imperfect people who are in the process of reclamation, restoration, and a new beginning. That is a fitting image for the temple of God. Jesus is able to take us in our imperfect state and transform us into strong and functional building blocks that work together to make a holy structure.

Church architecture should follow the model of the Creator. In Genesis 2:9 it is said of God's work that it was "pleasing to the eye and good for food." This forms the theological basis for building places of worship. They should be beautiful (pleasing to the eye) and functional (good for food).

⌘

ARMY OF GOD

Paul graphically portrays Christians as spiritual soldiers who put on the armor of God to do battle with a powerful and cunning enemy. That image has long been a favorite metaphor woven into the language and hymnody of the Church.

> *Therefore put on the full armor of God, so that when the day of evil comes, you may be able to stand your ground, and after you have done everything, to stand. Stand firm then, with the belt of truth buckled around your waist, with the breastplate of righteousness in place, and with your feet fitted with the readiness that comes from the gospel of peace. In addition to all this, take up the shield of faith, with which you can extinguish all the flaming arrows of the evil one. Take the helmet of salvation, and the sword of the Spirit, which is the word of God. And pray in the Spirit on all occasions with all kinds of prayers and requests.*
>
> *(Ephesians 6:13-18)*

Make no mistake about it. The Church fights a real battle against a real enemy. It is accurate to perceive ourselves as warriors, defending against an enemy who is like a roaring lion moving about the earth, seeking his prey. Just as we think we have the enemy pinned down, he slips from our grasp and attacks from the rear. Sometimes he even gains entry into our own camp and attacks when we are unaware and where we are most vulnerable.

However, in our zealous energy as Christian soldiers, we must be careful not to fight against ourselves or attack each other. Sometimes armies turn inward, weakening themselves with quarreling and failing to focus on the real enemy where the battle needs to be fought. Wounding from friendly fire is especially painful. It is a double tragedy when we forget who the enemy is and turn on one another.

Churches often have been identified as institutions lacking compassion, places where we tend to "shoot our own wounded." Churches can be so focused on outward activities, they forget to take care of their members who have been hurt along the way. We must learn how to pick up our brothers and sisters and carry them when they need us.

I would hate to go into battle with an army that believes a medical corps is an unnecessary expenditure. It would be tough to be in the trenches with no medics available to help. In every church, there must be caregivers who bind up the wounded, encourage the discouraged, and lift up the lonely. But the church can't be a successful army if all the people in the army are in the medical corps. Such an army would never go to battle. It would stay put and take care of itself. No one would ever be ready for the fight.

⌘

BRIDE OF CHRIST

The Church becomes the bride of Christ through His sacrificial love for it, and through His activity in nourishing, cherishing, and sanctifying it.

Husbands, love your wives, just as Christ loved the church and gave Himself up for her by the washing with water through the word, and to present her to Himself as a radiant church, without stain or wrinkle or any other blemish, but holy and blameless.   (Ephesians 5:25-27)

In the first century, the parents of the bride and groom customarily arranged marriages. It was something of a business arrangement, frequently with the help of a marriage broker whose job it was to negotiate a good match. Oftentimes the bride and groom would not even meet until the wedding ceremony began.

When the prospective bride was brought before the groom's parents for their approval, it was difficult to determine the girl's appearance. By tradition, young women remained heavily veiled from head to foot. The groom's parents could see only the forehead and the eyes of the prospective bride. Consequently, they would look very closely at what they could see. If the young woman's brow was wrinkled or blemished, it might mean that she was sickly or given to anxiety and would not make a good wife. If the brow was smooth and blemish-free, it was more likely the girl was healthy, even-tempered, and would make a good wife.

Paul presents an image of the Church as the bride of Christ whom Christ has personally washed with the word of God, fully cleansing her to be presented to Himself without stain or blemish, fit to be His bride. John the Baptist testified to the coming of Christ as "the bridegroom" whom he would joyously serve.

> *". . . I am not the Christ, but am sent ahead of him. The **bride belongs to the bridegroom**. The friend who attends the bridegroom waits and listens for him, and is full of joy when he hears the bridegroom's voice. That joy is mine, and it is now complete. He must become greater; I must become less."* *(John 3:28-30)*

The Church wants to please the bridegroom through righteous acts. Reverence, respect, and service express life as Christ's bride. The bride renounces every other allegiance and seeks holiness through a faithful relationship.

> *Let us rejoice and be glad and give Him glory! For the wedding of the Lamb has come, and the **bride** has made herself ready. Fine linen, bright and clean, was given her to wear.* *(Revelation 19:7-8)*

*I saw the Holy City, the new Jerusalem, coming down out of heaven from God, **prepared as a bride** beautifully dressed for her husband.*   *(Revelation 21:2)*

Having performed many marriages as a pastor, I can attest that there is a wonderful moment common to every wedding ceremony. When the bride enters, dressed in a beautiful gown, and she walks down the aisle on the arm of her father, the groom's eyes light up with delight and he breathes a sigh of loving anticipation. Brides are beautiful—and that's the way God sees His Church. We are not worthy to be seen that way but that is how He sees us.

I began thinking one day about people who say they love Jesus but don't like the church. They say Jesus is wonderful and we should all try to be like Him, but they can't stand the church because it is full of hypocrites. The German philosopher Arthur Schopenhauer once said, "I could tolerate Jesus Christ if he didn't insist on bringing his leprous bride, the church, along with him."

That statement may sound pious. One is elevating Jesus and recognizing that Jesus is different from and better than His Church. But I have a feeling Jesus feels about His Church the way I feel about my wife, Rosemary.

Imagine that someone would say something like this to me: "Charles, I really like you and you're doing a wonderful job, but I don't like your wife. I think she's a real handicap in your ministry."

I believe I would reply, "You will do better with me if you figure out how to love my wife. I'd rather you brag on her than me."

I don't think Jesus takes kindly to those who criticize the local church, neglect the church, act like the church is not worth their effort, won't help in the work of the church, and won't do anything but sit on the sideline and find fault. Some folks are going to be in for a rude shock when they discover how much Jesus loves His Church. The Church is the bride of Christ.

⌘

ARK OF GOD

The Ark of God is another beautiful metaphor for the Church. The idea is borrowed from the Old Testament story in which God instructed Noah to build an ark in which to save his family from destruction when God caused the great flood to wipe out decadent humanity. Early Christians began to use the ark (or ship) as a symbol of God's saving grace and provision of safety for the Church of Jesus Christ.

> *For Christ died for sins once for all, the righteous for the unrighteous, to bring you to God. He was put to death in the body but made alive by the Spirit, through whom also he went and preached to the spirits in prison who disobeyed long ago when God waited patiently in the days of Noah while the ark was being built. In it only a few people, eight in all, were saved through water, and this water symbolizes baptism that now saves you also—not the removal of dirt from the body but the pledge of a good conscience toward God. It saves you by the resurrection of Jesus Christ, who has gone into heaven and is at God's right hand—with angels, authorities and powers in submission to him.*
> *(1 Peter 3:18-22)*

As a symbol for the Christian Church, the ark is conceived as the vessel in which God's righteous people ride out the storms of life amid the turbulent water of a sinful world. Many of the beautiful stained glass windows in European cathedrals depict *the Ark of God* as a ship sailing the high seas, sometimes with a cross for a mast signifying that it is not the ark of the Old Testament, but the ark of the New Testament Church.

We should remember that Noah's ark was not a ship designed for navigating the seas. Rather, it was more like a big floating houseboat drifting perilously on the ocean swells, designed primarily to allow its passengers to survive disaster. That image has merit for many people who have survived persecution or escaped the catastrophe of dysfunctional family circumstances by taking refuge in the ark of the Church. God has often used the Church to protect His people while the vessel, no matter how imperfect, has been adrift in the sea of life.

On a more humorous note, the local church is sometimes more like Noah's Ark than we would like to admit—if it weren't for the storm on the outside, it would be impossible to put up with the smell on the inside! Churches have problems and the circumstances aren't always pleasant. We bump up against people who have different opinions and are obstinate in their personalities. When we labor against each other, our emotional perspiration makes it very difficult to get along.

I'm always amused at people who keep looking for the perfect church. They say they want to be a part of a church just like the Church Jesus started. If we read the New Testament, we find that first church had a betrayer as a charter member and several members who showed cowardice under pressure. Many of those early church members seemed to be slow learners in discovering who Jesus really was. They argued among themselves about how money was to be spent and about who would be most honored.

If we study the church in Corinth, we wonder how anyone could find peace with God amid such dissension and difficulty among the members. In Antioch, the church struggled to overcome prejudice and old traditions in order to accept the Gentile Christians.

No church is ever perfect, and living up to the demands of Christian discipleship is never easy. The Ark of God is a wonderful symbol of refuge for pilgrims on a stormy sea, but we must be honest in admitting the typical trials of life aboard ship. To be useful, the church has to be in the world as the ark was in the sea, but if too much world gets into the church, just as a ship that takes on too much water, it will begin to sink. Passengers and crew must work through the fears and discord so common among those who share the danger of stormy crossings.

⌘

BODY OF CHRIST

The Body of Christ is the most dominant image of the Church in the New Testament. Christ is the head of the Body, the source and locus of authority which the whole Body must honor and obey. Speaking of the authority of Jesus Christ, the apostle Paul said:

> God placed all things under his feet and appointed him to
> be head over everything for **the church, which is his body**,
> the fullness of him who fills everything in every way.
>
> *(Ephesians 1:22)*

When Jesus was born in Bethlehem and God brought Himself to earth as flesh, God made His journey into a far country. We call that event the incarnation. Incarnation means God took human flesh and wrapped it around Himself. He became a man—God made visible.

So, as the Body of Christ, the Church is the continuing incarnation. Jesus died, was buried and rose from the dead. He went to be with the Father. Jesus Christ is absent from this world in the flesh but He sent the Holy Spirit into the world that He might empower the Church to be Christ's continuing presence in the world.

> **The Holy Spirit empowers the church to be the continuing presence of Christ in the world.**

At the heart of this image is the mystery of how the many parts of the Body function together in unity through the power of the Holy Spirit. Every Christian is a member of the Body with shared dependence and shared suffering; yet all members function together in the power of God's love. The distinct spiritual gifts and individual ministries of each person are important to the whole. Christ reconciles all people—in Him there are no distinctions of race, class, or gender.

> *Just as each of us has a body with many members and these members do not have the same function, **so in Christ we who are many form one body**, and each member belongs to all the others.* *(Romans 12:4-5)*

Becoming a part of the Body of Christ requires an individual commitment of one's entire being—body, mind, and soul. We lose ourselves to find ourselves in the will and purpose of God. Some folks seem to be able to make that full commitment at the time of conversion. But many Christians would say our experience with God is a slowly growing process across the years.

As we learn to depend on Christ as our Savior, we begin to discern that God wants us to grow and He is prepared to help us in our faith and walk with Christ.

The body of believers that surrounds the new Christian is the fellowship where new believers begin to discover the pattern and shape of their discipleship. Like the young duckling who must receive the needed *imprinting* from its mother to learn what it is to be a duck, the young Christian needs the imprinting of the Body of Christ to emerge as a functioning and integral part of the Body itself. If the Church is consciously seeking to be the presence of Christ in the community, then new believers learn that the goal of the Christian life is to grow to be like Jesus. The agenda for a church today is the same agenda Jesus had when in the world.

> **The goal of the Christian life is to grow to be like Jesus.**

The apostle Paul encourages Christians who want to grow to hear and internalize this truth.

I urge you . . . in view of God's mercy, to offer your bodies as living sacrifices, holy and pleasing to God—this is your spiritual act of worship. Do not conform any longer to the pattern of this world, but be transformed by the renewing of your mind. Then you will be able to test and approve what God's will is—his good, pleasing and perfect will.

(Romans 12:1-3)

A church in which the Holy Spirit is not alive and at work is a dead body. That's why the Holy Spirit is always looking to create a people gathered in unity, faith and love. When unity is present, He can inhabit our lives and give us power and energy to be the continuing presence of God in this world in a very literal way. We are the Body of Christ. That means we are the presence of God in any community.

We are a Body - not a Bunch

The image of the church as the Body of Christ is especially helpful when we consider that the church is an organism, a living thing. It is not a bunch of people but a body of people. Onions are gathered together in bunches, held together by a string. One tender onion can be removed from the bunch without a sound being made by the other onions. But try to pull a finger from the hand, or a toe from the foot, and a howl of anguish breaks forth.

The church is not a bunch of people haphazardly thrown together. We are a body, and every member of the body is precious and valuable. When one of us cries, the others taste the salt.

As the Body of Christ, the church does not easily let one of its members go away. We part only with a degree of pain. There are three occasions to say good-bye to members:

♦ When it is time for a member to move to another town, we should send them on their way, praying that God will use them to be a healthy addition to another body of believers.

♦ Although parting is always a sorrow, it can also be a blessed time when the body can reproduce itself by sending some of its members to serve in another place—to reach out to others who could not be reached by the original body.

♦ When there is damage being done to healthy members by one of the body who refuses to heal and who has become a cancer, destroying the life of the body, that member must be asked to go. This is most painful. Congregations must pray for the skill and judgment of a surgeon to perform such a delicate and sensitive operation. As long as possible, the healthy members must seek to find reconciliation with the troubled, angry, or hurting member. Pray for one another. But do keep in mind the mission of the church as well as the fellowship. Move forward.

The Body of Christ needs all its members, functioning, healthy, and harmonious. The church cannot be healthy without healthy people. The church will not be harmonious without happy people, and the church will not be helpful if its people are not committed to being useful to God and getting His work done.

When a church is working together, it can get more done collectively than it could if everyone was doing his or her very best in isolation. The Holy Spirit fills the body with purpose, anticipation, and unity. He brings to the body the grand triplets of faith, hope, and love. Each member of the church is called to value his or her place, function, and gifts, and prayerfully seek to encourage every other member to faithful and joyful service.

We have different gifts and abilities, but we are all about the same task. One of us may find expression for God's will through teaching, while someone else finds expression through the gift of encouragement. One may serve best through extraordinarily generous giving, while another serves best through the gift of leadership.

Whatever our gifts, we should all serve for one reason, not to call attention to ourselves but to call attention to God's power to change lives. God knows how to use ordinary people in extraordinary ways.

⌘

CHURCHES WITH PURPOSE, PRESENCE, AND PASSION

The local church as the Body of Christ has a simple **purpose:** to do the will of God. Jesus was fully devoted to doing God's will and that should be our unwavering devotion as well. Individually and corporately, we must go where Jesus would go, see what Jesus would see, and respond in love to the needs of all those we encounter.

To fulfill our purpose to do the will of God, we must individually and corporately work to establish a Christ-like **presence** in the world. Who is going to love people if the church does not? Who is going to care for people whom no one else cares for if the church does not? We are the Body of Christ walking through Samaria, taking time to talk to a woman at a well. We bind up the wounded and broken-hearted and restore them through love. We teach and train individuals as they grow in discipleship. We worship, praise, build fellowship, and courageously minister—secure in our identity as the Body of Christ, doing God's work in the world.

As we work together to respond to God's call, each of us is an integral part of the Body. We are grateful for and proud of all the members. We cheer each other on as we seek to be like Jesus.

Love, encouragement and commitment to the task breed a wonderful **passion** to do the will of God as we are equipped by the Holy Spirit to be instruments of God's grace in the world.

⌘

⌘
JESUS PRINCIPLES
FOR UNDERSTANDING THE CHURCH

⌘ A church is not free to be or do whatever it wants. It is called to be like Christ and do what Jesus would do.

⌘ We are Christ's Church only as we individually and corporately do God's work in the world.

⌘ When we take on a servant attitude and live the spirit of God's love and grace, each experience in life becomes a moment of opportunity to live out God's purpose for creation and reap the blessings He has for us.

⌘ Followers of Christ share the inheritance of the Kingdom of God and become part of God's household. We become the children of God—the family of faith.

⌘ The Church is built on the foundation of Jesus Christ. We are the building blocks of a temple in which the Spirit of God lives. We must protect the sanctity and integrity of this holy dwelling.

⌘ The Church is the army of God comprised of warriors against evil. Christian warriors defend ourselves with righteousness, peace, faith, and salvation. We arm ourselves with truth and the word of God.

⌘ The Church as the Bride of Christ has been made holy and pure for union with Him. Christ loves, supports, and defends His Church.

⌘ As the Body of Christ, the Church is the continuing incarnation, empowered by the Holy Spirit to be Christ's presence in the world.

⌘ The Body of Christ is a living organism with Christ as its head. In Christ, those who are many form one Body. Each member belongs to all others. If we live in isolation, we are not the Church.

⌘ The Body of Christ has a simple and basic purpose: to do the will of God.

DEAR FATHER OF US ALL:

YOU HAVE SO RICHLY BLESSED AND EN-COURAGED US THROUGH THE MANY NEW TESTAMENT IMAGES OF YOUR CHURCH. WHAT A PRIVILEGE IT IS TO BE HELD IN THE SAVING GRACE OF CHRIST JESUS AND TO WALK IN FELLOWSHIP WITH THOSE WHO FOLLOW HIM AS LORD OF THEIR LIFE.

AGAIN AND AGAIN WE ARE REMINDED OF HOW JESUS HAS SAVED US FROM SIN, RE-NEWED OUR SPIRITS, AND IS EQUIPPING US FOR HOLY SERVICE IN YOUR KINGDOM. HELP US TO RESPOND TO YOUR LOVE IN OBEDIENCE AND FAITHFUL SERVICE. HELP US TO LIVE THE FRUITS OF THE SPIRIT— LOVE, JOY, PEACE, PATIENCE, KINDNESS, GOODNESS, FAITHFULNESS, GENTLENESS, AND SELF-CONTROL. MAY OUR LIVES SO RE-FLECT THE CHARACTER OF OUR LORD THAT ALL WHO SEE OUR GOOD DEEDS WILL GIVE PRAISES TO YOU, OUR FATHER IN HEAVEN.

AMEN

Life Application

⌘

WHAT IS THE CHURCH?
Descriptive Images from the New Testament

1. This chapter defines a local church as a "called-out Body of believers," and presents the idea that we are the church only as we individually and corporately do God's work in the world.
   - What does it mean to be *called-out*? Are all Christians called, or only those with a call to vocational ministry?
   - Why is it important to do God's work in the world both individually and corporately?

2. Which of the New Testament images of the Church discussed in this chapter has particular meaning for you?

3. Focus on the image of the church as the Body of Christ. *(See Romans 12:4-5)*
   - The apostle Paul says, *"In Christ we who are many form one Body, and each member belongs to all the others."* What does this mean?
   - Discuss the responsibility of Christians in the church to relate to one another in unity, faith, and love.

4. If the goal of the Christian life is to grow to be like Jesus, where are you in terms of your commitment to pursue that goal?
   - What temptations do you find most difficult to overcome?
   - When do you feel most strong and competent as a Christian?

5. Over the next twenty-four hours, try an experiment to sharpen your awareness of how to establish a Christ-like presence in your world. In every event and relationship you encounter, consider your role as a member of the Body of Christ. Adopt a servant attitude to live the spirit of God's love and grace. Be aware of how this purposeful experience changes the way you think and act.

SECTION
TWO

FUNCTIONS
OF THE CHURCH

⌘
FUNCTIONS OF THE CHURCH

The social ferment that swept through America during the 1960s produced anguished soul-searching about who we were as a nation and what we were to be about as a leader among the great nations of the world. During that same period, many Christians seriously questioned the role of the church in society by evaluating whether churches were in tune with God's purpose in the communities they served.

As a result of that introspection and fear that the churches had been sidetracked into social and political causes, a major movement developed among churches in the early 1970s to get back to what many considered to be the "main thing"—evangelism. Churches restructured their programs and their schedules to give evangelism their primary focus.

Putting evangelism in the number one position was a real change for some churches who had not emphasized evangelism much at all. That was good! Evangelism is the toughest function to focus on as a church. Not many people want to do it, including a lot of pastors. Churches seem to schedule many rewarding, interesting and inspiring activities throughout the week, few or none of which include talking about Jesus to an unbeliever. Consequently, not much evangelism gets done in American churches even today.

As a young pastor, I sympathized with the idea and intent of the "main thing" movement but I couldn't be comfortable saying that the church has just one main task. I knew that it couldn't be that simple.

In 1970, after completing my second seminary degree, I was called to be pastor of the First Baptist Church in Enid, Oklahoma. I remember saying to a reporter who interviewed me there, "I believe the church moves on two tracks, evangelism and ethics." That was the best way I knew at the time to express my conviction that the Christian life is about believing, but it is also about behaving. Evangelism and ethics have to be held together if we are to be faithful to what Jesus

> *Finding the balance between believing and doing is the challenge.*

taught. Finding the balance between believing and doing is the challenge.

Emphasizing theology without action brings imbalance on the side of intellectual belief. Focusing on performance without understanding the reasons for our actions puts a church out of balance on the side of behavior. Buddhism, for example, is about behaving, but not much about believing since it has no theistic base.

In the years following, I articulated that two-part focus to my congregation in Enid and sought to lead them as a church to where both John 3:16 and Matthew 25:40 are heard and acted upon.

BELIEVING *(Evangelism)*	BEHAVING *(Ethics)*
❧ *For God so loved the world that he gave his one and only Son, that whoever believes in him shall not perish but have eternal life.* *(John 3:16)*	❧ *I tell you the truth, whatever you did for the least of these brothers of mine, you did for me.* *(Matthew 25:40)*

As I served a few more years as pastor, the "believing and behaving" approach grew less adequate. I was aware that the behaviors or "ethics" we express as Christians grow in large part out of the quality of our worship, Bible teaching, and love for one another. I was beginning to understand that the church is not as simple an organism as it might first appear.

In 1976, when I came to be pastor of the First Baptist Church, Arlington, I undertook a renewed effort to clarify what a church should be about and what shape our ministry should take in Arlington, Texas. As I pondered, it seemed to me that there were five major functions necessary to fulfill the task of reaching people and addressing the individual needs of the people of God. I enlarged my earlier list to five items.

To be healthy, a church must:
- ♦ Worship
- ♦ Evangelize
- ♦ Disciple
- ♦ Minister
- ♦ Create Fellowship

These five areas of emphasis seemed logical, practical, and true to my experience as a pastor in all the church life I had ever known. And they put in place a balance between the church's commission to make new disciples and the church's command to love others in Jesus' name.

The frustrating thing about that list is articulating five interrelated functions to a congregation so they understand what the main focus was to be. I have had church growth consultants tell me to shorten the list because people can't remember five things. They told me the church vision has to be focused on one thing, or at the most, two.

I kept thinking. There are many wonderful Christian churches who seem to concentrate on one of the five functions as their major emphasis. That is fine. But I find that most people who join special-focus churches receive what is there for them for a time and then move on. They may need the special emphasis for the short term but need something more for the long journey.

My heart's desire was to build a church that would meet the needs of people from birth to death, similar to a full-service general hospital which handles all kinds of cases

> **A full service church is one in which people can find Christ and stay involved all of their lives.**

from emergencies to long-term rehabilitation, has both an obstetrics and a geriatrics wing, both a cardiovascular and oncology center. I believe a full-service church is the kind of church through which people can find Christ, become a part of the family of faith, and stay involved all of their lives.

To begin communicating this concept to the congregation, I preached a series of sermons outlining how the five functions could be expressed in the life of our church.

Later, Dr. Kenneth Chafin, professor of evangelism at two seminaries, and at that time pastor of South Main Baptist Church in Houston, came to First Baptist, Arlington to speak to our Sunday school leadership. He spoke on the five functions of the church and emphasized the exact list that had been our focus. That was both affirming and encouraging to me. But the new insight Chafin brought was that the Sunday school, with its ongoing small group Bible study organization, was essential to the church because it

provides the structure through which the church effectively per-
forms *all five* of those essential functions.

◆ **Worship** - A church's Sunday school prepares people through
Bible study to be more disciplined about personal devotions
and to be more consistent and thoughtful participants in corporate worship.

◆ **Evangelize** - Christians involved in Sunday school reach out to
people in the community who do not have a church or a knowledge of Christ. It provides a small group structure to welcome,
encourage, and bless those who come to the church. It is a
place where the gospel can be presented in a personal and non-
threatening way.

◆ **Disciple** - The Sunday school has a primary task to disciple
believers—to teach people how to study the Bible, how to pray,
how to teach and serve, and how to be responsible for each
other in a caring way. People grow in Christ best when they
have a small group of people with whom they can study, apply
the Scripture, and share in practical ministry experiences.

◆ **Minister** - The Sunday school network makes it possible to put
people into situations where they can help others effectively.
One of the needs Christian folks feel is to be involved in service to others. Sunday school classes can mobilize their resources to meet human needs in Jesus' name.

◆ **Create Fellowship** - The Sunday school builds loving relationships among members of the church. Ask church members
what they like most about their church, and their typical response will be "The fellowship. My friends are there! When I
go there, they know who I am. When I am sick, someone
comes to see me. When I have a need, people pray for me and
offer to help."

After hearing Chafin speak on this theme, I realized more than
ever why the Sunday school is so important to the life of a church.
It helps the church achieve its purposes of reaching out to people

so they too can become followers of Jesus Christ. And, it ministers to the needs of people as Jesus did when He was on earth.

Sometime later while we were trying to determine how best to implement these five functions, several church members expressed their concern that an emphasis on five areas might diminish our effectiveness as a church. They feared we would lose our focus unless we could establish a primary objective.

My problem was that I didn't want to give up any of those five functions. I believed they were all important. We might focus on one more than another for a period of time because it needed special attention. But as a hand needs five fingers in order to be fully functional, I believe a church needs those five functions to be a healthy, vital and vibrant church.

In the process of trying to figure out what the primary focus of the church might be, it became clear to me the purpose would have to grow out of its basic nature.

> *The primary focus of the Church is to do what Jesus did.*

♦ **What is the Church?** *It is the Body of Christ.*

♦**What is the Church's function?** *It is to act as the Body of Christ—to do what Christ did while He was on earth.*

Everyone has basic human needs that cannot be fulfilled apart from a relationship with God. The truth about God's incarnation into human history is that Jesus came so mankind could have life, and have it abundantly. As we live in Christ and He lives in us, our doing comes out of our theology. We are the church and our purpose is to be the presence of Christ in the world. I began to ask what Jesus would be doing. It became clear that He certainly would be doing now what He did then.

Jesus Worshipped. He loved God in such a profound way that when He spoke, the people around Him heard the voice of God. He inspired others to love God, to sing praises and to pray. He affirmed that God's greatest commandment was to love God with all one's heart, mind, soul and strength.

Jesus was a Witness to the Gospel. He taught people that God loved them and through repentance and faith, their lives could be changed. He brought them hope for salvation and eternal life. He finally died, a "ransom for many."

Jesus Taught His Disciples. By example and by word, He equipped them for practical godly living in the world. He trained them and sent them out into the world to witness and to minister.

Jesus Ministered to People. He was loving and compassionate. He healed people in body and in spirit, whether they followed Him or not. He overcame evil with good. He fed people. He cared for those whom others ignored. He called people to act with justice and integrity.

Jesus Created Fellowship. He said to His followers, *"By this they will know you are my disciples, if you love one another."* He turned a group of men into a band of brothers. He taught them how to love. They learned to serve one another and to bear each other's burdens in kindness and gentleness. They became one in His Spirit.

It is from this insight into the person of Jesus Christ that these five essential functions of the church came into focus. The functions are more than a descriptive analysis of what Christians should be doing. Rather, they are the "fleshing out" of the heart and soul of Jesus Himself—to show us how truly to live the abundant life God wants for us. *When the church, the Body of Christ, worships, evangelizes, disciples, ministers, and creates fellowship, it is doing what comes naturally.* It is doing what Jesus did when He was here on earth, and what He is doing today as He fills the congregation of believers with His Holy Spirit. *As we seek to be like Him, our nature flows out of His nature. The church learns to behave as Jesus behaved. That is "The Jesus Principle."*

Some years later I was pleased to find that church growth expert Rick Warren also was saying that the primary issue is not just church growth, but church health! In his book *The Purpose Driven Church,* Warren uses a chart to illustrate the comparative focus of various types of churches as they seek to be true to God's purpose. He emphasis is on the "purpose-driven church" which can provide the necessary balance of functions so the Body of Christ truly can be what Christ created it to be. I join Warren and others in this on-going dialogue about keeping the church true to God's full purpose as we work together to meet the needs of people in each succeeding generation.

The following adaptation of Warren's chart should provide a helpful overview of what I believe the church is all about and how its functions grow out of who Jesus is and what He did in His earthly ministry. Our task is to apply THE JESUS PRINCIPLE and become the *continuing incarnation of God in our world.*

Type of Church	Soul Winning Church	Experienc- ing God Church	Family Reunion Church	Bible Classroom Church	Social Conscience Church	Jesus Principle Church
Primary Focus:	Evangelism	Worship	Fellowship	Edification	Ministry	Balance All Five
Pastor's Role:	Evangelist	Worship Leader	Chaplain	Instructor	Reformer	Equipper
People's Role:	Witnesses	Worshippers	Family Members	Students	Activists	Ministers
Primary Target:	The Community	The Crowd	The Congrega- tion	The Committed	The Core	All Five
Key Term:	Save	Feel	Belong	Know	Care	Be & Do
Central Value:	Decisions for Christ	Personal Experience	Loyalty & Tradition	Bible Knowledge	Justice & Mercy	Christ-like Character
Tools Used:	Visitation & Altar Call	Music & Prayer	Fellowship & Shared Meals	Books & Notes	Petitions & Volunteerism	Life De- velopment Process
Source of Legitimacy:	Number Baptized	The Spirit	Our Heritage	Verse by Verse Teaching	Number of Needs Met	Changed Lives

The following five chapters (one on each of the five functions of the church) reflect what Jesus Christ did when He was here on earth and what the Body of Christ is doing on earth today.

⌘

4

WORSHIP
Honoring the First Function of the Church

> **Wor•ship –**
> To bow down, obey, show veneration, give homage, and demonstrate extreme devotion or love.

Worship is a stirring of the human spirit, a fusion of emotion and intellect in an outpouring of expression toward God. Worship is as broad and variegated as the soul is deep. Our lives are enriched and blessed when we regularly meditate on the word of God, acknowledge and repent of our sin, seek His thoughts, offer our prayers, sing His praises, and lose ourselves in the glory of His presence.

When we experience God, we cannot keep from loving and praising Him. For centuries, the beauty of Psalm 100 has inspired and enriched worshippers coming before our Lord God.

Shout for joy to the Lord, all the earth.
Worship the Lord with gladness;
come before Him with joyful songs.
Know that the Lord is God.
It is He who made us, and we are his;
we are his people; the sheep of his pasture.
Enter his gates with thanksgiving
and his courts with praise;
give thanks to him and praise his name.
For the Lord is good and his love endures forever,
his faithfulness continues throughout all generations.
(Psalm 100)

This exuberant Psalm encourages us to come in joyful worship, to shout, to sing with a full heart and joyful spirit, to give praise and thanksgiving to a loving and faithful God.

THREE REQUIREMENTS OF TRUE WORSHIP

In Isaiah 6:1-8, the prophet Isaiah experienced a life-changing event in his worship of God.

- ◆ He truly saw the Lord.
- ◆ He truly saw himself.
- ◆ He responded faithfully to the needs of God's world.

1. Focusing First on God

In true worship, the first focus is on God. Jesus said the first commandment is to "love the Lord your God with all your heart, and with all your soul, and with all your mind" *(Matthew 22:37)*. That is the very first responsibility of the human heart. I like the paraphrase Carlyle Marney gave to that commandment: *"What Jesus is saying is this—we are to love God as we love nothing else."*

Do we love God as we love nothing else? Establishing priorities is a tough business. Keeping love of God first place in our hearts and minds is an issue we deal with continuously. Putting God first means we must adjust every other allegiance or love in order to be true to our highest calling. We are dishonest if we don't admit it is a struggle. The powers of darkness are wily and insistent, seducing our hearts away from our central commitment to God. Jesus told us to mark it down. The most important commandment of all is to love God as we love nothing else in all of life.

Isaiah understood devotion to God first in terms of fear and reverence. He knew no man could see God and live, unless God in His grace allowed it to be. Isaiah experienced life-threatening fear in the temple of God where he saw a vision in which heaven was open with the angels of power gathered around, showing reverence to the Father. *"Holy, holy, holy is the Lord of hosts. The whole earth is full of His glory."* Isaiah trembled as an earthquake shook the building. He fell to his knees in anguish and fear, crying out, *"I have seen the Lord and I am lost, undone and unclean."* But God sent the seraphim angels to cleanse his life and allowed Isaiah to live.

We search our hearts to understand the fear and reverence that Isaiah felt. God is loving and forgiving, but He does not patronize us in our weakness and sin. When we encounter the majesty of God's love, we experience an awesome sense of belonging to Him. We owe everything to Him. He is the Lord of life. He is the Lord of death. He is the Lord of all. We live by His grace. We die in His presence. He is worthy of all we can give.

If God's people go week after week with never a searching, soul-searing look into the face of Holy God, then our worship is lacking in seriousness and honesty.

When we focus on God, we also understand we must put aside every other human distraction that might become our god. Wealth, power,

> **God's righteous anger is sharp, but it is cleansing.**

fame, pleasure—all are seen as superficial when compared to the eternal God of all creation. God's righteous anger is sharp, but it is cleansing.

There is an emptiness within each of us that draws us to worship that which is above and beyond ourselves. Many people, with good intentions, give bland acknowledgment and allegiance to a nebulous "higher power" or "creative force." But the God of the Bible wants nothing of that kind of generalized all-inclusive worship. The worship of God as taught in the Scriptures calls for a very specific kind of commitment. It is the worship of the God of Abraham, Isaac, Jacob, Moses and David. The God of our Lord Jesus Christ, the only God, is the one to whom we come in love and reverence, casting our lives before Him. He wants us to give Him our hearts, our wealth, our ambitions—all we are.

Men and women often deal with lesser gods. Isaiah the prophet cautioned people about consulting mediums and wizards who chirp and mutter.

> *Should not a people consult their God? Should they consult the dead on behalf of the living?* *(Isaiah 8:19)*

Isaiah is saying that never can one who worships God be satisfied to listen to the empty promises of mind-readers, palm-readers, fortune tellers, wizards, witches or any of those who claim to have supernatural psychic wisdom. What an indictment on our current generation that seems to be so obsessed with the occult, new-age mysticism, and appeals to discover their future by calling the psychic telephone hotline!

Christians have been called into abundant living through relationship with the God of life. Why would anyone want to continue to live out of the past and focus on the dead? Isaiah insists we are to have nothing to do with that kind of darkness.

> *They will look toward the earth and see only distress and darkness and fearful gloom, and they will be thrust into utter darkness.*   *(Isaiah 8:22)*

Those who play the games of astrology or the Ouija board, and who dabble in the occult, will finally find themselves in confusion and anguish of heart. They will reach a dead-end road and finally darkness. Contrast that with the vision Isaiah has of the people who walk with God.

> *The people walking in darkness have seen a great light; on those living in the land of the shadow of death, a light has dawned.*   *(Isaiah 9:2)*

True worship focuses fully on God—who He is, what He is, how He loves us, and how in His holiness He calls us to righteous living. We worship the one God, fully revealed, three in one:
- **God the Father** - Creator and Sustainer
- **God the Son** - Savior and Redeemer
- **God the Spirit** - Comforter and Equipper

This is the mighty God we worship when we come to raise our voices in praise and thanksgiving. This is the righteous God we worship when we open our hearts for His judgment and healing. This is the loving God we worship as we are humbled by His forgiveness and grace.

2. Honestly Facing Ourselves

If the first step in true worship is to love God with our entire being, the second step is to look within and honestly evaluate who we are in relationship to God. Like Isaiah, we must recognize our predicament and our sin—a view of ourselves we avoid as much as possible. We can look in the mirror of our own ego, and by rearranging certain patterns, make ourselves appear amazingly attractive. We choose to look into mirrors that give us the most pleasing image—held by people who seek our favor, who stroke us so we feel greater than we know in truth we are. Depending on our motivation, looking in mirrors can be a helpful reality check, or it can be an excuse for constructing a facade.

Some of us who attend worship services regularly want to go away from every service feeling that all is well in the earth. We want a God who is all-forgiving and will control things the way we want them controlled. We want to believe it doesn't matter who we are or what we do as long as we express our love for God. We'd prefer a God who won't ask us to be responsible for our thoughts and behavior. We'd prefer a God who doesn't require us to look within for the sin that needs rooting out. However, if we do not turn our eyes inward to search the paths of our walk, we miss the cleansing and renewing which worship can bring to our lives.

In true worship, it can feel as though the heavens open and God appears. We see our emptiness. We come face to face with our prejudice, guilt, pride, unloving spirit, critical attitude, jealous ways, greediness, unconcern for people who are hurting, laziness and indulgence in the diversions of the flesh that destroy us. We confront our carelessness for being poor stewards of the life and time God has given us. Unless we are willing to admit our sin, we journey through life in denial and arrogance.

> *Unless we are willing to admit our sin, we journey through life in denial and arrogance.*

Experiencing the holiness of God through worship serves to illuminate our sin and unworthiness and awaken us to the glory that is reflected in a holy God. Facing the truth of our condition frees us to respond in humility to God's call to be His servant.

The burden of unresolved guilt can block us from true worship and deprive us of the glory of contact with God. Sometimes we feel guilty because some preacher or authority figure has reminded us of our evident shortcomings. But usually, our guilt is the result of recognizing our own waywardness or carelessness. Guilt can be legitimate—a healthy warning that we are headed toward disaster. But often, our guilt becomes counter productive. We hold on to it with a sense of helplessness as we grow weaker and weaker. We can't save ourselves.

There is a better way to deal with guilt. We can accept the unbelievable God-given grace freely available to us. Some of us carry heavy burdens and hurt because of things in our past, having survived traumatic experiences, hurtful people, evil influences, and unwise decisions. Some of us have heard again and again how worthless we are and how wrong our life has been. We respond in sinful patterns of judgment, bitterness, unforgiveness, and hardness of heart. We react to our hurts with anger and resentment, and the guilt of sin sets in.

> **When we come into God's presence and confess our sin, He forgives us.**

We don't get rid of sin and guilt by ignoring our wounds, pretending we aren't bitter and unforgiving, or rationalizing our wrongdoing by saying we aren't nearly as bad as some people we know. When our heart condemns us and guilt lives in our soul, there is only one remedy for the sickness. Seeing the love and mercy of God, we must turn repentantly from our sin and sorrow, trusting Him for forgiveness. Healing and renewal come only through the forgiveness of Jesus Christ who loves us while we are sinners, and loves us just like we are *(1 John 1:9; 4:10)*. When we come into God's presence and confess our sin, He forgives us. Jesus takes the burden of our sin upon Himself and sets us free. We become new creatures in Him.

Part of our problem is that we have never quite understood what it means to confess our sin. So often when we pray to ask God to forgive us, we fail to do the most important thing—confess our sin. Confession of sin means that we are finally willing to admit to ourselves and to God that our attitudes and deeds are wrong. We are ready to quit trying to call sin by some other name or excuse it away.

The New Testament Greek word for this is *homologeo.* Break it down: *homo* means *the same. Logeo* means *to speak or to say.* Then *homologeo* means *to say the same thing, to agree with.* In legal terms, a person who confesses guilt agrees with the judge that the accusation brought against him is true. In essence, the person is saying, "I agree with you, judge. What you say about what I have done is true. I did it."

When we confess our sins to God, we are finally willing to agree with God about what we have done. We quit rationalizing away our behavior or justifying ourselves. We face up to our sin and admit to God and others that we have done wrong. We look into the presence of God and say as Isaiah did, *"I am undone. My lips are unclean. My mouth is full of foulness. I live in the midst of people who have ignored You. I am lost."*

It is only when we have admitted our sin and said, *"Yes, God, what You have been saying about what I am doing is true. It has been true all along. I confess. I agree with You. Oh God, in my sin and weakness, can You do something to help?"* At that moment, God descends into our very presence with His cleansing power and takes our sin away.

In true worship, we focus first on God, then zero in on the human heart. True worship causes us to quit praying like the self-righteous Pharisees,

> *God, I thank you that I am not like other men—robbers, evil doers, adulterers—or even like this tax collector. I fast twice a week and give a tenth of all I get.   (Luke 18:11-12)*

Jesus clearly said that kind of prayer goes nowhere. God does not hear the prayer of the haughty and self-righteous. He hears the simple prayer of those like the tax collector, who came with all the knowledge of his guilt and sin. He stood hesitantly in the back of the temple. He raised his heart to heaven and bowed his eyes to the Father, asking simply, *"God, have mercy on me, a sinner."* That prayer was heard and he went home justified before God.

Unfortunately, many proud Christians walk into church sanctuaries Sunday after Sunday with an attitude that says, "All right, pastor, entertain me! All right, musicians, impress me! I have come to see if I will like what you have to offer today."

That kind of attitude will never lead anyone into true worship. Rather, we must come with humble expectancy, seeking the awesome presence of God, trembling at His greatness, marveling at His love and ready to be transformed by the power of His holiness. In the melting of our pretensions, we lay our malleable spirits before Him so we might be re-shaped more and more into the image of the Lord Jesus Christ.

3. Responding to God's Call

True worship lifts our hearts, gives us courage to go on and puts joy back in our lives. After Isaiah had a vision of his true self, he heard the voice of God saying, *"Who will go?"* God's question was an awesome word. Although it must have been difficult, Isaiah's humbling experience with God equipped him to be able to answer, *"Here am I, Lord. Send me."*

When we hear God's word in Scripture and sermon, we must participate and respond. I saw a poem recently that ended with a line describing two images that are inseparably related: "Dust on the Bible and drought in the heart."

Never reading the Bible and never really hearing God's word in worship leads to a parched heart. We bring drought into our life when we turn off our mind and spirit at the reading of God's word. When we awaken to hear God's word with gladness, blessing comes like cool rain to revive a withered and dying flower.

Worship lifts up the heart when, in all the ways of worshipping God, we finally come in response to answer His call. We say with Isaiah, *"Here I am, Lord. Send me!"* We say with Samuel, *"Speak Lord for thy servant is listening."* We say with Jesus, *"Not my will but thine be done."* Worship brings us into the presence of God. It shows us who we are and then fills us with confidence that He takes us as we are, cleanses our lives and sends us out to be His ministering servants.

The worship service or the worship style never defines true worship. Styles come and styles go. True worship is a matter of the heart. It confronts us, lifts us and changes us. It leaves the mark of God on us, written in the folds of the heart.

⌘

How Did Jesus Worship?

Jesus worshipped regularly. He worshipped in the temple. He worshipped in the synagogue. He worshipped with His band of followers. He worshipped alone. Out of His heart He lifted a life of prayer to His Father. We do not know the content of Christ's prayers except as a window is opened for us in several Scriptures.

The recorded prayers of Jesus reveal:

- ◆ **Petition** *(Matthew 26:36-44)*
- ◆ **Intercession** *(John 17)*
- ◆ **Mercy** *(Luke 23:34)*
- ◆ **Anguish** *(Mark 15:34)*
- ◆ **Trust** *(Luke 23:46)*

Jesus worshipped not only when it was expected and easy, but also during times of great trial and anguish. Jesus wanted to be sure that His will was the Father's will. He did this through continual prayer. In Jesus' humanity, He had to keep constant contact between His heart and the Father's heart. It is interesting to note that the disciples didn't ask Jesus how to love others, to teach, or to minister, but they did ask Him how to pray *(Luke 11:1)*. His response to them *(Luke 11:2 and Matthew 6:9-12)* is what we know as the "Lord's Prayer":

> *In Jesus' humanity, He had to keep constant contact between His heart and the Father's heart.*

Our Father in heaven, hallowed be your name. Your Kingdom come, your will be done on earth as it is in heaven. Give us today our daily bread. Forgive us our debts, as we also have forgiven our debtors. And lead us not into temptation but deliver us from the evil one. *(Matthew 6:9-12)*

The format of the Lord's Prayer tells us much about what worship should be. Jesus taught us to:

- ◆ Address God, not man *(verse 9)*.
- ◆ Praise God and affirm the righteous authority of His will over heaven and earth, and over our lives *(verse 9-10)*.
- ◆ Ask for God's provision while acknowledging our sinfulness in an attitude of repentance and humility *(verse 11-12)*.
- ◆ Ask for God's protection against temptations and harm *(verse 13)*.

When we truly worship, we come in thanksgiving and gladness to praise God. We are drawn in expectancy to lift ourselves up to God in prayer. There are different kinds of prayer we may offer in corporate worship.

In the **invocation,** we acknowledge what we ought to know, but sometimes forget, that unless God is with us, our worship is in vain. In this prayer, we say, *"God, we need You. Please hear our prayer. Fill us with Your presence."*

We pray the **prayer of confession**, acknowledging our sin and expressing thanks for the way God pours out His grace through forgiveness.

The **pastoral prayer** is an intercessory prayer for others. During the worship service, this time is precious to pastors who, for a few moments, bring the needs of the people before the God of heaven who is in our midst.

The **offertory prayer** praises God as the source of all we have and expresses our gratitude for the way He lovingly provides for our needs. This prayer also seeks God's help—that we might respond to His grace through cheerful and generous giving, becoming partners with Him through our money and our lives to spread the Gospel of Jesus Christ. Giving of our offerings can be a time of joyful participation in the great plan of God for the spread of His Kingdom. Our money is only a reflection of what we have. Our willingness to gladly share our wealth to further God's work is a reflection of who we are. When we joyfully and generously give in a spirit of worship, it is as though we write the word "myself" on a slip of paper and place it in the offering plate when it goes by.

The **benediction** is a glad moment in worship. The word means a "good saying," a blessing of God upon us, followed by our going out to serve Him in response to His call.

Not all services will have all these prayers but these are the markers that guide us along the path of sincere devotion to God in corporate worship. When these prayers are thoughtfully prepared and earnestly prayed, not only does God respond, but the congregation is caught up in the spirit of prayer as well.

I experienced a poignant and life-deepening moment in worship as a missionary to South Africa gave her testimony during a service in our church. She told of a young man who had come to seek work in the city where she was assigned. The young man began to attend the Bible study for young adults sponsored by the mission, and after a while he committed his life to Jesus Christ.

Because he had made a sincere profession of faith in Christ, the missionary thought he would begin to attend the Sunday morning worship services regularly. But he didn't. After a few weeks of expecting him to show up, she asked, "Why are you not here on Sunday for worship?" He said, "I must go on weekends to visit my family in the village. I am trying to explain to them about Jesus."

Some time later she noticed bruises on the young man's arms and face and asked him if anything was wrong. He answered, "When I go to see my family, they curse me and beat me because they believe I am bringing evil on the family since I can't pray to the old gods anymore. Even my grandmother, as well as my brothers, sisters, mother and father, throw rocks at me." The missionary was horrified and exclaimed, "Well then, you must not go to see them anymore . . .you need to be with your new family in worship on Sundays."

To that, the young man answered, "But I have to go! I am the only Christian in my family. If I don't tell them about Jesus, how will they ever learn?" The missionary concluded: "That brave young man revealed a stinging truth to us. We can get so comfortable worshipping in our own church that we forget how important it is to take the good news of Jesus Christ to those who will never know unless we go to tell them."

As the truth of that story pierced our hearts, an oboe began to play a haunting melody, wafting like a fragrance across the congregation: "Take the name of Jesus with you . . ." Then the congregation picked up the song:

> *Take the name of Jesus with you,*
> *Child of sorrow, child of woe;*
> *It will joy and comfort give you,*
> *Take it then where'er you go.*
> *Precious name, O how sweet,*
> *Hope of earth and joy of heaven;*
> *Precious name, O how sweet,*
> *Hope of earth and joy of heaven.*

In that moment I was weak in the knees with a new sense of the price some pay to take the name of Jesus to others. And shivering with a renewed determination to help our church be a people who take His name everywhere we go, I prayed, "Oh God, here is my life, here is my ministry, fully committed to taking Jesus' name to everyone!"

Others that morning were touched in the same way and told me later how much the service had meant to them. Worship experiences such as that make Jesus more precious, God's will more delightful, people's needs more real, and the hearts of worshippers more malleable to the leading of God's Holy Spirit.

⌘

WORSHIP PREFERENCES AND PRACTICES

So often our ideas about what makes corporate worship meaningful are determined by our experiences of worship as we grew up. We develop attitudes about what is appropriate and styles of expression in which we feel comfortable.

It might amaze you to learn that 300 years ago Baptist churches would not have allowed a piano, organ, or orchestra in their worship service. In fact, they were not interested in hymn singing either. A tradition had taken hold in the early part of the Reformation in which hymn singing was forbidden. Singing a song written by a contemporary composer was considered unnecessary, disrespectful and irreligious.

In 1691, Benjamin Keach, pastor of the Horsley Down Baptist Church in London, published a hymnbook entitled *Spiritual Melody*, containing nearly three hundred sacred hymns. Very few Baptist churches were ready to sing the songs in his hymnbook. He wrote several papers stating his belief that opposition to congregational singing was hurting the growth of Baptist churches. In part, Keach said:

'Tis a hard case that any Christian should object against that duty which Christ and his Apostles, and the saints in all ages in their public assemblies were found in the practice of it; but 'tis no easy thing to break people of a mistaken notion, and an old prejudice taken up against a precious truth of Christ. The Lord will, I hope, satisfy all his people about this heavenly ordinance in due time, and they shall not call it a carnal nor a formal thing anymore.

It was through Keach's visionary espousal of congregational singing that Baptist churches have become fervently committed to singing the gospel into the hearts of saints and sinners alike.

Worship style has always been a matter of debate because the way we personally view worship is very similar to the way we view art. Our response is a matter of taste. We can go to an art exhibition and see a painting we think is absolutely wonderful, then talk to someone else who can't understand what we like about it. Or, we can go to the theater and thoroughly enjoy a play, only to read later that the critics panned the production.

In regard to worship, most people know what they like and know what elements produce a positive response in them, but they have a difficult time describing their experience. Responses to unfamiliar forms of worship are highly individual and are often heavily affected by the emotional state we are in when we enter into worship.

Sometimes when we talk about worship and try to explain what we feel, it is a bit like attempting to grab hold of a butterfly instead of just admiring it as it flutters in the sunshine. If we try to capture, analyze, and explain our worship experience, suddenly the joy, beauty, and life are lost.

Occasionally, we may experience wonderfully serendipitous moments when the atmosphere, emotion, and circumstances are just right to catch us up in worship when we least expect it. However, worship experiences do not usually just happen. Effective, meaningful worship services most often are the result of careful planning by those leaders who are sensitive to the needs, experiences, and tastes of those in the congregation.

Even among churches of the same denomination, there are a variety of worship styles. If you have been a member of more than one church, you may have noticed that each church seems to have "their way" of worshipping. Churches tend to gravitate toward the style that seems most effective or comfortable for them. The danger comes when a church begins to think that their way is the only right way.

A pastor friend of mine said to me years ago, *"It is not given to any preacher to ring every person's bell."* The same can be said of the worship services we plan. Not any one style will meet every person's need. That is a principle of life. God must have intended it that way. I believe God loves and encourages variety and diversity. He made all different kinds of flowers, trees, and animals—and He made every one of us unique individuals.

The Difference between Taste, Quality and Style

We often mix up the terms *taste, quality*, and *style*. These words are often used interchangeably but they are really quite different.

♦ **Taste** is a matter of what we like or don't like. It is purely personal preference.

♦ **Quality** is a subjective evaluation, although it may not be as subjective as we might think.
Quality has much to do with how well something is performed or executed. Even if something doesn't suit our taste, we still recognize whether it is done well or not.

♦ **Style** defines the historical period, tradition, or methodology on which the music or worship form is based.
Style has nothing to do with qualitative, personal evaluation or judgment. It is simply a category that classifies.

Let's take a look at these three elements which seem to cause much concern in the area of corporate worship.

Taste in Worship
If we let ourselves get too narrowly defined in what we are exposed to, or participate in, we will cut ourselves off from all the variety of worship forms that are available in our wonderful world.

Learning to appreciate new worship forms is not unlike children learning to eat new foods they have never before been served. It may take several exposures before there is a willingness to try something new. And it may take a while to develop a taste.

Tastes in foods often change over the years. The same is true of our personal taste in worship forms.

Our personal preferences change over the years, so we should be able to appreciate that others' personal preferences differ from ours. A church is like a family, made up of different people with different tastes at different stages of their lives.

Quality in Worship

Anything we offer to God ought to be the best we have to give. Careless efforts offend sensitive people and distract from the focus on God in worship. Quality of presentation and carefulness of execution is a reflection of the devotion and reverence we show toward God and the respect we have for the experience of our fellow worshippers.

There is a place in congregational worship for the offerings of members of the family of God who are not as skilled as we might like. The sincerity of their effort and their willingness to share of themselves can elicit appreciation from the congregation and succeed in helping people worship. When this happens, certainly God is pleased. But this needs to be carefully monitored lest it become an excuse for poor, unprepared offerings of praise.

Styles of Worship

Because of the personal nature of worship and the infinite variations in the way worship is carried out in congregations, it is difficult to classify specific worship styles. However, many observers of contemporary worship in American evangelical churches agree that there are five broad categories of worship style under which most churches fall: liturgical, traditional, revivalist, praise and worship, and seeker. It may be helpful to evaluate where your congregation fits in these categories so you become aware of and appreciate the differences between your church and that of other Christian brothers and sisters.

Liturgical Worship Style - Liturgical worship styles are characteristically formal, solemn and majestic. The services are altar- and pulpit-oriented, often with robed clergy and the use of processionals and recessionals. The music is usually provided by a pipe organ with a choir singing traditional hymns and classical anthems. The vocal music is almost exclusively choral arrangements with very few solo presentations. Participation of the congregation is limited to the singing of standard hymns and reading responsively from Scripture or prepared litanies.

The purpose of the liturgical style is to lead the church in giving corporate recognition to the transcendent glory of God. The greatness of God is the focus. A biblical model for the liturgical style is

Isaiah 6 in which the prophet is described as coming into the presence of the glory of God. He bows in reverence, repentant for his sins, and waits upon the Lord as a willing servant. The liturgical model has guided Christian worship in many churches for centuries.

Traditional Worship Style - Traditional style creates a mood of subdued and orderly worship that is both majestic and contemplative. The sanctuary is seen as a place for gathering the family of faith and for reverent response in the order of worship. Biblically-based preaching is often thematic and inspirational. Organ and piano provide music with an emphasis on traditional gospel hymns and contemporary anthems sung by a robed choir from hymnals. Vocal solos are common.

The purpose of the traditional worship service is to lead the congregation into spiritual reflection, to praise God and thank Him for His goodness, to be thankfully aware of the rest of the Body of Christ gathered as a congregation, and to hear God speak through the Scripture and the preached word. A scriptural model is from Colossians:

Let the word of Christ dwell in you richly as you teach and admonish one another with all wisdom, and as you sing psalms, hymns and spiritual songs with gratitude in your hearts to God. *(Colossians 3:16)*

Revivalist Worship Style - The revivalist worship style is exuberant, celebrative and informal. The purpose is to save the lost and encourage believers to witness. Preaching is central and focuses on evangelism and recommitment to discipleship. Congregational singing plays a significant role. The emphasis is on hymns, especially gospel songs testifying to God's saving power in the individual's life. Choral and solo music also have a prominent place in the worship format. Solo music is often a highly personal testimony to what God has done in a life.

A biblical model for the revivalist style is based on the day of Pentecost described in Acts 2:1-41. In this rich passage, the descending of the Holy Spirit is followed by personal testimony, an evangelistic sermon, and a direct urging of the people to repent and be baptized.

Praise and Worship Style - The mood of this worship style is expressive, celebrative, contemporary and informal while praising God through the singing of Scripture-based songs. Contemporary, by definition, means this style will change at a rapid pace as worship leaders seek to provide meaningful experiences for people who no longer are comfortable in traditional cultural patterns.

It is popular to project the lyrics of choruses on a screen or wall using a projector instead of using hymnbooks. The Scripture songs contain many references to "I" and "me," creating a very personalized approach to worship. Many of the songs are praise and adoration addressed directly to God. Electronic keyboard synthesizers, guitars, and drums are popular along with several singers who make up a "worship band" or "praise team."

The "praise and worship" musical sound is similar to what worshippers hear daily on the popular music radio shows. It is the vernacular—what worshippers are most comfortable hearing. The solo voice or close harmony of a few singers is preferred over choral works. Music is usually played in major keys. Participants in the service respond best to music with an upbeat tempo, and the style is very personal and informal.

It's interesting that many people who prefer the praise and worship style of music may be reacting against what we know as "gospel songs" which have been included in evangelical hymnbooks. Yet when gospel songs were first introduced, one of the big differences between them and the traditional hymns was the use of "I" and "me" in the lyrics. Gospel songs, like praise and worship choruses, use the personal pronouns in expressions of feeling toward God or personal expressions of faith. A biblical model for the praise and worship style is Psalm 150:

Praise the Lord.
Praise God in his sanctuary.
Praise him in his mighty heavens,
Praise him for his acts of power,
    praise him for his surpassing greatness,
Praise him with the sounding of the trumpet,

praise him with the harp and lyre,
praise him with tambourine and dancing,
praise him with strings and flute,
praise him with the crash of cymbals.
Let everything that has breath praise the Lord.
(Psalm 150)

Seeker Style - The "seeker church" is the name commonly applied to churches whose focus is on people who have not grown up in the church and have no past tradition about what worship is or should be. The worship service in these churches is often scheduled for a time other than on Sunday when believers gather to be taught through expository preaching. In the seeker service, religious symbols and terms are minimized. The purpose is to present practical help in meeting life's problems: family issues, personal choices, business ethics, how to develop one's personal life in a meaningful and mature manner. Biblical principles are taught, Scripture is introduced, and the way of Christ is shown to be reasonable, practical, and meaningful.

Seeker churches attempt to present the Gospel in clear terms through contemporary forms that will not "put people off" with old or unfamiliar traditions. Worship centers in seeker churches usually are more like auditoriums than sanctuaries. Theological or ecclesiastical language is kept to a minimum, even to the point of de-emphasizing any denominational names or affiliation. Sermons focus primarily on praise, thanksgiving, and inspiration. Worship services in seeker churches are usually very friendly and encourage a "come as you are" attitude toward dress.

Blended Worship Style - A sixth category, made up of elements from the other five, might also be added. The blended worship style utilizes a combination of forms, like walking through a flowering garden and selecting blossoms along the way that can be gathered into the most attractive and fragrant bouquet to serve the church's purpose. A blended service might include a high church processional mixed with hymns sung from a hymnal, contemporary choruses and Scripture songs, choral anthems, and instrumental music all woven together in an eclectic format to accentuate a biblical sermon.

Blended worship is open to innovation and choice of forms. It's like a streetcar with lots of handles to hold on to as you ride. Each church creates its own unique ways of worship. This blended style is what most characterizes worship at First Baptist Church, Arlington, a

> **Blended worship is open to innovation and choice of forms. It's like a streetcar with lots of handles to hold on to as you ride.**

big church with a broad spectrum of backgrounds and tastes among those in the congregation. Every person can't be pleased every time, but the worship team thoughtfully and prayerfully puts together a mixture of worship elements that will stir a broad cross section of people.

At First Baptist, Arlington, Sunday morning services are more traditional, although choruses and dramatic vignettes are mixed in to create a more informal mood and to involve the congregation in the worship themes. An orchestra is utilized with frequent solos and vocal ensembles to supplement both classical and contemporary anthems sung by the choir.

Sunday evenings are much more informal, both in dress and presentation. Those services might vary to include old-fashioned gospel singing, contemporary choruses accompanied by a band, dramatic presentations, musical concerts and sermon dialogues.

I have always been moved by worship services when the choir enters the sanctuary joyously singing with steady and strong-measured stride. They make the words of Psalm 100 come alive for me: *"entering His gates with thanksgiving and His courts with praise"*. As they process down the aisle, I ride their song. My spirit takes flight. This worship element is not used often enough for me.

Music must be special to God because the Bible is full of references to music—the playing of instruments, dancing and singing. Our response to mediums of expression such as music, drama, poetry and

> **Music touches a part of the human soul that moves us to deeper levels of worship and spiritual devotion.**

the visual arts transcends our ability to describe how they move us emotionally. Music, perhaps more than any other medium, touches a part of the human soul that moves us to deeper levels of worship and spiritual devotion. Music involves us. It has emotional power and allows us to release energy. Music can make us laugh or cry. It can inspire and motivate us. It can even change our heartbeat and metabolism. Music is something we can all do together. It can unite us as a worshipping congregation, link us across denominational lines and even give us a sense of connection with our history. Using music literature that lasts from generation to generation gives us the ability to identify with the worship experiences of our grandparents.

The majesty of sacred hymns and the pageantry of the processional are only two expressions of worship that lift me. I can be as deeply moved by the quiet sharing of personal testimonies in a small group, the burden-bearing for fellow Christians through prayer, or even the hilarious fun of singing choruses with hand movements at Vacation Bible School or youth camp. The depth of meaning of worship is in the honest celebration and involvement of our spirit with a loving and receptive God.

⌘

ACCOUNTABILITY IN WORSHIP

Congregational worship needs to be a participative, reciprocal event in which each person supports the experience others are having. We seek to approach worship with a sense of love and belonging so we can empathize with and encourage each other. That is a Christian principle applicable not only to worship, but to all of life. We need to support each other because we see the worth and value in each individual, and we sincerely respect his desires and tastes.

One of the most destructive things we can do during a worship service is turn to our neighbor and grumble about what we don't like. Doing this can spoil the other person's entire experience because what we don't like may be moving her at a great emotional depth. That very moment may be a time of connection between that person and God in which a real need in their life is being met. When we impose our dislikes on another person, we introduce an element of peer pressure and rob them of an opportunity for personal expression.

God has given us a vast variety of worship elements and styles from which to choose when we are attempting to create formats for meaningful worship experiences. He certainly must desire that we enjoy ourselves, be creative, and stretch to reach new and meaningful levels of expression.

God made us different yet gave us an underlying unity. Surely He delights in any expression of worship if it is done faithfully, according to biblical truth, sincerely, honestly, without guile, and regularly (including every Lord's day).

Style of worship doesn't impress God one way or the other. He looks past worship forms to see into our hearts. In the opinion of Christian writer

> **Style of worship doesn't impress God one way or the other. He looks past worship forms to see into our hearts.**

C. S. Lewis, it makes little difference to God whether the church organist plays Bach or Beethoven or some simple popular chorus. What does matter to God is the spirit in which the music is played and the spirit of the worshippers who receive it. Lewis, an English professor and literary critic, didn't like most of the hymnody of the Anglican Church. He called it fifth-rate poetry. But in a marvelous passage regarding congregational worship, he wrote:

> There are two musical situations on which I think we can be confident that a blessing rests. One is where a priest or an organist, himself a man of trained and delicate taste, humbly and charitably sacrifices his own desires and gives the people humbler and coarser fare than he would wish, in a belief (even as it may be, erroneous belief) that he can thus bring them to God.
>
> The other is where the stupid and unmusical layman humbly and patiently, and above all silently, listens to music which he cannot, or cannot fully, appreciate, in the belief that it somehow glorifies God, and that if it does not edify him this must be his own defect. Neither such a High Brow nor such a Low Brow can be far out of the way. To both, church music will have been a means of grace—not the music they have liked, but the music they have disliked.[1]

One of the real challenges in the church is to raise the accountability of individual worshippers in the congregation as they participate in worship experiences. Members of the Body of Christ should not be passive receivers of something served on a silver platter. Ideally, people come to services as real participants, accountable for being there with a ready spirit, and seeking the mind of Christ. People come reverently and expectantly, asking for God's help, and appreciatively acknowledging the work that has been done in the planning and preparation of the service. What individuals bring in the way of personal preparation for worship will invariably be reflected in what they receive from the worship experience.

> *What individuals bring in the way of personal preparation for worship will invariably be reflected in what they receive from the worship experience.*

⌘

WAYS CHURCHES MISS THE MARK IN WORSHIP

Prayer and worship are inseparably linked because both seek communion with God—a sense of holy presence in which giving and receiving takes place in open and honest intimacy. Our prayers and our worship can miss the mark when we fail to keep communion with God as our singular focus.

Being Careless with our Prayers

- ◆ In our prayers, we sometimes preach sermons, scold the congregation, or try to enlist people in our pet causes.
- ◆ We often fail to give thanks for our blessings and ask for God's help only in time of need.
- ◆ We hastily seek God's forgiveness without being truly repentant or confessing our sins.
- ◆ We don't always pray from the heart, expressing our true feelings.
- ◆ We don't think carefully and prayerfully in advance about the prayers we are asked to lead in corporate worship services. Consequently, our spontaneous prayers can become trite, ritualistic, and without meaning.

Making Worship a Performance

- ◆ We are tempted to rate worship experiences only for the entertainment value of the service.
- ◆ We participate in worship only on an emotional level without being willing to allow our thinking to be challenged.
- ◆ Or, we participate in worship only on an intellectual level without becoming involved emotionally.
- ◆ We value preaching primarily for the preacher's skill of presentation and the music primarily for the quality of its performance.

Worshipping in a Box

- ◆ We negatively define ourselves: "I don't do choruses," or "I don't do Bach." Who we are becomes what we don't do.
- ◆ We define ourselves on the basis of what some other church does that we don't like, rather than on what we are called to do or what moves us to worshipful devotion.

Basing Worship on Likes and Dislikes
- ♦ We base our worship planning as a leader or a participant simply on what we personally like or dislike.
- ♦ We lock on to a familiar or favorite style and are unwilling to be open to any variations that others might propose.
- ♦ We are more concerned about comfort than we are with challenge and calling.

Withdrawing from openness to different worship
- ♦ We vote with our feet—if we don't like something, we just don't show up.
- ♦ We allow matters of taste in music styles or worship formats to become value judgments on others, and we withdraw from Christian fellowship with them.

Dissension over Worship Forms
- ♦ We become judgmental and critical of others for a worship form they choose which we don't like.
- ♦ We argue among ourselves about what to do or not to do and about who should be in charge instead of focusing on meaningful ways to worship God.

Most of us are confident that we know what helps us all to worship God best. In many areas of the country we can choose from a variety of churches and worship opportunities. But if we are in a place with few choices, it is better to attend and worship, asking God to teach us a new thing or to help us see the work of God in other people's lives, rather than to absent ourselves from worship.

> **Satan takes great pleasure when Christians argue, especially over how they should worship God.**

We need fellow Christians, although they may be different, and apparently God believes they need us or He would not have led us to live in that community. We all have something to give and something to receive.

One of Satan's greatest pleasures is corrupting and perverting God's good gifts. We usually can recognize something purely evil. But when a good thing can be corrupted to cause dissension and ill will, Satan catches us unaware, our unity is destroyed, and God's good gifts are used for Satan's purposes. Satan takes great pleasure when Christians argue, especially over how they should worship God.

⌘

CHALLENGES OF WORSHIP LEADERSHIP

God created men and women in infinite variety. Apparently, it is not God's intention that we should all be alike. We come from different cultures, families, and backgrounds. We respond differently, and that is a God-given characteristic of human nature we should celebrate.

There is no room for either elitism or carelessness in worship planning. When we are too quick to say we like or don't like something, we run the danger of invalidating another person's worship experience. At First Baptist Church, Arlington our Minister of Music, Barry Rock, reminds us that for every worship experience we plan—every anthem performed, every song sung, every prayer prayed, every sermon preached—there are at least four different people listening.

♦ The first person absolutely loves it and wishes we'd do it that way every single time.

♦ The second person hates it and thinks doing it that way is an absolute waste of time.

♦ The third person is ambivalent—part of it he got and part he didn't get. He can take it or leave it.

♦ The fourth person is asleep or miles away in a "daydream" and doesn't even know it is happening.

Worship leaders in churches have the role of sorting out the congregation's needs, balancing those findings against their own preferences and motivations, and making decisions on a week-by-week basis to plan worship experiences that will be interesting, inspiring, and developmental.

In a church congregation of any size, there are four-year-olds and ninety-four-year-olds. Hopefully a church's worship ministry will reflect the diversity of its members. Going through a

> *Hopefully, a church's worship ministry will reflect the diversity of its members.*

variety of worship forms over the course of a few Sundays is necessary in order to give all the people something that will touch
them at the level of their needs. People come to rely on that range
of variety and relax in the fact that what is happening in worship is
for the purpose of reaching out to everyone. Churches can choose
to be a church for all people, to embrace diversity and not limit
themselves to a narrow focus of preferred styles or tastes.

Many churches have the opportunity to work with internationals
of multiple language groups, children, youth, college students, single adults, young families, median adults and senior adults. Members of the church are regularly out in the community through their
vocations and through mission activities. I believe the worship
leader's role is to mix and match, blending all kinds of music,
drama, and worship forms to meet the needs of these widely diver-
gent audiences.

We might not be able to sustain all of those people all the time
and it's not reasonable to expect that we will meet every need that
every possible group might have. But we can identify large groups
and their needs, determine what we can do well, and utilize our
strengths to be as effective as we can in leading the Body of Christ
to worship.

If the Body of Christ is healthy, worship will draw us closer to
God, closer to one another, and send us out into the world to make
a difference.

[1] C. S. Lewis, *Christian Reflections*, (Grand Rapids: Erdmans Publishing
Company), 1967

⌘

JESUS PRINCIPLES FOR WORSHIP

⌘ Worship is the first function of the church and is necessary for the health of the Body of Christ.

⌘ In worship, we love God as we love nothing else. God experiences joy when we love and praise Him.

⌘ When we focus on God, we must put aside everything and everyone so that nothing except God can be God.

⌘ Worship confronts us. It causes us to face ourselves honestly, confess our sins, come in repentance before God, and trust in His mercy and forgiveness.

⌘ Worship lifts our hearts with joy and gives us the courage to go on. We respond to God's love by serving Him.

⌘ Congregational worship needs to be a participative, reciprocal event in which we seek the mind of Christ, with each person supporting the experience others are having. We can delight in the variety of worship offerings even as we delight in the many colors and textures of creation.

⌘ Music touches a part of the human soul that moves us to deeper levels of worship and spiritual devotion. The music we offer in worship should flow from our lives as the Spirit of God moves in us and helps us give voice to praise and song.

⌘ Prayer and worship are inseparably linked because both seek communion with God—a sense of holy presence in which giving and receiving take place in open and honest intimacy.

⌘ Preparation and diligence are required for the church to worship God faithfully and fully.

⌘ Worship draws us closer to God, binds us closer to one another, and sends us out into the world to make a difference.

LOVING FATHER IN HEAVEN, CREATOR & SUSTAINER OF THE UNIVERSE:

YOU ARE SO MUCH GREATER THAN WE CAN EVEN IMAGINE. HEAVEN AND EARTH REFLECT YOUR GLORY. EARTH, SEA, AND SKY GIVE WITNESS TO YOUR BLESSED NAME. YOU ARE THE GREAT "I AM." YOU HAVE ALWAYS BEEN, AND WILL FOREVER BE. WE CONFESS YOU AS THE ONLY GOD, THE HOLY ONE WHO REIGNS OVER ALL THERE IS.

WE MARVEL THAT YOU LOOK ON US WITH LOVE, AND SEEK US OUT FOR HOLY FELLOWSHIP. WHO ARE WE, THAT YOU ARE MINDFUL OF US?

WE COME IN REPENTANT CONFESSION OF OUR SINS. LORD, WE ARE THANKFUL FOR THE GIFT OF JESUS CHRIST AND WE PRAISE YOU FOR YOUR LOVING-KINDNESS. THROUGH HIS SACRIFICE WE HAVE BEEN FORGIVEN AND CLEANSED. WE LIFT OUR EYES TO YOU FOR MERCY AND FOR GRACE.

LORD, WE PRAY FOR YOUR PRESENCE IN OUR LIVES. FILL US WITH YOUR HOLY SPIRIT. LIFT US OUT OF SIN. TRANSFORM US WITH YOUR LOVE AND EQUIP US FOR FAITHFUL SERVICE IN YOUR KINGDOM. GRANT US THE GLORY OF YOUR PRESENCE THAT YOUR SPIRIT'S SONG MAY BE SUNG JOYFULLY IN OUR HEARTS THROUGHOUT ETERNITY.

AMEN

Life Application

⌘

WORSHIP
Honoring the First Function of the Church

1. This chapter suggests three requirements for true worship:
   - ♦ Focusing first on God
   - ♦ Honestly facing ourselves
   - ♦ Responding to God's call

   How would you characterize your own ability to fulfill these requirements of worship?

   With which are you most successful?

   Which gives you the most difficulty?

   Where are your greatest obstacles to worship?

2. Among the worship styles described (liturgical, traditional, revivalistic, praise and worship, seeker, blended), which is most comfortable or meaningful for you?

   Describe why you think that style best suits your taste.

3. To what degree do you perceive yourself to be open to participate in worship styles that differ from your own taste?

4. How would you describe your usual worship experience?

   Is it more of a religious ritual or a true meeting with the Holy Spirit of God?

   Take time now to think through and write out a prayer, inviting God to fill your life and your worship experiences with the transforming power of His Holy Spirit.

5. What specific actions could you take to deepen your personal experience of worshipping God?

6. What could you do to improve and deepen the experience of others through congregational worship in your church?

5

EVANGELIZE

Intentionally Reaching Out With the Gospel of Christ

> E·van·gel·ize -
>   Bring good news; proclaim the gospel
> Gos·pel -
>   Good news concerning Christ, the message
>   of God and personal salvation; absolute truth

My father was a Baptist preacher. I literally grew up in the church. One would think with that kind of background, I would have known what the gospel was. During my growing up years in Oklahoma, I heard the word *gospel* used in many different ways. Frankly, some of the ways it was used left me cold.

I've always liked *gospel music*. I enjoy the syncopated beat and the personal and intimate nature of the lyrics. In many churches when I was growing up, there would be all-day gospel singing on the fifth Sunday of the month. Those were the heydays of old time gospel quartets. But the offstage attitude and private conversation of the members of these groups were not always consistent with what they sang before the crowds.

I also knew preachers who called themselves "gospel preachers." The only thing I could figure out about a gospel preacher was that he was a screamer who didn't have a lot to say unless he loudly repeated himself, beat the pulpit and waved his Bible in the air. I figured those gospel preachers marked their sermon notes with "loud" and "louder" sections. To me, gospel preaching was a matter of style. Those experiences left me with a negative impression of the word *gospel*.

When I felt God's call to vocational ministry as a teenager, I wasn't very excited about being labeled a "gospel preacher." I believed the gospel was the good news of Christ, but I didn't want *gospel* to be the title assigned to my occupation. I wanted to be a preacher, a Bible preacher, but not a *gospel* preacher.

WHAT IS THE REAL GOSPEL?

My attitude about the word *gospel* stayed with me for several years. It wasn't until I was in seminary that I realized what the gospel really is about. Those were some of the most important days of my life. In the seminary classroom, my professor of preaching outlined for us what the gospel is and what it is not.

The gospel is not:
- ♦ Every word that comes out of the preacher's mouth.
- ♦ A style or way of saying something.
- ♦ A unique type of music.
- ♦ Found in the Old Testament, except for a foretaste in the writings of the prophets.

The gospel is:
- ♦ A definitive word about the heart of the Christian faith.
- ♦ What the earliest preachers preached as recorded in the New Testament.

Elements of the Gospel

I still have my classroom notes from the session in which my professor described the gospel. He said it is defined by what the Apostles actually said when they sought to proclaim the "good news" to a lost and desperate world. The gospel is made up of at least these eight elements:

- ♦ **Good News Foretold:** The revelation by Old Testament prophets that God would send a Messiah, a personal representative of His grace *(Acts 2:16-21; 3:12-13)*.

- ♦ **Fulfillment of Prophecy:** As described in the New Testament, Jesus, the Son of God, the Messiah, came to earth to live and work among us *(Acts 2:22, 25-31; 3:18, 22-26)*.

- ♦ **Jesus' Death for Our Sins:** Jesus took upon Himself the guilt for the sins of all humankind so that through our faith in Him we are able to stand before God, free of the stain of sin *(Acts 2:23; 3:15)*.

◆ **Jesus' Resurrection from the Dead:** God conquered sin and death by raising Jesus from the dead. Through faith in Jesus, we have the promise of eternal life *(Acts 2:24-32; 3:15)*.

◆ **Presence of the Holy Spirit:** When Jesus ascended into heaven, God sent His Holy Spirit to live among us. The Holy Spirit comforts, sustains and equips us to do the work of Christ in the world *(Acts 2:33-36, 38; 3:19)*.

◆ **Call to Repentance:** We all are guilty before God. Men and women must repent of their sins to come into new relationship with God *(Acts 2:37-39; 3:19)*.

◆ **Forgiveness of Sins:** God forgives the repentant sinner. Through Jesus, our guilt is removed and we are saved. God makes us His children. He accepts us into His family *(Acts 2:38; 3:19)*.

◆ **God's Ultimate Victory:** God is coming again in Jesus Christ to gather all His children home *(Acts 2:33; 3:21)*.

As I heard my professor line out the elements of the gospel, my heart swelled within me. The proclamation of good news about Jesus Christ is what my ministry is all about. Sharing the good news with men and women, boys and girls, is my life's commitment—wherever I go and whenever I have the opportunity.

That very day after class, I rented a trailer to move some household goods. On the rental agreement form, there was a blank asking for "occupation." For the first time in my life, I realized what it meant to describe myself as a **"Minister of the Gospel."**

Today if you asked me *what I do,* I would tell you I serve as Executive Director of the Baptist General Convention of Texas. But *who I am* is a minister of the gospel of the Lord Jesus Christ. I am a gospel minister. It is my task to tell what I have been given to tell. Jesus is God's Son, God's great and good gift of Himself to the world. Believe in Him, turn from sin, and the One who has died for us and has been raised up for us will save us now and forever.

That conviction truly defines the core purpose of my existence. That sense of who I am contributes to decisions I made as pastor every day and now as denominational leader, husband, father, grandfather, co-worker, teacher, friend, counselor, and neighbor.

⌘

INTENTIONAL OUTREACH ISN'T EASY

As a church leader, I believe it is important for each member of the Body of Christ to have a strong sense of who he or she is in Christ in order to really represent Christ in this world. Waiting for the paid staff of a church to make all the decisions and act on them is passive admission by the members of the Body that they don't sense their responsibility to share the gospel.

One of the essential functions of a church is **intentional outreach**, reaching out *on purpose* because people need God. Years ago, while I was serving as pastor in Alex, Oklahoma, there was an old man in the town who was dying. Every preacher of every denomination in Alex tried to explain the gospel of Christ to this man, but his heart was hardened to hearing the good news.

As a young pastor I knew it was my responsibility to talk to people about their relationship with God. Most of the time I had not found it difficult to answer people's questions and explain the gospel. I often had the joy of helping them to receive Christ as their Savior. But as I began meeting with this man, I realized how ill prepared I was. He had participated in numerous discussions with many preachers, and he remained unconvinced of the merits of the gospel and uncommitted to Christ.

I was attending Southwestern Baptist Theological Seminary in Fort Worth, Texas, at the time and was taking a personal evangelism course taught by Dr. Ken Chafin. I probably have never paid as close attention in a class as I did that semester. I was focused on finding every possible idea that would help me understand that man and successfully explain the good news. Chafin taught us how important it is to listen carefully to people—to be their friend and build a relationship out of which comes an honest and personal witness to Christ.

I would attend this class on Tuesdays and Thursdays, listening to every word from Dr. Chafin and reflecting on its meaning. Then

I would go home to Oklahoma on the train late on Thursday nights and visit with my elderly friend two or three times over the weekend. For many weeks there seemed to be little progress made. But he seemed happy to see me and wanted me to come back, so I kept going to visit him.

One spring afternoon, the window was open in the front room where he sat most of the time. The grass outside was showing green. Trees were beginning to bud and birds were singing. I explained to him once more that faith is what saves us. Salvation is not achieved through anything we can do, not even baptism. Salvation is a free gift from God when we trust Him to love and save us, and when we repentantly open our lives to receive the forgiveness of our sins through Jesus Christ.

Finally, he got the idea—he broke through a lifetime of confusion and misunderstanding that he somehow was responsible for earning his own salvation by what he was able to do. He finally understood that God doesn't want to trip us up. God knows everything about us and He is a gracious, loving, and forgiving God who wants all of us to be saved.

My friend prayed with me that afternoon and gave his life to Christ. He was dying and one of his questions was about baptism. His family had taught that one had to be baptized to be saved. I explained again that baptism was not necessary to be saved, but if he could be, it was right to be baptized because Jesus expected all His followers to be baptized *(Matthew 28:18-20)*. He indicated he would like to be baptized, so we made plans for the following Sunday.

That week at seminary, I received a phone call telling me my friend had died. When I went back home to visit with his family, they said he had left a message for me before he died. He wanted me to know that I wouldn't be able to baptize him on Sunday—but all was well. He would like to have been baptized, but he wasn't trusting that act to save him.

In the years since, I have often thought about that experience. Prior to taking that seminary evangelism class I had almost given up on the idea of persistent, persuasive, personal evangelism. But accompanied by the element of building friendships and relationships, the idea of intentional outreach takes on an entirely new meaning.

Our Heart's Desire

In Romans, the apostle Paul bares his heart as he speaks of his deep passion for his brothers and sisters in his own community, the children of Israel. He yearned for them to come to know God through Jesus Christ.

> . . . *my heart's desire and prayer to God for the Israel-ites is that they may be saved.* (Romans 10:1)

If you were to express to someone your heart's desire, what would it be—not one desire among many, but your deepest desire? Paul is saying his deepest desire is for those who know about God to come to know Him fully in Jesus Christ.

> *I can testify about them that they are zealous for God, but their zeal is not based on knowledge.* (Romans 10:2)

Many people have a great desire to know God, but their zeal is off center. They are not focused. Before Paul's conversion, he exemplified great zeal for God. He was religious to a fault. After his encounter with Jesus, he came to understand what misdirected zeal is about.

> *Since they did not know the righteousness that comes from God and sought to establish their own, they did not submit to God's righteousness. Christ is the end of the law so that there might be righteousness for everyone who believes.* (Romans 10:3)

People who are self-righteous think the way to be right with God is to do good works and to create a righteous appearance in their life. That way God can look at them and say, "My, aren't you good. You are acceptable to me because you are so righteous in yourself." Some people think righteousness is earned and they give themselves to good works. Then when they fail, make a mistake, or get off target, they feel condemned by their sin and their obvious lack of righteousness.

> *Moses describes in this way the righteousness that is by the law: "The man who does these things will live by them."*

But the righteousness that is by faith says, "Do not say in your heart, 'Who will ascend into heaven?' " (that is, to bring Christ down) "or 'Who will descend into the deep?' " (that is, to bring Christ up from the dead). But what does it say? "The word is near you; it is in your mouth and in your heart," that is, the word of faith we are proclaiming: That if you confess with your mouth "Jesus is Lord", and believe in your heart that God raised Him from the dead, you will be saved. (Romans 10:5-9)

We are not saved by fulfilling all of the lists of the law—the righteousness we can create in our flesh. Moses said if that's the way we are going to live our life, then we have to keep the whole law. If we make one mistake and fail in even one way, we are a total sinner and a total failure.

We cannot earn salvation by keeping the law because no one keeps it fully. If we miss in one part, we miss the whole. That was the burden Paul had for his people. They were moral. They were godly. They sought to justify themselves before God through their works related to the law. Now Paul is saying that the righteousness that comes to us by faith, not by works, is a faith that believes God has come to us offering salvation. We don't have to go get Him. He has come to us. We don't have to go dig Him up. He has won the victory for us by rising in triumph from the grave. In faith we receive Him. If we will confess "Jesus is Lord" and believe in our heart God has raised Jesus from the dead, God will save us.

For it is with your heart that you believe and are justified, and it is with your mouth that you confess and are saved. As the Scripture says, "Anyone who trusts in him will never be put to shame." For there is no difference between Jew and Gentile—the same Lord is Lord of all, and richly blesses all who call on him, for everyone who calls on the name of the Lord will be saved. (Romans 10:10-13)

We cry out in faith, "Lord, save us!" And He does.

How then can they call on the one they have not believed in? And how can they believe in the one of whom they have not heard? And how can they hear without someone preach-

ing to them? And how can they preach unless they are sent? As it is written, "How beautiful are the feet of those who bring good news!"   *(Romans 10:14-15)*

The people Paul was writing to were searching for God. They needed and wanted God. Sometimes they thought they really knew God, but there was still a deep disquiet in their hearts. The children of Israel believed they would be made worthy to be saved by their good works in obedience to the Old Testament law, so they had to work and work and never stop working. They never knew for sure if they had worked enough. They kept score on themselves and each other, and they were constantly afraid of what might happen if they messed up. They had no lasting joy or confidence in God. They felt stressed and lost.

Many people raised in a Christian tradition feel the same way because they have not yet grasped the marvelous gospel truth revealed through the writings of Paul.

For it is by grace you have been saved, through faith— and this not from yourselves, it is the gift of God, not by works, so that no one can boast.   *(Ephesians 2:8-9)*

⌘

EVERYONE HAS A GOD-SHAPED EMPTINESS

All people have an empty place in their hearts placed there by God. As Augustine said, ***"The emptiness in us is God-shaped."*** Until God fills the emptiness in our hearts with Himself, we are restless and unfulfilled. It is no accident that we find rest and peace only in Him. The Christian knows that finding Jesus is to find the reason for living. God intended it that way. He wants us to love Him. He wants for there to be a place in our life where He can connect with us—so there is this place at the heart of our life that needs God.

Many members of the church come to Christ as children. At the very first indication in their heart that they are separated from God by their sin and alone in the world, they reach out in faith. Someone loves them enough to tell them about God and they are saved.

For those of us who have been Christians and have lived in the confidence of God's love, mercy, grace and forgiveness from childhood, it is

> **The Christian knows that finding Jesus is to find the reason for living.**

very difficult to understand how helpless many adults feel who are alienated, alone, hopeless, afraid and angry.

Hurting people seek after God even when they don't know who to seek. After futile attempts to grab on to the nearest divine possibility, they become discouraged because all the gods of this world are idols and the answers people give don't satisfy for very long. So they continue seeking.

Attempts to Fill the Emptiness

The Christian understands that life is at its best when living in Christ. The world does not understand this and spends billions of dollars each year trying to convince the rest of us what things in life to embrace. That which they say will make us popular, smell good, feel good, and look good has no lasting relationship to a happy and fulfilled life. "Having it made" in this life is a misnomer.

People who do not know God fill their lives with any substitute they can latch onto, hoping it will fill the emptiness and mute the pain. People go after money, lovers, exotic vacations, intellectual ideas, popular psychology, social causes, artistic expression, alternative lifestyles, gang involvement, drugs, or high-risk behavior. Or they may pursue spiritual fads such as cosmic mysteries, channeling, UFOs, fortune telling, yoga, mind control, or the telephone psychic hotlines, to name a few.

The so-called New Age movement has captured tens of thousands of adherents. That tells us there is a hunger in people. If God is not filling their emptiness, people will seek after alternatives, perhaps trying out a lifelong series of options, only to discover that none fills their emptiness. Each failed attempt brings them back to the beginning. Then another god is temporarily fashioned out of the materials at hand. Worship at that new altar may satisfy for a while, but sooner or later the ever-present emptiness reasserts its lonely pain.

Success as a Substitute for God

Success is a false god that many people search for to fill the emptiness. Bob Buford in Tyler, Texas, made millions of dollars by getting in on the ground floor of the cable television industry. After making huge sums of money, he came to a crisis in his middle life. Out of it, he wrote a book called *Half-time: Changing Your Gameplan from Success to Significance.*[1]

Buford perceives life for many people to be divided into two parts. The first part is that early time in life when we work to make money, make our mark, and become successful.

Having achieved success, we go into a half-time transition in which we may enjoy the financial fruits of our labor, but we begin to realize there must be more to life than money. It's hard to convince younger people of that, and those of us who haven't made a lot of money have a difficult time believing that anybody who has millions of dollars does not find it satisfying.

Buford says that by the time we get into our middle forties, most of us have begun to figure out that money is not where it's at, even if we have not made as much money as we wanted. We may enjoy success, but we really seek significance. We want our lives to make a difference. We want to have meaning and purpose. We want what we are doing to be in line with our values and principles. We don't just want people to tell us that we are a success; we want to feel significant. Then we will spend the rest of our lives acting on those values we have learned to define and pursuing a course of life that has real meaning.

Work as a Substitute for God

There is a cultural emptiness pervasive in Japan today, emptiness in the hearts of many Japanese people. The word *otaku* describes a young person in Japan who is obsessed with personal performance to the point of being asocial—almost communally autistic or veritably isolated.

Otaku describes a whole generation of children for whom family life barely exists. Fathers are always at work. Children are at cram school preparing for the next exam. Social relationships are minimized. The father often works so hard because he remembers the desperation and deprivation in Japan just after World War II.

He believes only money and success can take away that pain. The child goes along with it because society says he must.

Sometimes this self-perpetuating system seems to work, turning out efficient, next generation, salaried men. But when some of these children reach adulthood, they begin to ask questions for which their narrow training provides no an-

> **We don't get to life abundant by trying to create it with our own hands.**

swers. The Japanese word for them is *majemin*, translated as "earnest". A recent *Time* magazine article concluded they are in search of meaning but unequipped with the tools to discern it. They seem to latch on to any world vision they are offered. Once attracted, they pursue their new faith with the stupendous energy of the lost.

That last idea haunts me. When people have lost their way, they do not know God in their life. They have an empty place and a deep hunger to fill it. They are incomplete in the deep caverns of their soul and they know no peace. They search for God with stupendous energy. That energy, unguided, may lead them into paths of destruction.

Jesus says, *"I am the way and the truth and the life. No one comes to the Father except through me" (John 14:6).* We don't get to life abundant in this world or in the next trying to create it with our own hands, or latching onto it greedily after we have shaped it in our own image. God made us to be like Him. We do not need to manufacture other gods that look like us.

Cult Involvement as a Substitute for God

Seeking to fill the emptiness, some people move toward cultic authorities like David Koresh in Waco or Jim Jones in Guyana. Many cults grow out of faulty views of Christianity, Hinduism, Buddhism or other beliefs. Cults focus themselves on a little piece of the truth and then cover it with misdirected answers and energy. A cult is a religious group that exhibits an essential difference in belief or practice from the parent faith of which it claims to be a part.

In the Christian faith, a cult is a group that calls itself Christian but deviates in its theology and practice from Biblical doctrines that are accepted by orthodox, traditional Christianity. Some of these groups are focused on the end of the world. Other cults em-

phasize human potential and the importance of the mind in religion. One thing all cults have in common is that they stand apart
from orthodox Christianity. They do not view Jesus as the unique
Son of God, fully God, fully man, who died for our sins and arose
in power that all who believe in Him can be saved. Biblical faith
teaches that we need no extra revelation beyond Jesus Christ to be
made fully right with God. Jesus is the ultimate and final revelation
from God and the Bible is the superlative witness to Jesus Christ.

> **Churches should identify
> and critique cults.
> But it is also important to
> understand why people are
> attracted to cults.**

Churches should identify and cri-
tique cults. But it is also important
to understand why people are attracted to cults. People are drawn to
cults because they need somewhere
to connect, somewhere to get an-
swers, someone with authority who can tell them what to do. Cults
offer simple answers to life's difficult questions. They involve
people in time-consuming activities, helping people gain a feeling
of importance. People are warmly received and feel a strong sense
of belonging.

All people have that God-shaped emptiness in their lives.
Through organized outreach, cults appear to provide the answers to
the emptiness. Hurting and seeking people respond to others who
pay attention to them and meet their needs. The members of the
Body of Christ can choose to extend themselves to those same
people in the community, or the church can sit back and let other
groups provide the influence and the "answers."

The True Meaning of a Fulfilled Life

The Gospel teaches us not to count on our earthly success to
form the meaning of our lives. The meaning of life comes from the
significance God places on us because He loves us. He sees us as
persons of worth.

> **God believes in us before
> we know how to believe
> in ourselves.**

Our lives take on significance
when we begin to understand the truth
of how much God values us and when
we learn how significant it is to serve
God as the Body of Christ. God be-

lieves in us before we know how to believe in ourselves. We begin to fill that empty shape in our lives with the imprint of Jesus, His principles, His love, His courage and His commitment.

Sometimes even churches start out doing what they believe they have to do to be "successful." They spend a great deal of their energy on implementing the latest "growth programs" and on raising the funding to be able to do them. By outward appearances they may appear successful, with fine buildings and comfortable congregations. But somewhere along the way, churches may reach a half-time transition in their lives, trying to decide whether their "success" really equates to significance.

> **Churches may need to decide whether their "success" equates to significance.**

Are the people coming into your church really experiencing transformation in their lives? Is the community really being impacted for good by their ministry? Is the church really reflecting the character of Jesus?

⌘

GOD REACHED OUT INTENTIONALLY
AND SO SHOULD WE

God has come to us intentionally and sacrificially. He changes lives in a powerful way. His gift is for anyone—Jew or Gentile, male or female, slave or free. It doesn't make any difference who we are or from where we come. The gospel is for everyone.

One of the main functions of a church is to reach out intentionally to people. God's church is not content to build a building and passively wait for people to show up, or to announce the services on a sign and hope people will come. Church is about intentional outreach—not occasional, not seasonal, not accidental, but regular, year-round and on purpose.

God's people get outside the walls intentionally—reaching out to others, inviting people to meet Christ. That means we intend to touch others. We plan how to reach others. We don't just think and talk about it, we step out and go into the community, inviting and encouraging people to join us. The church is not neutral about this. We care about sharing the good news of God's grace. Furthermore, we care enough about introducing people to God's love that we help people find God whether or not they ever come inside one of our buildings.

> *Church is about intentional outreach—not occasional, not seasonal, not accidental, but regular, year-round and on purpose.*

One of the most consistent ways First Baptist, Arlington has been able to reach out beyond the walls of the church is through a ministry called *Mission Arlington*. (More about this mission outreach in Chapter 7.) The church realized there were many people in Arlington who needed Christ but would never get out of their community or comfort zone to find a church where they could be discipled. So, we decided to take the church to the people where they live.

Mission Arlington began by starting Bible studies and worship services for people who live in apartments, mobile home parks, and the old "weekly" motels across the city. As Tillie Burgin, director of Mission Arlington says, *"We hover around John 3:16 and hang out on the property"* through the week. Volunteer Ministry Teams make these Bible study groups their place of evangelism and ministry. They get acquainted and then get involved in the lives of people they never would have met in the ordinary traffic patterns of their lives.

Mission Arlington intentionally goes to places where people have human needs, with volunteers giving of themselves and giving the gospel we have been trusted to share. People's lives have been changed. With all the things we have to share, like food, clothing, furniture and household goods, dental and medical help, day care, safe shelter, transportation and employment counseling, we always give our best gift—Jesus Christ, who loves and saves and gives abundant and eternal life. Since the first year of Mission Arlington's existence in 1987, the original five Bible study groups grew to two hundred points of ministry across the city, serving over 3,000 people in weekly Bible study. Year after year, the ministry continues to expand.

We Christians need to be reminded that the most common means of leading people to salvation is through the personal testimony of a Christian friend. According to Christian researcher George

> **The most common means of leading people to salvation is through the personal testimony of a Christian friend.**

Barna, 44% of Christians surveyed said they had been led to faith through personal or family witnessing. Church services and sermons were rated second at 13%. Evangelistic crusades, personal evangelism by clergy, and experiences of physical healing were rated next with 5% each. Sunday school classes, youth camp events, and the death of a relative or friend were rated with 4% each. "Other means" were indicated by 16% of the respondees.[2]

These statistics speak loudly of the power of personal relationships in the witnessing process. Church sermons, evangelistic crusades, and Sunday school lessons do their part as the church corporately seeks to bring unbelievers into the fold. However, the real power of effective evangelism lies with individuals as we live our every day lives. All of us have personal relationships with family members, friends and neighbors, but not all of us take advantage of our opportunities to speak openly and honestly about God and what Christ is doing in our lives.

Invitation Evangelism

One of the most effective evangelism techniques among lay people is what I call "Invitation Evangelism." Invite people to come to church and special events. Invite them whether you know them or not. That may seem to be a small thing, but a lot of people say they originally came to church simply because someone asked them to come.

Many Christians assume that if a church puts a welcome sign out on the street corner, everyone will feel welcome. People out in the community don't think of the church as belonging to them. They think the church belongs to church members. They feel a bit like intruders in someone else's space. That's why it is important to do public advertising. Through the media, churches are saying to the community we really do mean it when we say "welcome." We want everyone to come. When people see an ad in the newspaper or on TV or hear a radio announcement, they understand that the church is not targeting one group or another. The invitation is open to all. That kind of advertising prepares people to respond positively to a personal invitation.

In invitational evangelism, church members demonstrate openness to the entire community by sharing the good news, by having a gracious attitude toward guests, and by inviting friends and neighbors to church. Visitors feel welcome and find out that Christians are gracious people and some of them are interesting as well. That makes for a powerful drawing to Christ. We understand, however, that it takes more than one contact, one ad, one sign, or one direct mailing to get people's attention enough for them to actually come inside the church doors. That's why we must keep on inviting for however long it takes.

⌘

WHY DOESN'T THE CHURCH REACH OUT ON PURPOSE TO ALL PEOPLE?

The hardest thing the church does is evangelism. The world doesn't want us to convert them to Christian faith. Most church members don't really want to talk about their personal faith and ideas. So, the church is pretty content not to evangelize. Satan devil has us right where he wants us. The world doesn't want us to do it and we don't want to do it. Everyone breathes a sigh of relief.

General Norman Schwarzkopf said, *"The truth of the matter is that we always know the right thing to do. The hard part is doing it."* So, in our personal lives, our families, and our churches, why is it that we know what we should do but we don't do it? That is a question churches need to ask and answer for themselves. There are many areas in the life of a church where the members of the Body of Christ know the right thing to do, but somehow we don't always do it. We rationalize and justify our position.

Many Christians subscribe to the idea that only a few specially gifted members of the Body of Christ have the gift of evangelism. They think that if they don't have the "gift" of evangelism, they are excused. That's wrong—all of us are called to be witnesses.

Some do seem to have a gift for casting the net and drawing people to Christ. Their success seems amazing. Yet, it usually takes many Christians bearing

> **Each Christian should have a current good news story of how Christ is at work in his or her life.**

witness over a period of time before somebody is ready to respond to the boldly given invitation. Those gifted ministers who are particularly anointed by God to lead and encourage people to publicly make professions of faith build on the quiet, consistent witness of others who have come before them. Each Christian should have a current good news story of how Christ is at work in his or her life.

That's why I'm not surprised when I am told that it takes 40+ members of Baptist churches to lead one person to Christ. It takes a lot of people investing themselves in personal witness. If Christ is in us, our good news story is in us. The question is, are we willing to be aware and to share? Wouldn't it be great if the 40+ members were praying and serving in such a way that they would win four or five people to Christ each year?

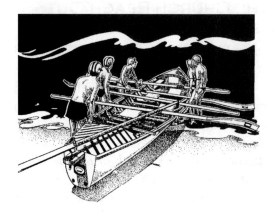

Church: The Lifesaving Station

Consider this parable written by Theodore O. Wedel in 1953:

On a dangerous seacoast where shipwrecks often occur, there was once a crude little lifesaving station. The building was just a hut, and there was only one boat, but the few devoted members kept a constant watch over the sea, and with no thought for themselves, they spent day and night tirelessly searching for the lost. This wonderful little station became famous because so many lives were saved.

Some of those who were saved, and various others in the surrounding area, wanted to become associated with the station and give of their time, money and effort for the support of its work. New boats were bought and new crews trained. The little lifesaving station grew.

Some of the members of the lifesaving station were unhappy that the building was so crude and poorly equipped. They felt that a more comfortable place should be provided as the first refuge of those saved from the sea. So they replaced the emergency cots with beds, and put better furniture in the enlarged building.

Now the lifesaving station became a popular gathering place for its members and they decorated it beautifully and furnished it exquisitely, because they used it as sort of a club. Fewer members were now interested in going to sea on lifesaving missions, so they hired lifeboat crews to do this work. The lifesaving motif still pre-

vailed in this club's decoration, and there was a liturgical lifeboat in the room where club initiations were held.

About this time, a large ship was wrecked off the coast and the hired crews brought in boatloads of cold, wet, half-drowned people. They were dirty and sick, and some of them had black skin and some had yellow skin. The beautiful new club was in chaos. So the property committee immediately had a shower house built outside the club where victims of shipwreck could be cleaned up before coming inside.

At the next meeting, there was a split in the club membership. Most of the members wanted to stop the club's lifesaving activities as being unpleasant and a hindrance to the normal social life of the club. Some members insisted upon lifesaving as their primary purpose and pointed out that they were still called a lifesaving station. But they were finally voted down and told that if they wanted to save the lives of all the various kinds of people who were shipwrecked in those waters, they could begin their own lifesaving station down the coast. They did.

As the years went by, the new station experienced the same changes that had occurred in the old. It evolved into a club, and yet another new lifesaving station was formed. History continued to repeat itself and if you visit that seacoast today, you will find a number of exclusive clubs along that shore. Shipwrecks are frequent in those waters, but most of the people drown. [3]

SEVEN EXCUSES FOR NOT EVANGELIZING

What kind of excuses do churches and church people use to avoid doing the job of evangelism God expects us all to do?

Excuse # 1: Fear

One of the main reasons we church people hang back is fear—fear of the unknown, fear of embarrassment, fear of making a fool of ourselves. We need to ask ourselves what Jesus would do if He were in our community.

Who are we afraid might come to our church? Who are we afraid of talking to? Really bad people? Some of us were really bad people before we invited Jesus to be the head of our life. We need a lot more bad people to join the rest of us bad people. The only difference between those of us who belong to the Body of Christ and those who don't is that someone cared enough about us to help us understand how much God cares! They "fleshed out" God's grace by their graceful way with us. Now it is our turn to do the same for someone else.

Excuse # 2: Satisfaction with the Status Quo

Sometimes churches get so focused on satisfying their own needs, hosting social events and feeling good about the fellowship, they get satisfied. It's as if their personal needs are being met, so they don't take time to consider other people in the community who do not have a church home and who are still lost from God.

Excuse # 3: Too Busy Doing Other Important Things

Another excuse we church types use is that we have so much to do inside the church that we don't have time to reach out. There are lessons to study, meetings to attend, papers to shuffle, meals to prepare and music to rehearse. We hide in a holy huddle inside the church and don't realize there is a community of hurting people down the street and across town.

Excuse # 4: Protecting Sacred Turf

Another version of this selective isolation occurs when people finally get inside the church and feel good about being there. Then they want to close the gate and say, "Enough! The church is big enough. Sunday school attendance is big enough. Now that I'm in, we don't need anybody else."

I was preaching recently in a lovely hill-country Texas town. One woman was really upset that the area was growing so rapidly. She had lived there for six months, but now that she was settled, she didn't want

> *The church should never be considered just fine as long as there are people outside who do not know Jesus.*

anyone else to come. Sometimes Christians are that way. Thankfully her pastor and most of the church members don't feel that way. The church should never be considered just fine as it is as long as there are people outside who do not know Jesus.

A healthy church exists in the community for the benefit of everybody. We are glad when new people come. We know God loves them. We know God sent them to us. We know their life will never be significant until they find God. Healthy churches help people know God.

Excuse # 5: Laziness - Let the Hired Staff Do the Outreach

Most church members do not perceive their personal role as evangelists sharing the good news. They think that responsibility is only for preachers or others who have been called by God. Sometimes church members get lazy and rely on their paid leadership staff to do everything. Visitation nights are scheduled and hardly anyone shows up to help the staff go visit church prospects.

In moments of true honesty, church members might even say, "That's what we're paying them for, and besides, they're probably better at witnessing than we are." If the church staff are the only people who do intentional outreach, then the church is not a church which believes one of its corporate functions is intentional outreach. If only the deacons and the Sunday school leaders are the ones who do all the reaching out, then we really can't say the church is involved in intentional outreach.

Not everyone wants to be visited at home—and especially not on a drop-by "weekly visitation night." But many people do appreciate the effort church members make to welcome them to the church and to share their faith. Churches need to carefully study their own community and decide the best approach.

I encourage churches to use a variety of visitation methods: quick door-step visits, telephone calls, appointments to visit, drop-by visits with cookies or slices of pizza, offers to take people to lunch for an opportunity to talk about church. Whatever church members do, we have to be willing to get personally involved with people we don't already know.

Excuse # 6: Aversion to Gun-Notching Evangelism

Sometimes in evangelism, we get narrowly focused on how many people we can win to Christ. When this happens, we can develop a psychology that I call "gun-notching." The gunfighters of the Old West bragged about the notches on their gun handle marking the number of men they had killed. I have seen a few "professional" Christians in my time who, it seemed to me, were only interested in how many people they had won to Christ—no matter how they went about it, no matter how much pressure they placed on people, and no matter how they sought to manipulate others into belief.

Some well-meaning people who have ineffectively blundered through their attempts to share the good news have given witnessing and evangelism a bad rap. Evangelism is simply the telling of God's good word. But some people hear the word *evangelism* and immediately think of pushy people running around, button-holing everybody they can, wherever they can find them, pushing strangers up against the wall to find out whether they have been saved, and passing out tracts to everyone they meet. Many Christians shy away from witnessing because they don't want to be perceived like those who have been abrasive and insensitive in their evangelistic zeal.

It's important that I am understood here. There are people to whom God has given special gifts—people who know how on first encounter to bring others face-to-face with their personal need for Jesus Christ and to tell them how to come to life in Him. This is a beautiful gift.

However, there are Christians who don't have that gift but are trying to manufacture it. With pumped-up courage, they blunder toward a person and succeed in doing no more than antagonizing someone who would actually like to know something about Christ but keeps being put off because of rudeness and inappropriateness.

Manipulative gun-notching evangelism is not the kind of evangelism the church is called to do.

Evangelism should not to be abrasive or scary; it is simply the telling of
God's good word. I believe God leads
us to encounters with people who are
ready to receive witness. As we are

> **Evangelism should not be abrasive or scary; it is simply the telling of God's good word.**

sensitive to His Spirit, He leads us into sensitive conversation with people and helps us bring them to Jesus Christ.

Excuse # 7: Selective Evangelism

Selective evangelism occurs when a church decides that they are going to try to reach the people in the community who live on "this side of town," or those who speak our language, whose eyes look like ours, whose skin color matches ours, or whose background is similar to ours. I have heard of churches taking a census to expand their witness in the community, and then choosing to leave out certain sections of town when they go visiting in order to control the type of people they want to invite to church. That is an abomination to the meaning of evangelism.

Jesus made a habit of hanging around with sinners, and He got a lot of criticism for it. A few years ago, our church decided we would run short advertising messages on the screens in the movie theaters in Arlington as an outreach activity. We also decided that we should not monitor which movies our ad would accompany. If Jesus hung out with the so-called wrong crowd, we figured He would give us the go-ahead to run our ad in all the movies, not just selected ones. We trust that God will use those messages to speak to the hearts of whomever He has prepared to hear.

⌘

THE CHURCH IS CALLED TO
TELL THE GOOD NEWS TO ALL PEOPLE

Evangelism is the Greek word *evangel*. It is the same word as *gospel* or *good news*. The good news is not good when we decide that some people will hear it and some will not—or that some people will be overlooked, left out, or excluded and kept outside the church doors.

A spurious doctrine of selection may give some Christians "permission" to overlook those who they believe God has overlooked. Whatever predestination means, it doesn't mean that Jesus died for only a few!

Evangelism is being sensitive to God, meeting people and sharing about what is happening in our life right now. When we share what God is doing in our life, we do not embarrass the other person and we try not to place the other person in an uncomfortable situation. We are sharing from our own experience what God is doing and inviting the other person into the conversation about what God could do in his or her life.

> **Evangelism is being sensitive to God, meeting people and sharing about what is happening in our life right now.**

To be sure, when people come under conviction of their sins and their distance from God, they will be uncomfortable until they respond to God's love for them in repentance and faith. But this is the convicting work of God's Spirit, not something we manipulate by being rude or demanding.

We people who are the "good guys" love to hear stories about Jesus' radical deliverance of some of the "bad guys." We love to hear testimonies of people who have lived a life of tragic and terrifying sin, and to learn how God has delivered them from the bondage of drugs or immorality or rebellion.

> **God's grace is for bad guys, but it's also for ordinary sinners like you and me!**

God's grace is for so-called "bad guys" but also for ordinary sinners like you and me. His grace is ideally suited to people whose sins are rather common, people who can't find anything to brag about in their righteousness *or* in their sins. His grace is for the ordinary problems of ordinary people like you and me whose lives aren't so terribly bad but aren't fully alive either.

However, these ordinary people often justify their lives by finding a lot of other people they are "better" than. But millions of these ordinary people are still empty, wandering around looking for a reason for living and a purpose for each day. In Jesus Christ, men and women finally begin to find that they don't have to live for themselves. They can choose to die to self and come more fully alive in Him and begin to live for others in their world.

God's News is Good News

The gospel is all the good news that men and women need to know. All the other news we may seek to tell will not be enough if we do not tell God's good news. The greatness of the gospel is not man's wisdom or man's creation.

> *The message of the cross is foolishness to those who are perishing, but to us who are being saved it is the power of God.* *(1 Corinthians 1:18)*

Man's wisdom is foolishness before God, and what seems to be foolishness to us is the wisdom of God. The weakness of God is so much wiser and stronger than anything we know. His folly is our wisdom and His weakness is our strength.

In Romans 5:1-6, Paul draws a contrast between faith in Christ Jesus and the works of the law. He says the law cannot save, and we cannot save ourselves through good works. Again, it is through faith alone that men are brought into a right relationship with God. It is in the wisdom of God, not in man's wisdom, that the cross becomes our way to salvation.

Give the story of Jesus and the cross to a philosopher and he can make no sense of it. Give the story of the significance of the cross to a historian and he can make no sense of it. Give the story of a shamed and weakened man dying on a cross, hanging between two criminals, to anyone who is designing a great new religion, and that person would say the cross is certainly no foundation upon which to build a worthy or successful religion.

Yet God chose to empty Himself of all His royal prerogatives, and send His Son to earth to live among us and teach us how to love and to serve *(Philippians 2:1-11)*. He loved us enough to allow His Son to be sacrificed for our sins, abandoned and tortured to death on a cross. He allowed Jesus to suffer the agony of separation from God in order to bear our sins. He allowed Jesus to die so that His death might become our way out of emptiness and into life through the resurrection *(1 Corinthians 15:1-22).*

Does all that make sense to you? Does it sound foolish? Is it unreasonable that a mighty God would carry out such a plan? It may be all those things, but it is the good news. As we see humanity at its worst—killing Jesus, we see God at His best—loving us, reaching out to us, forgiving us, saving us.

> *As we see humanity at its worst—killing Jesus, we see God at His best—loving us.*

The Church Has Work to Do

God has given the church the keys to the Kingdom. When we go out into the world with grace and mercy, preaching the gospel, living life in Christ, forgiving and touching lives, heaven's doors open. God uses our lives to reach out to others and to bring them to Himself. When we get lazy, self-satisfied or pre-occupied, and forget to pay attention to the people around us who need Jesus, we close the doors of God's Kingdom. If we really believe our churches have the key that can unlock the Kingdom's doors so people can come out of the darkness and enter the light, why aren't we constantly looking for locks to put the keys in?

Practice Invitation Evangelism

Provide fellowship, worship and study opportunities through the church to help people be receptive to the gospel. Pray that God will raise up a host of people in your church who will develop the gift of personal witnessing so that wherever they are—in the work place, school rooms, airports and homes—they are committed to introducing people to Jesus. The church is the one group in the world that has been given the job of telling the good news. If we fall down on the job, there is no one else to pick up the slack.

> *The church is the one group in the world that has been given the job of telling the good news.*

⌘

[1] Robert P. Buford, *Half Time: Changing Your Game Plan from Success to Significance.* (Grand Rapids, Mich.: Zondervan, 1994).
[2] Quoted in *The Baptist Standard* from the premier issue of the *Barna Report*, evangelical Christian newsletter.
[3] Originally appearing in an article by Theodore O. Wedel, "Evangelism—The Mission of the Church to Those Outside Her Life," *The Ecumenical Review*, October, 1953, p.24.

⌘
JESUS PRINCIPLES FOR INTENTIONAL OUTREACH

⌘ God has created all people, yet all suffer separation from Him because of sin. God loves all people and desires that all might repent of their sins and relate to Him in love.

⌘ People who are out of relationship with God have a God-shaped emptiness in their hearts that only God can fill.

⌘ God desires to establish a love relationship with every person. He prepares people to be ready to hear the gospel message as He prepares His people to use every opportunity to share it.

⌘ God provides Christians with encounters in which people are ready to receive a witness about Jesus. If we are alert, we can share the gospel naturally out of our own experience and in the normal traffic patterns of our life together.

⌘ The ministry of invitation is one of the most effective methods of personal evangelism. When we invite people to participate with us in church ministries and in our lives, they feel included, significant, and cared for.

⌘ Intentional outreach is both planned and spontaneous. It is both corporate and personal.

⌘ Each member of the Body of Christ is a witness, but we do not all have to witness in the same way.

⌘ It is our privilege and responsibility to establish a ministry of presence with people who are not members of the church and those who are not yet believers. We have an opportunity to be there for them in the ordinary times of life as well as in times of joy, crisis, and grief.

⌘ Worship services, Bible study groups and community ministries can be highly effective in reaching out to new people.

⌘ Seeing God change lives energizes the church as nothing else can do.

LORD OF LIFE:

WHAT A JOY IT IS TO KNOW YOU LOVED THE WORLD SO MUCH YOU SENT YOUR ONLY SON, THAT WHOEVER GIVES THEMSELVES IN FAITH TO JESUS WILL NOT PERISH BUT HAVE ETERNAL LIFE.

YOU ARE THE GOD OF OUR SALVATION. IN YOUR SON, JESUS CHRIST, WE FIND TRUE MEANING, HOPE, AND ABUNDANT LIFE. THANK YOU FOR GRANTING US THE MERCY OF FORGIVENESS. WE PRAY THAT YOU CONTINUE TO CLEANSE US AND EQUIP US FOR SERVICE IN YOUR KINGDOM.

GIVE US A VISION OF HOW WE MAY DO YOUR WORK IN THE WORLD BY BEING LIVING WITNESSES OF THE GOOD NEWS OF SALVATION THROUGH JESUS CHRIST.

LORD, EMPOWER US WITH COURAGE. GIVE US THE WISDOM TO SPEAK OUR WITNESS WITH SENSITIVITY AND GRACE. LET THE LIGHT OF YOUR LOVE SHINE SO BRIGHTLY THROUGH US THAT OTHERS SEE OUR GOOD DEEDS AND RESPOND WITH PRAISES TO YOU, OUR FATHER IN HEAVEN.

AMEN

Life Applications

⌘

EVANGELIZE
Intentionally Reaching Out With the Gospel of Christ

1. Pretend you are a member of your community with no affiliation to your church. From an outside point of view, how does your church communicate to your community its good news?

2. As a member of the Body of Christ, write out your answers and share with someone.
   - What do you do?
   - Who are you?
   - What is your heart's desire?
   - What is your good news?

3. Discuss how our performance-oriented society reinforces good works as a false way to earn *worthiness*.

4. How do people tend to "keep score" on the works of other Christians?

5. What are some substitutes for God you have attempted to stuff into the God-shaped emptiness in your life? On a daily basis, what can you do to make sure it is God who fills the core of your being?

6. What are some specific ways you can improve your ability to relate to people who are hurting, alienated, alone, hopeless, afraid and angry? Who are these people? Where are they?

7. Make a list of ways your church already reaches out beyond the church walls into your community. Think about the parable of the Lifesaving Station. What happens when church members come to the church on Sunday mostly to "celebrate property rights" and to evaluate the damage done to the building by the community? Who should you be reaching out to?

8. List ways individual church members can get beyond themselves to share their good news.

9. Evaluate yourself on the following:
   ♦ When was the last time you asked someone to come to church with you?
   ♦ When was the last time you made a follow-up call to a visitor to your church to make him or her feel welcome and to seek to meet his or her needs?
   ♦ When was the last time you visited someone outside your close circle of friends for the purpose of reaching out with the gospel of Jesus Christ?

10. Think about your congregation. What groups of people does your church apparently include in your church? What groups of people does your church apparently exclude, whether consciously or unconsciously?

11. Survey your group to find out how old each person was when he or she received Jesus Christ.
    ♦ Ask those who made their conversion decision as an adult to write down words or phrases to describe the emptiness in their life prior to deciding to follow Jesus.
    ♦ Those who made the decision to follow Jesus as children may take for granted the presence of Christ in their lives as far back as they can remember. Ask them to write down words or phrases they think would describe the God-shaped emptiness had they not accepted Christ as their Savior when they did.
    ♦ Share these feelings with others. Compare the feelings of emptiness without Jesus with feelings of fulfillment that come through having a relationship with Jesus as Savior.

12. Pray that God will reveal the God-shaped empty places in the hearts of people around you so you have the opportunity to introduce them to new life in Christ.

6

DISCIPLE
Nurturing Spiritual Growth

Dis•ci•ple
> **v.** To teach or train someone in Christian disciplines, to nurture a student
>
> **n.** A follower or pupil of Jesus Christ.

When I was a boy, I asked my preacher father, "If God created light before He created the sun and stars, where did the light come from?" Kids often ask questions like that and we don't have to be around a class of bright and curious children very long before we hear other questions that are equally puzzling.

"What did God have in mind when He created creatures like mosquitoes and chiggers and fleas?"

"What happened to the dinosaurs—were they too big to get on Noah's ark?"

"Why does God allow good people to die of terrible diseases?"

My father would often respond to questions like those by saying, "Don't worry about it, son. If God intended us to know that, He would have told us. Someday when we get to heaven, we will find out. In the meantime, be patient."

Although there was wisdom in my father's counsel (who can know the mind of the Lord in all matters?), I have never been satisfied to put my questions permanently on hold. It seems clear to me that if God doesn't want me to know something, He is certainly able to keep it from me. In the meantime, I will attempt to find out everything I can without deciding in advance that the question puzzling me is something God doesn't want me to know.

One criticism often leveled against Christians is that we are anti-intellectual—we are accused of placing so much emphasis on faith and believing that we often neglect the hard work of logic and reason. In truth, that charge often has been accurate. In the face of hard questions, well-meaning Christian friends or counselors might say, "Don't worry about the questions

> **The search for truth needs no apology.**

you have. Just believe." Or "If you only believe strongly enough, you won't worry about those kinds of problems." Personally, I have always resisted that advice. The search for truth needs no apology.

⌘

HONEST QUESTIONS DESERVE HONEST EXPLORATION

How do we deal with troubling intellectual questions that sometimes cross our minds? If we have the intelligence to formulate the question, surely there is someone with the intelligence and wisdom to explore the dimensions of the issue with us. We shouldn't have to bury our doubts, or to feel guilty because we have questions that might create discomfort in others. Neither should we be made to feel that some questions are wrong to ask.

I am suggesting that we can love God with a question as well as with an answer. If we refuse to let blinders be placed on our minds as we search the unfamiliar and the unknown, we often will be rewarded with delightful new perspectives through which God will bless us. If we shield ourselves from the big questions in life, we erect walls that can become prison cells for the mind. We may believe we are protecting ourselves because we love God and want faithfully to serve Him. In reality we are making ourselves captive to simplistic and perhaps petty answers. God wants us to love Him with minds that refuse to be limited, are courageously stretched and trustingly dependent on Him to equip us to handle the most challenging of life's questions.

What should we do with those questions for which we can't find immediate answers? Some people get very disturbed and confused. Some people opt out of loving and serving God. I have found that in the midst of questions and concerns that trouble me deeply, I can steadfastly continue to love God with my mind. In due time, God will deal with my questions if I am faithful to read, study, listen, and inquire.

Great men and women of faith throughout Christian history have been able to serve God, even when they did not have all the answers to issues that puzzled them. This has been true of mathematician Blaise Pascal, philosopher Soren Kierkegaard, English critic and writer C.S. Lewis and evangelist Billy Graham. One sign of true Christian maturity is being able to live with unanswered questions and with ambiguity.

> **One sign of true Christian maturity is being able to live with unanswered questions and with ambiguity.**

⌘

DISCIPLESHIP IS A PROCESS, NOT A DESTINATION

For many people, the term "spiritual growth" has a certain mystery to it. We may wonder, "How do I know if I am growing spiritually? What disciplines must I follow? What kind of a person will I be when I am spiritually mature?"

The Apostle Paul wrote to his friends in Corinth, assuring them of God's involvement in their lives and confirming that God will equip them to grow into full maturity in Christ.

> *I always thank God for you, because of his grace given you in Christ Jesus. For in him you have been enriched in every way—in all your speaking and all your knowledge—because our testimony about Christ was confirmed in you. Therefore you do not lack any spiritual gift as you eagerly wait for our Lord Jesus Christ to be revealed. **He will keep you strong to the end** so that you will be blameless on the day of our Lord Jesus Christ. God, who has called you into fellowship with His Son, Jesus Christ our Lord, is faithful.*
> *(1 Corinthians 1:4-9)*

If we seek God, He will not let us down. He keeps His promises. God's vision is for us to join Him in the work of His Kingdom, giving thanks for His provision and ready to enjoy Him forever in the fellowship of the saints, now and in the life to come. From the time we first come to trust in Jesus, and are born into the family of faith, He provides the nurture we need to grow into the fullness of Christ.

As a pastor, I always rejoiced with parents as they experienced the birth of a child and the beginning of their family. It is genuine joy to witness the healthy growth of babies from infancy to childhood to adolescence to adulthood. But one of life's saddest experiences is to see a baby who does not grow.

Unfortunately, some of us have experienced thwarted growth on a spiritual level. Born anew in Christ, we gave our life to Him in such excitement, stepping forward in faith and expectation—but for whatever the reason, we have not grown much since then. That which once was joy and celebration has become sadness, pain, discouragement, frustration and/or boredom. We intended to grow much more than we have. We wanted to live a more knowledgeable, self-assured, and satisfying Christian life—to be mature in our witness and commitment. Instead, we still feel like "babies" in the faith, with too little knowledge, limited experience, too many uncertainties, and a faltering devotional life.

> *The good thing God is working out in us is very specific— that we grow to be like Jesus, even in adversity.*

When we find ourselves experiencing these feelings, how do we get back on track? We must not give in or give up. Spiritual growth is a process that requires effort and is rarely achieved without some setbacks and some pain. God has given us the example of His Son to encourage and inspire us. The apostle Paul tells us that God works in everything that happens to produce good among those who are called to His purpose. The good thing God is working out in us is very specific—that we grow to be like Jesus, even in adversity.

And we know that in all things God works for the good of those who love him, who have been called according to his purpose. For those God foreknew he also predestined to be conformed to the likeness of his Son.   (Romans 8:28-29)

⌘

THE CHURCH AND THE INDIVIDUAL — ESSENTIAL PARTNERS IN CHRISTIAN DISCIPLESHIP

Individual Christians must assume primary responsibility for their own discipleship. If we are to be true to the high calling with which God is entrusting us, we must be diligent in learning all we can about the ways of the Lord and seek to be guided by His Spirit in all things. However, Christians cannot be expected to learn and grow in isolation. The church must provide the willing learner a framework for instruction and practical opportunities to grow through first-hand experiences in service. Personal discipleship requires four basic disciplines in which the individual's commitment to learn is bolstered by the church's commitment to teach.

1. Show Up.

I worked for decades leading inquirers classes and new church member orientation sessions as new Christians began their journey. Out of this experience, I reduced my message from *"Twelve Things a Christian Should Know and Do"* down to a two word sentence — *"Show up."* That may sound superficial, but if a church is really doing what a church is supposed to do, then everything that is important for young Christians to learn and do will become clear if they show up.

I have great confidence in the life of the church and its teaching and preaching ministries, in the power of influence when people worship and work together, and in the work of the Holy Spirit in making all that come together for spiritual growth. So show up! Pay attention! That sounds simple—but it's biblical.

> *Let us consider how we may spur one another on toward love and good deeds. Let us not give up meeting together, as some are in the habit of doing, but let us encourage one another—and all the more as you see the Day approaching.*
> *(Hebrews 10:25)*

If people get into a good Sunday school class, we are going to learn. We will be encouraged to pray. We will be encouraged to study the Bible regularly, develop Bible skills, become familiar with Scripture, and apply lessons from Scripture to their personal lives. (See Chapter 13 on *Living the Jesus Principles*.) Through worship experiences, we will be inspired, encouraged, and confronted with God's word. As we are exposed to human need, we will have opportunity to respond in ministry. We will deepen interpersonal relationships and improve our communication skills. As we grow spiritually, we will be encouraged to give of ourselves and our resources.

I believe in small groups whether we meet in the church house on Sunday or somewhere else at other times. But I know of no approach to Bible study that involves more people, develops more leaders, and is more consistent than a well-organized Sunday school. The Sunday school class is the original "small group".

The steady building of knowledge and wisdom as a person studies the word of God and interacts with other Christians in a healthy Sunday school class, in my opinion, is better than sending new Christians through ten weeks of discipleship training class. A new member orientation is very helpful to most new members of a church. But it should be brief—no more than four weeks—so that people do not lose touch with the small group that is best equipped to nurture them in Christ.

> **Withdrawal is the first hindrance to spiritual growth.**

Withdrawal is the first hindrance to spiritual growth. If we have a Sunday school department or class that is self-centered, status conscious, and reluctant to include outsiders, it will be difficult for newcomers to break into that closed group. In that case, a new class may have to be started.

As new Christians "show up," the healthy church will befriend, support, encourage, bless, and hold them accountable as they begin to grow in Christ. One of Satan's goals is to keep Christians from showing up and getting involved in doing God's work. He will try to keep us from getting our priorities right. He will tempt us to become frustrated because people we meet at church are not as friendly as we would like them to be. He will tempt us to get irritated when we observe a church member behaving hypocritically. He will tempt us to become discouraged when we recognize our own sins and failures, to condemn ourselves and to withdraw from Christian fellowship. I tell new Christians that if they get discouraged because they fail to be as good as they want to be, Satan has them right where he wants them. "Please remember," I have told new church members over the years, "if you goof up, don't give up. Keep showing up. We're here to help each other."

Carol Bowman shared a story about a Christian friend, Charlotte, from California whom I had met briefly. This friend, who had grown up in a Baptist church in Texas, had been judged and wounded by her church youth leadership as a high school student. Having put her own Christian church involvement on hold during her marriage, she had not been a member of a church anywhere for over twenty years. Recently, after experiencing some personal inner healing, forgiveness and a time of spiritual recommitment to the Lord, she decided to "show up" at a Presbyterian church near her home. An awareness of her personal need for active Christian fellowship was rekindled. Her testimony is "life is changing for the better now."

Miracles can happen wherever people meet to worship God and allow the mind of Christ to shape us. Every Christian needs a healthy church in which to become involved —a church that teaches God's word, that helps people grow, and that does things in the community that Jesus would be doing.

> **Miracles can happen wherever people meet to worship God and allow the mind of Christ to shape us.**

2. Grow in Christ Daily.

A regular discipline of spiritual nurture is extremely important to Christian growth. Scripture reading, prayer, fellowship with other Christians and ministry to others are essential to well-rounded personal spiritual growth. I found this wonderful counsel paraphrased in *The Message* as Paul instructs the Ephesian church.

> *No prolonged infancies among us please. We will not tolerate babes in the woods, small children who are an easy mark for impostors. God wants us to grow up, to know the whole truth and tell it in love, like Christ in everything. We take our lead from Christ, who is the source of everything we do. He keeps us in step with each other. His very breath and*

blood flow through us, nourishing us so that we grow up healthy in God, robust in love.

Since we do not have the excuse of ignorance, everything (and I do mean everything) connected with that old way of life has got to go. It is rotten, through and through. Get rid of it and then take on an entirely new way of life, a God-fashioned life. A life renewed from the inside, working itself into your conduct as God accurately reproduces his character in you.

Don't grieve God. Don't break his heart. His Holy Spirit moving and breathing in you is the most intimate part of your life, making you fit for himself. Don't take such a gift for granted.   *(Ephesians 4)*

3. Learn by Doing!

Effective discipleship requires hands-on experience and on-the-job training. Everyone I know who has ever been a teacher has said, "I've learned more teaching than I ever learned by just listening." Pastors and other leaders in churches need to quit worrying about how much people know before they begin serving, and simply give them opportunities to serve alongside someone more experienced. They will grow and be effective with that mentoring. But don't put them to work and forget about them.

> **Individual church members need more opportunities to apply their knowledge and commitment.**

Individual church members need more opportunities to apply their knowledge and commitment. My observation is that most people who have been in churches a long time know more than they think they know, and can do a lot more than they think they can do. The experiences of church people in the work of Mission Arlington provide a good example. When they volunteer to help, many of them don't think they know much about how to teach and minister. But when they begin to teach and relate to people through the apartment ministries, they discover they know a great deal about the Christian life.

It is not more training that church members need to encourage their spiritual growth, but more opportunity and direction to apply what they already know. That's why lay network mobilization and volunteer ministry have become so important in churches. When churches do a better job of enlisting, assigning, encouraging and rewarding people, we will get a whole lot more done and Christians will feel a whole lot more useful. In *doing*, people recognize spiritual growth in their lives and have a deeper sense of their own worth.

Discipling others or ministering to others can become disheartening if there is no support system. People directly involved in ministry need a source of af-

> **Discipleship rarely happens in isolation. Christians need each other to learn and to grow.**

firmation, encouragement, correction, access to resources, and a quick response to needs. If they can't get that support, they will quickly burn out. With support, they will keep going. Discipling people is mostly a matter of helping them do what they know they should do, encouraging them, answering their questions, helping them solve problems, assisting them in making their own decisions, and allowing them to make mistakes along the way. Discipleship rarely happens in isolation. Christians need each other to learn and to grow.

Bottom-line, the Sunday school is the best source of spiritual training for the Christian who wants to learn and grow. It provides an environment for teaching and learning, for dealing with people's problems and needs, and for equipping people to expand their interpersonal relationships. It is flexible. It provides opportunities for service for great numbers of people. Best of all, it is ongoing. Discipleship programs like *Experiencing God, MasterLife* and others have been life-changing for so many churches and church members. They can be very helpful, but they work best as *extra* options for growth, and not as a substitute for the steady, systematic small group, gathered around a caring teacher with an open Bible in hand.

4. Apply the New Learning.

Small groups such as the Sunday school class historically have been helpful in building those important intimate relationships among Christian friends. But realistically, one needs more than a small group for well-balanced growth in discipleship. We all need to see that our world is bigger than the controlled environment of like-minded people in our Sunday school class. We need to interface with a broad range of people, including those who may be very different from us in temperament, experience and religious ideas

I remember receiving a letter from a person who was helped to get on his feet through Mission Arlington outreach.

> *"Dear Dr. Wade:*
>
> *This is just to thank you again for making your church and Mission Arlington as visibly helpful to everyone in need as you do.*
>
> *Your church helps regardless of why people need help, and in ways that are truly helpful toward getting them to become self-sufficient to whatever degree that is possible . . ."*

When the church is doing what it should be doing, it will help individuals get in touch with all kinds of human need. Giving ourselves to serve others is where most of us learn best. As we share our lives and the love of God flows through us in practical ways, we experience our greatest growth as Christians.

> **Giving ourselves to serve others is where most of us learn best.**

A deacon who helps faithfully in Mission Arlington said to me, "The reason I love to be involved is because I have never seen people change like they do in this work, including me!"

So it is fairly simple—show up, grow in Christ daily, learn by doing, and apply our new learning. If all Christians practiced these simple actions, our world would be a different place.

⌘

RESPONSIBILITIES OF THE CHURCH
TO DEVELOP DISCIPLES

The New Testament portrays teaching as a basic ministry of the church. In Acts, the apostles would not cease teaching about Jesus, even when they were warned to stop. Thrown in prison, they continued to preach and teach. Teaching the Word of God is an anointed privilege. We are instruments through whom God chooses to enlighten the dark places of people's minds and bring them into mature discipleship.

Unless the church member is open and available for instruction and relationships, growth cannot occur. But the church must provide opportunities for instruction and mentoring. As a church works at discipling believers, the following five ideas are extremely important.

1. Accept the Challenge to Disciple.

Jesus was a teacher. In fact, in the New Testament, the word *teacher* is used over 60 times. More than half of those times, the word is used in reference to Jesus Himself, the master teacher. Jesus taught by words and by example. Ultimately, He was crucified, not because of what He taught, but because He insisted on living what He taught.

Walking the talk should be the paradigm by which we gauge the effectiveness of a church's teaching ministry. If a church teaches missions, are church members

> *Walking the talk should be the paradigm by which we gauge the effectiveness of a church's teaching ministry.*

personally involved in missions? If the church teaches evangelism, are church members actively witnessing to people outside the congregation who are in their sphere of influence?

One of the great tasks of the church is to teach God's truths in order to counter the pressures of a hostile, materialistic, and cynical society. The church must nurture members of the Body of Christ so as to develop their ability to radiate the light of the gospel wherever they live and work.

When we teach as Jesus taught, we will have to pay attention to both our words and our deeds. A teaching church helps people learn to make decisions seven days a week based on the ethics and

principles of Jesus Christ, rather than the ethics and principles of
the world. Fortunately, some of the ethics and principles of the
world have been influenced by Christ. Business leaders are talking
more and more about servant leadership. The compassion displayed by those with power to those without is a spillover from the
gospel. But to our shame, more often the ethics of the church have
been influenced by the ethics of the world—performance-
orientation, obsession with success, preoccupation with comfort
and convenience, greed, instant gratification, selfishness, self-
promotion, image-consciousness, and exclusivism.

We must do the hard task of teaching little children even before
they formulate verbally their own ideas. We must teach children
when they start school, teenagers as they grow up, college students
as they become more adult-like in their decision-making, and
adults who need to re-learn and more deeply understand God's
principles by which to guide their lives.

2. Decide what Disciples Should Learn.

The church has a corporate responsibility to take periodic inventory of the kind of Christian nurture that is being offered and of the
quality of presentation. There are basics of Christian understanding
and life-skill training that must be a part of any church's discipleship efforts. These would include:

- Living in relationship with God: Father, Son, and Holy Spirit
- The nature of sin and God's call to salvation
- The basics of prayer and private devotion
- Bible study: understanding the nature of Scripture, organization
  of the Bible, and outline of biblical history
- A Christian's responsibility as a member of the Body of Christ
- Principles of Christian stewardship
- Christian principles of personal morality and ethics
- Christian history, including the negative as well as the positive
  episodes
- How to share one's Christian faith
- Discovering and doing God's will.

Many people think discipleship is a method of learning what
you should know about the Christian life. They focus on memoriz-

ing verses, reciting facts about the Bible and repeating principles of spiritual growth. That kind of learning is helpful, but not complete. People can even talk a lot about spiritual matters, their "great faith," and their assurance of heaven, yet be ineffective witnesses. The "language of Zion" does not help much on Main Street. As is sometimes said, *"People can be so heavenly minded that they are of no earthly good!"* Real learning will transform the soul. Real discipleship begins when we take what we learn and begin using it, in believable ways, every day and everywhere.

> **Real learning will transform the soul.**

Mastering basic information contained in a study curriculum does not cover the full scope of Christian discipleship. We always need to look beyond one's exposure to facts to determine how learning penetrates the inner person and works a transformation on the soul. The question must be asked: *"Is our church's discipleship training producing people who give evidence of being genuine followers of Jesus Christ?"*

To illustrate, let's look at the first section of the discipleship study areas in my list above and move past factual information to personal application.

Living in relationship with God, the Father - We can be taught and intellectually affirm that God is three-in-one, Father, Son and Holy Spirit (the Trinity). But what does that mean as we relate to God? Christian counselors tell us that how we view Father God is almost always affected by how we viewed our earthly father in the formative years of our childhood. If our earthly father was mean-spirited, harsh or abusive, we likely will have difficulty perceiving Father God as loving, kind and forgiving. The God we "know" will tend to be harsh and judgmental.

> **How we view Father God is almost always affected by how we viewed our earthly father.**

If our earthly father was undemonstrative, emotionally distant or absent from the family, our perception of Father God likely will be one of an unavailable or unapproachable figure who does not provide us with a sense of security or dependability.

However, if our earthly father was a warm, loving, steadying influence in our life, we are likely to transfer that positive image to our Father God. We will have developed a basic trust in God and in our fellow man. Jesus paid Joseph a high compliment when He used the image of "father" in describing the character of God. Even though Joseph was the "adoptive" rather than the biological father of Jesus, he did provide the nurturing of a father which could be positively affirmed by Jesus.

Sometimes we have to look beyond our experience with our human father (or mother) and ask God to make His fathering so real to us that we can re-learn what a father's love should be and forgive our human parent who may have terribly wounded or neglected us.

When we are able to forgive our earthly parents for their sins or inadequacies, and repent of our own judgments against them, then we become free to relate to God unhindered by our earthly wounds.

Living in relationship with God, the Son - Just as we must learn to see God the Father for who He truly is, we must be able to move past an impersonal belief about Jesus Christ as one who lived in a distant history. Although to say we believe Jesus is the Son of God, as an orthodox affirmation, it is not enough. We must come to an intimate relationship with the living Christ, our personal Savior, who loved us enough to take our sins upon Himself so we can have an open and free relationship with the holy Father God. We must stop trying to save ourselves and enter with humility into God's unmerited grace, bestowed upon us through Jesus Christ.

This personal relationship is given directly to us as we sincerely pray for God's mercy and forgiveness. Jesus Christ brings our wounded and needy heart directly to Father God and we are saved by His intercession on our behalf. Thus we move from knowledge *about* Jesus to a life in which *we live in Him* and *He lives in us*.

Living in relationship with God, the Holy Spirit - Jesus told His disciples that He would not abandon them as orphans, but that He would send another Counselor, the Spirit of truth, to be with them forever. This Holy Spirit, sent by the Father in Jesus' name, would live in them, remind them of what Jesus had told them and teach them all things *(John 14:15-18; 26-27)*.

The Holy Spirit is the presence of God living within us, given to us as we are reborn through faith in Jesus Christ as our Savior. The Holy Spirit is the Christian disciple's equipper and sustainer, enabling us to do the work of Christ in the world—to be co-workers in His Kingdom and heirs in eternity.

What is the application of this truth beyond the knowledge that God's Holy Spirit lives within us as believers? It is that God's equipping

> *Christ cannot fill us with Himself if we are already full of ourselves.*

power is ours to the degree that we are willing to die to ourselves and allow Him to live in us. He cannot fill us with *Himself* if we are already full of *ourselves*. Until we want more of Him and less of us, there will be no great power in our life. The Holy Spirit is the one who knows what each of us has been created to be and to do. God wants only good for us and we can trust our lives to His control.

As we grow spiritually, deeper levels of application will appear. Discipleship demands that we move past a simple "belief in God's existence" to an understanding of God's true character reflected in Jesus Christ. Jesus provides the true image rather than the distorted image we may have from our life experiences.

The common thread for understanding these discipleship principles, and whatever others you may add to the list, is that following Jesus is not a matter of learning information about God or of

> *Discipleship begins with establishing a love relationship with God.*

following rules of behavior. Discipleship begins with establishing *a love relationship* with God, and responding to that love relationship by relating in Christ's love to all our fellow men. We are deeply and profoundly loved and we are asked to return that love with all our heart, soul, mind, and strength.

3. Utilize the Bible as the Textbook.

The teaching ministry of a church must be biblically centered. The Bible, God's word, is the textbook. God's word is like no other word available to us. In God's book, we find the mind of God about issues that affect us daily. The Bible speaks to the problems and concerns we have about our families and ourselves. It cries out for application in our lives. Frankly, I have never been able to read Scripture for five minutes without becoming aware of how it speaks to me personally.

Christians almost universally will say they believe the Bible should be at the heart of the church's teaching ministry. But if we do an analysis of how Christians teach or preach or live their lives, regrettably the Bible often is placed off to the side. Sometimes a Sunday school class can be so concerned about contemporary application and current issues that they only brush by the biblical revelation. We need to do careful thinking as teachers and as a church in this matter. The human issues we face every day point us to the problems. If we raise the human issues and simply gather the group's extemporaneous thoughts without a prayerfully understood word from the Lord, we fail to utilize the guidance provided for us in the truth and wisdom of the Bible.

> **The Bible is a treasure of revealed truth and wisdom waiting to be understood and applied to life.**

The Bible is a treasure of revealed truth and wisdom waiting to be understood and applied to life.

Jesus tells us to go into the world with the knowledge that He is going with us. We are to make disciples of all those who will believe, baptize them, and teach them all the things He has commanded us. That covers a lot of territory—all the world and all He has commanded *(Matthew 28:18-20)*. We must always go to the Scriptures to find guidance and answers. When we teach, we must use the Bible as our plumb line, the standard by which we evaluate our own personal opinions and attitudes about a given issue.

4. Commit to Learning as the Desired Outcome of Teaching.

Spiritual growth, or discipleship, is a process very similar to going to school to receive an education. It requires an ongoing process of teaching (effectively imparting information), and learning (receiving, understanding and applying what is taught). Unless the teacher and the student understand the two-sided nature of this educational process, and each assumes responsibility for fulfilling their respective roles, then true learning is not likely to happen.

I like what college professor Lee Bowman says about the importance of everyone assuming accountability for the part he or she plays in the educational process. When he goes into his college classroom on opening day of a semester, he sets the stage for what should happen there by saying to his students:

"I'm the teacher. It's my job to effectively communicate to you what I know. I'll be here, prepared to teach. And I'll do my best to help you receive, understand, and apply the information and to model the principles I have for you to learn.

"You are the student. It's your job to learn. If you are committed to learning, you will be present when teaching takes place, you will proactively participate by sharing and asking questions, and you will do your best to receive, understand, and apply the information and the principles being taught."

Students can't be made to learn, and certainly can't be made to apply the knowledge they receive. We want new Christians to accept responsibility for their Christian growth. Not all teachers are as committed and effective as they might be. Some teachers seem to get so immersed in the content of the lesson or in the teaching process itself that they never become aware of what the student does with the information imparted. We want teachers to understand that they do not teach lessons, they teach people. In most cases, the teacher is the lesson.

> *Teachers do not teach lessons, they teach people. In most cases, the teacher is the lesson.*

Learning is not complete until the student is able to translate information to knowledge and then apply the knowledge in a practical way to his or her life. Said another way, teaching people the right thing does not insure that they will understand, accept, and do the right thing. We must pray that God will be actively involved in the learning process as well as the teaching process to create in the heart of the student a desire to act on the teaching. If both student and teacher work together to accomplish the task of learning, growth will take place.

> **Learning is not complete until the student translates information to knowledge and applies it to life.**

5. Recognize Where We Are and Where We Need to Improve.

We need only to look around us to realize we have problems within our Christian educational systems. Studies have shown that many young people who have been raised in Christian churches have a tragic lack of basic knowledge about the Bible. They lack understanding of what the Bible is and how it was put together. They have little knowledge of many biblical characters or events and the flow of biblical history is a murky stream. They can't quote passages that an educated Christian should be able to quote. In responding to a questionnaire about the New Testament, some even mistakenly identified an epistle as the wife of an apostle!

Research has shown that a majority of Americans believe in God, have a high regard for religious institutions, and think that what the church is doing is important. However, with many of these people, their religious beliefs seem to have little effect on their everyday judgments of right and wrong and their moral behavior. Therefore, God in His highest ethical dimension is denied.

> **With many people, religious beliefs seem to have little effect on their everyday judgments of right and wrong or moral behavior.**

With many people, religious beliefs seem to have little effect on their everyday judgments of right and wrong or moral behavior. People can sit in a Bible study class on Sunday morning and discuss ethical issues addressed in Scripture. Then, during the week as they are confronted with essentially the same questions in their real world, there is a slip in their intellectual gears. In making decisions about business dealings, hiring practices, work commitments, integrity from employer or employee, voting issues, or school assignments, those ethical principles are forgotten. People fail to make the needed connections between their religious faith and the life choices they make. That inconsistency between belief and practice is a tragic judgment upon us.

As a pastor, I would swing between two extremes in judging the effectiveness of church discipleship training. When I would compare the moral and ethical condition of the world at large, and watch the people in the church make ethical vocational decisions and commit themselves to building strong Christian families, I would think we in the church are doing pretty well. Then at other times, I would become discouraged when I think of how we have been exposed repeatedly to powerful truths, yet fail to make personal application of the great themes in Scripture and theology.

For example, religious liberty, respect for the conscience of others, and separation of church and state are theological principles that have shaped my views about the role of the church in society. Christians are called to be light and witness to their community— but not lord and master of the community. The church is to approach its ministry as servants, leading through influence—not through wielding power as if it is our task to make everyone conform to our position. We are to confront, challenge and remind— but not threaten. Unfortunately, many Christians fail to consider these principles, much less put them into practice.

In the face of pivotal life issues, will we make decisions on the basis of Christian principles and teachings? Or, will we simply consider solutions that are the most profitable, expedient, beneficial, or attractive? Christians would be a more effective influence in the world if we would discipline ourselves to face decisions by asking:

1. *Is this the right thing to do before God?*
2. *What would Jesus do in this situation?*
3. *Will this action bring good or harm to people?*

These questions should always be the primary focus of both the church as a corporate body and of individual Christians seeking to do God's work in the world.

For example: One of the most difficult decisions in any kind of business is when and how to fire an employee. Christian business people often agonize over this issue. Here are some thoughts that might give perspective.

God sometimes has to "fire" people. God put Adam and Eve out of the garden. God did not allow Moses to take the Israelites into the Promised Land. Saul, the king, lost favor with God. David was not allowed to build the temple. Pastors and religious leaders sometimes lose their position of influence because God takes His hand off their ministry.

Jesus could be as redemptive as possible (note how He handled Peter after failure), but see how stern He was with James and John whose mother sought special positions for her sons *(Matthew 20:20-28)*. Note how Jesus blessed the firing of workmen or executives who were not faithful with their opportunities *(Matthew 25:14-30)*.

These considerations should be kept in mind. Is this firing necessary because the poor quality of the work is detrimental to the organization? What has been done to help the employee improve? One can hope that the firing will create a better attitude and lead to a better and more suitable job in the future. Care can be given so in the process of firing, the humanity of the person is protected, genuine help is offered to retrain or relocate, and appropriate appreciation is shown for the good that was done (such as a severance package).

Being a Christian manager in the working world does not mean carelessness in issues of quality, nor laziness in relation to work, nor cautiousness to the neglect of progress, nor fear in holding people accountable for their actions. Always, efforts need to be made to help people be the best they can be, to grow in their work, to be patient with those who are learning, to build up and encourage every associate. But, there will be times when you have to let someone go.

⌘

⌘
JESUS PRINCIPLES FOR DISCIPLESHIP

⌘ The key principle for church members who want to grow in discipleship is to "show up" and be willing to learn.

⌘ In a healthy church, all the essentials of Christian growth will be taught: prayer, Bible study, witnessing, stewardship, ministry, personal morality, and discovering the will of God. These will be supplemented by lessons in theology and Christian history.

⌘ A regular discipline of personal study and spiritual nurture is essential for Christian growth. God's word is central to Christian discipleship. The Bible is the primary textbook.

⌘ A church must be committed to equipping its members for effective, winsome Christian living at home, at work, at school, and in all relationships of life.

⌘ Churches should regularly take inventory of where its members are in their spiritual maturity and where they need to be.

⌘ Individuals learn best through hands-on experience and on-the-job training. As Christians begin to serve in specific ministry tasks, they discover they know more about God, the Bible, and the Christian life than they think they do! And they learn the questions and answers that are really important.

⌘ Small group interaction among trusted Christian friends needs to become more than a safe refuge where the individual needs of its members may be served. Healthy small groups will always let their love and energy flow out in ministry to others.

⌘ People have deep needs to be spiritually alive and growing. A healthy church will work at the task of creatively developing spirituality in its members.

WISE AND LOVING GOD:
YOU HAVE ALWAYS SOUGHT TO TEACH US.
THROUGH THE PROPHETS, SCRIPTURE, AND
THE LIVING WORD YOU HAVE REVEALED TO
US, YOUR WAYWARD CHILDREN, WHAT WE
HAVE NEEDED TO KNOW. WHEN WE WERE
SO FOOLISHLY BLIND TO YOUR WISDOM,
YOU SENT JESUS TO SHOW US HOW TO LIVE
AND TO SAVE US FROM OUR SINS. THANK
YOU FOR YOUR PATIENCE AND YOUR
GRACE.

NOW, LORD, AS WE ACT AS THE BODY OF
JESUS CHRIST IN THE WORLD, MAY WE
TEACH YOUR WORD WITH THE PASSION AND
WISDOM OF OUR SAVIOR SO AS TO BRING
MEN AND WOMEN, BOYS AND GIRLS, INTO
MATURITY.

HELP US TO MAKE THE SCRIPTURES COME
ALIVE IN THE HEARTS OF THOSE WHO SEEK
YOU. HELP US TO BE THE VESSELS
THROUGH WHOM OTHERS COME TO EXPERI-
ENCE A PERSONAL WALK WITH JESUS, OUR
LORD. MAY OUR LOVE BE CONTAGIOUS AND
OUR THEOLOGY BE TRUE. WE PRAY IN THE
NAME OF JESUS.

AMEN

Life Applications
⌘
DISCIPLE
Nurturing Spiritual Growth

1. The first personal principle of Christian discipleship presented in this chapter is to *"show up and pay attention."* What Christian learning opportunities are readily available to you for which you could take responsibility to *show up, listen and learn?*

2. A daily discipline of study and devotion is essential to Christian growth. Are you spending time each day in simple growth activities such as reading the Bible, listening in prayer for God's guidance, reading Christian books and magazines, and selectively tuning in to Christian radio and TV? Pause right now to plan how intentional learning activities could become part of your daily regimen!

3. We learn best by doing—by applying our knowledge in service to others, or by teaching others what we have been taught. Evaluate the effectiveness of your learning. In what ways have you been willing to go beyond just studying the Christian life, but to put your new awareness into practice through service and teaching others?

4. What basic areas of Christian understanding and life skill training do you think should be included in a church's discipleship curriculum? Construct your own list of those areas you consider to be essential. In what teaching format do you think these areas can best be presented for effective learning?

5. What area of Christian understanding or life skill development seems to be the weakest in your church? What can you do to personally grow in this area? What can you help your church do to strengthen this area of discipleship training?

7

MINISTER
Serving Courageously to Heal the Wounded

> **Min·is·ter -**
> To act in the name of Jesus Christ to give help,
> provide care, or render service to persons in need.

Tens of thousands of volunteers have made themselves available to do God's work through the community ministry of Mission Arlington in Arlington, Texas. We asked Tillie Burgin, Associate Pastor and Director of Missions at First Baptist Church Arlington, and founder of Mission Arlington, what advice she would give to pastors, church staff members or lay volunteers about ministering. Without hesitation, she answered, *"Be available, really available to be used by God. Start watching how He uses you. Learn the lessons He is teaching you."*

Tillie advises ministers to have their church building open every day. Be available and visible. Spend a lot of time outside the building, walking (not driving) around the community. From her decades of street ministry experience in Korea and in Texas, she believes ministry is taking the church to the people, rather than hauling the people to the church. As mentioned before, she talks about "hovering around John 3:16" and "hanging out on the property" where people live. Tillie shares:

> *When you are out and around in town, pay attention to what you see and hear. You don't have to go anywhere with a "presentation." You don't need to lead out with inviting people to your church. Most people won't understand how going to church can help them anyway.*
>
> *I have found that many unchurched people are suspicious of someone who immediately invites them to "church." Unchurched people question a "churchy" person's motivation. One of the things they are skeptical about is self-righteous Christians who just want another notch on their Bible. When people find out that we at Mission Arlington*

aren't trying to bus them to our church, and that we just want to hang out with them and help them, they realize our motivation is love. They realize there is really nothing in it for the people doing the ministry. Mission Arlington is for everyone, not just for people who have been "selected" to be ministered to by First Baptist Arlington. There's a big difference. Think about it.

TILLIE BURGIN'S TURNING POINT

We all have our own story of how God gets our attention and straightens out our off-based assumptions about how to live as people committed to do His work in our world. Tillie shared the following story of how she became fully available to God, how God changed her life, and as a result, touched the lives of thousands of people around the world.

As a young woman, there was a very frustrating time in my life when my kids were little. As I looked around my cul-de-sac in Arlington, my neighbors were actively involved in the community and so well respected by everyone. I lived each day just to be a part of their lives, to get invited to the upcoming party or just to be seen with them around town. As my relationships with these special people progressed, I would often be asked to baby-sit their kids and assist in other ways. Always included as the helper, it seemed I never became good enough to get invited to the really special parties or serve on the select committees.

I remember how down I was, on myself and on the situation. I thought about it all the time. My feelings were really hurt. I would sometimes sit on my front porch, look across the street and quietly cry tears of loneliness and rejection. Somehow, they seemed to be living the life I wanted to live, and I couldn't even get close enough to taste it.

Then I read A Taste of New Wine by Keith Miller. In his zeal for "success," he constantly tried his best to be part of the "in" crowd, working very hard to look and act the part. Miller tells how he bought expensive suits, carried an elegant brief case, even timed his day in order to get on the elevator with powerful business men in the community. He was always pushing to be part of someone else's life. His story sounded very familiar to me.

One morning, the elevator door closed before Keith could get on. Then the elevator man said, "Mr. Miller, you are the kind of man I would like to talk to." Keith listened to the elevator man and counseled him in a tough life situation. Through the rest of that day, other situations continued to leave Keith out of the "in group." The office guys left for lunch without him. So he went to lunch alone, and stopped for some gasoline on the way back. A fellow filling his gas tank said, "Mr. Miller, do you have a minute?" And so the story goes. God got Keith Miller's attention.

As I read the book, I reflected on my own situation of feeling left out of where I thought I wanted to be. I wondered if God wanted me to be still, in my house, with my one-year-old and three-year-old sons. I felt that God wanted me to slow down and switch gears in order to be available for the people He would send people my way, rather than feeling like I always had to invite someone else, constantly trying to make things happen.

At that point in my life, when I was really listening, God spoke to me clearly. Something visibly changed in me. I slowed down. I

> **When I was really listening, God spoke to me clearly.**

prayed. I turned the driver's seat over to God on a full-time basis. And the phone began to ring. People wanted me to be involved in what they were doing. People wanted to be involved in what I was doing. It began to happen.

*That was 1960 when God taught me that I didn't have to push things uphill. He showed me that all I had to do was **be available**. After committing to international ministry and serving in Korea for several years, I found myself once again back in Texas. Only this time, I was actively looking for ways to be a missionary in Arlington. God provided and still does each day. It is awesome to be a part of His plan to help the hurting and stand in the gap for people in need.*

People may look at Mission Arlington today (with hundreds of volunteers involved in community congregations made up of thousands of people in over 200 locations in our community) and wonder how they could begin this kind of ministry. You might be surprised to know that Mission Arlington all started with a phone call to our church from a woman who needed help. I went to her apartment, responded to her need, became her friend, started a Bible study in her apartment (which had no furniture), and began reaching out to the people who lived in the same apartment complex. And look what God is doing today.

Ministry is a natural expression of the Christian's social conscience. When members of the Body of Christ come alive to the reality of God's Spirit living within them, they will recognize human need wherever it is, respond with love to alleviate suffering, and work to establish justice in the name of Jesus Christ.

> **If we are to be the Body of Christ, we must attempt to see the world through His eyes.**

The social conscience of the church stems from the basic character of Jesus. If we are to be the Body of Christ, we must attempt to see the world through His eyes and courageously reach out to people as He did when He lived here on the earth. Simply stated, ministry is responding to needs. Ministry is not a program, an annual event or a scheduled tradition. As Tillie Burgin said, being a minister is being available, ready to respond.

Ministry is an important function of the church because we are called by God to fulfill four distinct roles as the Body of Christ:

- ◆ To speak out against evil and social injustice and to stand in defense of the oppressed *(Luke 4:18-19)*.
- ◆ To relieve human suffering by providing direct aid and comfort to those in need *(Matthew 25:33-40)*.
- ◆ To be an instrument of God's grace through whom people might learn of Jesus Christ—the Savior who can deliver them from the sin and evil that entraps them *(Matthew 28:18-20; John 17:20-23)*.
- ◆ To intercede through the power of the Holy Spirit to bring inner healing to the lives of wounded people, to facilitate spiritual transformation, and to promote forgiveness and reconciliation *(John 13:34-35; 14:15-17; James 4:13-16; Colossians 3:12-14)*.

I have often been asked where my social conscience came from. My answer is, *"From my parents and from the Bible."* As a child, I learned to sing, *"red and yellow, black and white, they are precious in His sight, Jesus loves the little children of the world."* In Vacation Bible School, we pledged, *". . . with liberty and justice for all."*

The mission sermons preached by my father called for compassion and involvement in the lives of people no matter what their race, language or nation. My parents taught me that it was wrong to use racial epithets, not because it was socially unacceptable, but because it showed disrespect for others who were also God's children and for whom Jesus died. As a youth, I was exposed to the moral problems and social issues associated with gambling, alcohol, drugs, tobacco, illicit sex, lying, stealing, and violence. Through God's grace and the teaching of godly parents, I was given guidance and blessing in dealing with each one.

The Scripture that really spoke to me as a young man is Luke 4:14-30. Jesus had returned to Nazareth early in his ministry, and was invited to speak to his hometown crowd. Out of all the Scriptures He could have chosen, He focused on this powerful passage from Isaiah 61:1-2.

> *"The Spirit of the Lord is on me, because he has anointed me to preach good news to the poor. He has sent me to proclaim freedom for the prisoners and recovery of sight for the blind, to release the oppressed, to proclaim the year of the Lord's favor."*   *(Luke 4:18-19)*

A THEOLOGICAL BASE FOR MINISTRY

Jesus' mission was to fulfill the will of His heavenly Father as the Father's will had been revealed centuries before through the prophet Isaiah. God calls for love and justice, for freedom and healing, for courageous proclamation of the establishment of God's Kingdom. The message was controversial in Isaiah's time, it caused Jesus to be rejected in His own hometown, and it remains controversial today. But the message is a clear call from God that cannot be ignored. If we as the Body of Christ are to be faithful to our calling, we must live our lives actively pursuing the mission claimed by our Lord.

Justice was a recurrent Old Testament theme. God's prophets repeatedly called the people to live righteously and to do justice.

Away with the noise of your songs. I will not listen to the music of your hearts. But let justice roll on like a river, righteousness like a never-failing stream.   *(Amos 5:24)*

The prophet Isaiah reminds us there are times in life when we sense God is not hearing our prayers because we are not living as He has taught us to live. We seek God with religious fervor, yet fail to treat our fellow man with love and compassion. We bring offerings as though our generosity can excuse our callous behavior toward people in need. But God will not be bought. God will not honor hypocrisy with His blessings.

> **We seek God with religious fervor, yet fail to treat our fellow man with love and compassion.**

"The multitude of your sacrifices—what are they to me?" says the Lord. "I have more than enough of burnt offerings, of rams and the fat of fattened animals. I have no pleasure in the blood of lambs and bulls and goats. When you come to appear before me, who has asked this of you, this trampling of my courts? Stop bringing meaningless offerings! . . . When you spread out your hands in prayer, I will hide my eyes from you; even if you offer many prayers, I will not listen."
(Isaiah 1:11-15)

And why is this true?

Your hands are full of blood; wash and make yourselves clean. Take your evil deeds out of my sight! Stop doing wrong, learn to do right! Seek justice, encourage the oppressed. Defend the cause of the fatherless, plead the case of the widow.

"Come now, let us reason together," says the Lord. "Though your sins are like scarlet, they shall be white as snow. Though they are as red as crimson, they shall be like wool. If you are willing and obedient, you will eat the best from the land; but if you resist and rebel, you will be devoured by the sword." For the mouth of the Lord has spoken.
(Isaiah 1:16-20)

True devotion toward God is demonstrated by how we choose to act toward others—the people who live with us, who work with us, who live in our neighborhood, state, nation and world. If we do not act with justice, God will ignore our prayers and pious platitudes. He will reject our tithes and offerings.

The eighth century before Christ was a time of moral and ethical ferment. God's powerful spirit moved on the hearts of men like Isaiah, Amos, Hosea and Micah to make them see what their compatriots and fellow-religionists did not see. There was awful abuse in the economic system. The poor were trampled and the rich paid no attention. Widows and orphans were left to their own devices while families who prospered did nothing to help those less fortunate.

The people could draw aside to worship with prayer, song and the playing of musical instruments, and then go out into the community to callously take advantage of the poor. In greed, selfishness, and pride, they turned their backs on the pleas of the needy. God spoke through the prophets to call the people to account for their sin.

> *He has showed you, O man, what is good. And what does the Lord require of you? To act justly, and to love mercy and to walk humbly with your God.* (Micah 6:8)

This message is as true for us today as it was for the people addressed by the Old Testament prophets. We ask God to take care of us, yet we cheat and steal and lie.

> **We live our lives of selfish non-involvement amid those who have great needs.**

We ask God to bless us, yet give little thought to share God's blessing with others. We live our lives of selfish non-involvement amid those who have great needs. Our hypocrisy is an affront to God. If we want God to hear us, the first prayer we need to pray is one of repentance.

In His time, Jesus addressed the self-righteous teachers and Pharisees, the leaders of the people of God, who had forgotten their calling. They lived as a privileged class, burdening the people with the requirements of religious legalism while being devoid of compassion and mercy.

*". . . you hypocrites. You give a tenth of your spice—
mint, dill and cumin. But you have neglected the more important matters of the law — justice, mercy and faithfulness.
You should have practiced the latter without neglecting the
former. You blind guides! You strain out a gnat and swallow
a camel."*   *(Matthew 23:23-24)*

The words of Jesus don't need much explanation. We may
strive to perform to the letter of the law by paying strict tithes on
even the little spices in our cupboard. But if we do not live the
spirit of the law, we are desperately out of step with God's will. If
immorality, cheating, stealing, lying, exploitation, prejudice, neglect of others and selfishness mark our lives, we must wake up to
the reality of our sin. If we have failed to listen to our conscience
or obey God's commands in Scripture, the first order of business is
to repent. We must stop doing evil and begin to do good.

That choice is ours, but it is not an easy task. In fact, it's virtu-
ally impossible unless we ask God's help to turn our priorities
around and to reshape our lives. The church is called to be where
people are hurting, left out, wounded, and guilty. We are to be
there with a ministry to the hungry, ill clothed, lonely, and afraid.
When the church is there for those people, we are there for Jesus.

It's one thing to know what needs to be done; it's another thing
for a church to make up its mind
to do something toward solving

> **If we truly love God, we must
> also love each other.**

the problems. If we truly love
God, we must also love each
other. It is important that we, as individual Christians, are meeting
needs by being there for people. It is also important for the church,
corporately, to put its resources and its life on the line for people
who need the grace and mercy of God.

**Ministry begins with sensitivity to human need and honest
seeking after God's will.** When we become aware of human need
around us, how do we know what to do? We must ask God for His
wisdom—that His will be revealed. Jesus prayed, *"Not my will but
thine be done."* God's will is that His values be put in place, that
the example of Jesus be followed, that His love be fleshed out
through the church.

When we try to make up our minds about what to do, what decisions to make, what service and ministry to undertake, we want to know the mind of Christ. That is our call—to think His thoughts, to have the mind of Christ alive in us *(Philippians 2:5)*.

Standing up to do what is right is not as fearful when we remember that God is on the side of those who seek love and justice. When we face trials and our faith is tested, we have the promise of God's wisdom as we persevere. There is joy in ministry.

> *Consider it pure joy, my brothers, whenever you face trials of many kinds, because you know that the testing of your faith develops perseverance. Perseverance must finish its work so that you may be mature and complete, not lacking anything. If any of you lacks wisdom, he should ask God, who gives generously to all without finding fault, and it will be given to him.* *(James 1:2-5)*

Do justice and love mercy. The prophet Micah said the Lord requires that we do justice and love mercy *(Micah 6:8)*. We all need mercy because if God dealt with us only in justice, who could stand? Thank God for His mercy. But before we pride ourselves on our mercy to others, we ought to do everything possible to obtain systems of law which yield justice.

Justice is about love and mercy and about holding people accountable. Carved into stone above the doors of the Supreme Court in our

> **Justice is about love and mercy, and about holding people accountable.**

nation's capital are these words: *Equal justice under law.* While visiting Washington D.C., I looked up at that solemn pronouncement cut in stone, and I thought, *"That's what we all say when we pledge allegiance to our flag—justice for all."* That's what we mean when we say we are a nation of laws and not men. No one has the authority to set the law aside for himself. Or, as is often said, *"No one is above the law!"* We are all bound by our justice system and by the provisions of our government's Constitution.

Law and justice protect us from abuse, but not everyone is happy with the concept of law applied all of the time to all of the people. Samuel Johnson, the great English lexicographer, may have gotten to the heart of it when he wrote, *"Justice is my being allowed to do whatever I like. Injustice is whatever prevents me from doing so.* " There are many people who feel that way about the law and the world in which we live. We want justice for the criminals we read about in the newspapers or see on TV, but if we should run afoul of the law, or if someone we love gets into trouble, we then want mercy. U.S. Supreme Court Justice Potter Stewart once defined justice in a very simple way. He said, *"Fairness is what justice really is."* Being fair can be a difficult issue in a world so prone to callousness!

As Christians, we often fail to see our own involvement in unjust practices, as though our general respectability is evidence of our total innocence. Unfortunately, ethical practices among church members often are more a reflection of our culture in general than they are of the high calling of Christ. Our sensitivity to unjust attitudes and behavior is often dulled when the issues are close at hand or involve us personally.

For example, many people come to America from other lands to find work—in the fields, in our homes and in other low wage jobs. Abused by many and unappreciated by most, these people live without much protection of the law, criticized and often despised by their employers who hire them to work. How are we to respond to this as people who are called to have the mind of Christ?

The debate over affirmative action is bitter and personally painful to many of my friends and church members. But we ought not to ignore that we have had affirmative action in our country for decades—it used to be that white males were the recipients of an informal but highly powerful system of preferential treatment. Justice is not easily gained in this matter, but a little bit of history and a lot of humility will go a long way in helping us work out this problem. This sensitive and troubling issue provides a modern day example of the truth of the biblical idea that the sins of the fathers are visited upon the children *(Exodus 20:5).*

What about justice in our school systems? Can we say that our schools consciously and carefully seek out what is just in all situations? Are all children treated equally? Or, is it a common practice for teachers to go into classrooms with preconceived ideas about which children can learn and which will be troublemakers? Do teachers begin the school year programming the children with what they expect the child can and can't do? It makes all the difference in the world for young people who have been counted as unworthy and worthless to find some adult somewhere in their life who believes they can really become something. We can all be that for some child in whom no one else believes.

My wife, Rosemary, was a schoolteacher for over fifteen years. She loved working with children, all the children. She was a tough disciplinarian but the children knew she loved them. They loved her compassionate spirit and infectious laugh. She tried to get the best out of every child. She was impatient with the reports on the children that relegated some to an inferior status. She, like any good teacher, could see potential in every child.

She often would have a child in her class whose mother was in the women's shelter or whose parents were temporarily staying at the community night shelter. It was easy to ask, "What are we supposed to do with these children? They are so far behind and will be moving on in a little while. How can we be expected to teach them anything?"

Rosemary said, "Maybe all we can do is love them and the next teacher can teach them."

How do we deal at home with our own children? Do we promise them we will do something and then don't get around to it? Do we demand that they live by standards of behavior different from our own? Is the punishment meted out for our children's disobedience consistent with the severity of their offense? Do we tend to set rules that are enforced only at our convenience or at our whim? Do we make the mistake of believing that loving our children means never holding them accountable? Do we think we can let them grow up doing as they please?

It is interesting that in Scripture, the justice most often called for is justice from the rich to the poor. It's hard for us to figure out how not eating the food on our plate relates to the starving children in China, as our mothers often chided. But somehow, we have to deal with the question of disparity between the "haves" and the "have nots." Out of our wealth and opportunities, we must give thought to what we can do to make a difference with the poor.

Justice is about protecting our families and ourselves from harm, but also about holding ourselves accountable to do what is fair and right toward others. God gives us a great compliment. He believes we are capable of making good choices. He holds us accountable when we make wrong choices. God will do justice in the world and He expects us to do justice as well.

In Luke 16, Jesus tells a story about a rich man who made a terrible mistake by thinking God was on his side. When the rich man died, he went to hell and found out that the poor beggar who had been lying sick and hungry outside his gate had gone to heaven. What's more, he discovered a great chasm between them. He could neither go up to heaven from hell, nor could mercy be extended from those in heaven down to him. God had revealed Himself and His demands for justice through Moses and the prophets. Those who do not listen suffer the consequences of their disobedience. God stands on the side of the poor. That is the message of Scripture. Justice will be had, in

> *Jesus said that we are all going to stand before Him someday and He will look into our hearts.*

this life or the next. Jesus said that we are all going to stand before Him someday and He will look into our hearts. He is going to say to some, *"I was hungry and you did not care. I was thirsty and there was no water for me. I was a stranger and you would not recognize me. I was in prison and you would not come to see me. I was sick and you did not come to care for me."*

We will say, *"When did we see you hungry or thirsty or a stranger or needing clothes or sick or in prison, and did not help you?"*

And He will say, *"I tell you the truth, whatever you did not do for one of the least of these, you did not do for me." (See Matthew 25:31-46)*

A Brazilian bishop of the Roman Catholic Church has been quoted as saying, *"When I give food to the poor, they call me a saint. When I ask why the poor have no food, they call me a communist."* We don't have the communists to kick around anymore. Judgment fell upon them. So why are there still hungry people? It's not because of communism or capitalism. It's mostly a problem of figuring out ways to get the food God provides distributed so that everybody everywhere gets some of it.

In Bangladesh several years ago, there was a famine. The government officials blamed it on the weather. Some time later it became known that there was plenty of food available from earlier harvests, but the problem was that those who controlled the food would not distribute it.

We live in a country where the welfare system has become a point of major controversy. People who have plenty of food and power can't seem to devise a workable plan to provide assistance to those who have few resources and even less power. The poor get hurt again and again. Some people think they are imposed upon because taxes must be paid to help the poor and needy. A close look at the money called "entitlement" in the US budget will show that Americans of all races and all socio-economic status receive special benefits from the federal government. We are finding better ways to provide assistance so that people are helped and not hurt by our society's attempts to do good. Someday, we will all stand before God and be asked what we were doing in the effort to help people find their way.

In 1997 I was asked to chair a committee for the Commissioners Court of Tarrant County to seek ways to help move people from welfare to work, from public assistance to self-sufficiency. It is a complex issue but one that is now being addressed with creativity and energy in communities all across America.

It is important in this effort to acknowledge there are people who will never be anything but poor and helpless, and they have a moral claim on the rest of us. There are people with mental limitations who would love to work but can't find jobs. Few employers know how to create special positions so the mentally challenged can be hired and become productive citizens. If we are not willing to hire them or help figure out a way they can make a living, we shouldn't complain about tax money spent to help provide them places to live. There are people with emotional difficulties who would love to have productive jobs, but they can't. It's not because they are lazy or don't care, but they will need special medical and spiritual attention if they will ever be able to work enough to provide for their own needs.

The church needs to sharpen its social conscience. I read of a survey which indicated that fewer than 10 per cent of the pastors in America have on their agenda a concern that their church help to make a difference in the lives of the poor. I'm grateful to be part of a church that has made a major commitment to intervene in the lives of people in our community who are broken, hurting, hungry and lonely. But I won't quit reminding and encouraging people to

> **God calls us out of our comfort zones.**

be involved. God calls us out of our comfort zones. Many people sit week after week in comfortable Sunday pews and never think, "I can make a difference." The fact is, they can help in many ways. In these cases, the preacher's job is to comfort the afflicted and afflict the comfortable.

The way I read the Bible, God was not terribly concerned about the rich receiving justice. He figured the wealthy and the privileged could handle justice on their own—and we mostly do unless we really mess up. Many people have more money than they want to admit. Someday we will give an account to God for where we stood when it was time to care for people who need what we have or what we can do. This is not about doing things for people they can do for themselves. It is about building bridges, making ways for people who have spent their whole lives in poverty to find ways to come out of poverty. Within the Body of Christ, there are those who are bright enough and care enough to find realistic solutions.

In the meanwhile, we are challenged by our Lord to do justice in our businesses—to pay a fair wage to those who work for us, to give our best effort to those for whom we work. We are challenged to do justice in our homes—to be loving and fair with our families. We must not take advantage of or abuse those who depend on us. God knows what's going on.

> **If it were not for God's mercy as well as His justice, where could we go?**

If it were not for God's mercy as well as His justice, where could we go? We love mercy because we are all guilty. We all stand before God, knowing there have been times in our lives when we have not done justice and we have not walked humbly with God. In arrogance and pride, we have pointed our fingers in judgment. We have shown our carelessness toward others who need us. We have allowed sin to grow in our lives.

If we do not have a merciful God who forgives and restores, where can we go? Our sin requires that justice be done. Our Lord Jesus took our sins upon Himself and suffered crucifixion and death on our behalf. But God raised Jesus from the dead and gives us hope of salvation and eternal life. Through this act, God provides both justice and mercy as we respond to His love in repentance, faith and commitment. We must be grateful for God's justice, as well as His mercy, for unless there is justice, mercy means nothing.

EVALUATING OUR MINISTRY PRIORITIES

As churches allocate time, money, influence, skill and abilities, it troubles me that we spend so much of our resources taking care of people just like ourselves, and so little of our energies and resources taking care of wounded and broken people outside our circle of influence. In trying to understand the mission of the church, we must constantly evaluate the focus of our ministry. Are we sensitive to the needs of those who are outside the fellowship of our church?

I have been in several churches during budget allocation discussions. A predominant statement during those discussions has been: *"I think we should take care of our own members. I don't see why we have to spend so much money on people who are not members of our church. How many people will join the church if we do that for them? How many new members do we stand to gain from that expenditure of money?"*

Those are perhaps legitimate questions. But at best, that kind of thinking means we are focused only on evangelism. At worst, it means we are focused on *churchism*—building up the numbers, which is not even true evangelism. Churches that have membership drives instead of calls to discipleship seem off the mark to me.

The church has a unique calling to feed, heal and care for people in the name of Jesus. I hear Jesus saying that ministry is doing good for people who need us and who may never be members of our church. They may never become Christians. They may never believe that God is good. They may take what we give and go their way without so much as a thank you. Are we obligated as Christians in those kinds of ways? I think that, under God, we are. We must develop a commitment to courageous service.

> **The church has a unique calling to feed, heal and care for people, in the name of Jesus.**

As a Christian and a minister of the gospel, I want the church to minister where there are open wounds of poverty, prejudice, and neglect. I want the church to speak out against conditions that push people down and cause them to lose hope in the world. I want us to find ways to bind up the broken hearted, take time to be a friend to the lonely, accept those who have not yet been able to accept themselves, and give people the freedom to find Christ because we are free enough to love them when they don't even love themselves.

We must allow the gospel to change the ways we relate to down-and-out people as well as up-and-outs, wherever and whoever they may be. Then we will earn the right to speak to them of the transforming power of the gospel. Some people have closed their ears and hardened their hearts to the gospel because they have not seen a consistency between what we Christians say and what we do. As we minister in Jesus' name, what we do takes on a new dimension of meaning for those we serve. They begin to believe that God's people care and that God cares. They begin to hear the good news for the first time. Darkness can turn to light because God is at work making us into new kinds of people—the kind of people Jesus was talking about in Matthew 25:40.

Doing the right thing may not shield us from times of real discouragement. One of the reasons churches have difficulty beginning community ministries is that the people we help often don't react the way we think they ought to react. We want them to have the good manners to say "thank you" and to act like they are grateful. We would do most anything for people who would say "thank you." But we need to remember that Jesus healed ten lepers and only one came back to say "thank you." That ingratitude wasn't easy for Jesus to accept either. That's the way it is with people. Jesus didn't take the healing away from the nine because they failed to express gratitude.

> *Caring with no expectation of dividends is doing ministry for the right reason.*

Sometimes people who receive goodness from others respond with anger rather than gratitude. Mature Christians understand that even as we do the right thing in the name of Christ, we should not necessarily expect anything in return. Whatever good comes back is serendipity. Servant-hearted Christians do not do good in order to receive an emotional high from the reaction of others. Caring with no expectation of dividends is doing ministry for the right reason. We do good for others even if they turn on their heels and walk away.

Wherever the hands of Jesus moved, that's where our hands are to move. Wherever the heart of Jesus carried Him in compassion for others, that is where the heart of the church must take us.

Healthy churches must be alert to ministry opportunities that God offers in the community. When the church recognizes a need and sends out a call for help, members of the Body of Christ will be moved by the Holy Spirit to respond. If we become sensitive to people in our city who need the Lord's love, we can trust God to help us as we seek to express that love in a variety of ways.

MINISTRY OPPORTUNITIES COME KNOCKING AT THE DOOR

There is no better way for a church to uncover ministry opportunities than for members of the Body to get involved in intercessory prayer. It opens the door for Christians to become the embodiment of Jesus Christ. Prayer that risks bearing the burdens of those in need also prepares the hearts of those in the congregation who are called by God to respond to need with loving support and service.

God's response to sincere intercessory prayer is to send His Holy Spirit to work in the Body of Christ. He will cause men and women to see and hear the plight of the broken-hearted, be compelled by His love to bind the wounds of the oppressed, and encourage those who want to serve the Lord.

> *Intercessory prayer opens the door for Christians to become the embodiment of Jesus Christ.*

I remember clearly when the Missions Committee at First Baptist Church, Arlington began gathering regularly to pray for new mission opportunities. We already had a Spanish-speaking congregation meeting in our building. The prayers of the committee for God to provide new opportunities were soon answered when a Chinese and, a month later, a Korean pastor came to me with the vision of starting a congregation for their language groups in our community. That work was enthusiastically supported and strengthened under our sponsorship. They met in our building for several years and now all three of those congregations have their own independent churches in Arlington.

The prayers of many in our congregation for our church to be involved in missions at home as well as abroad have been answered through a stream of sensitive people who have brought their visions of Christian ministry to us. They came, literally knocking on the church door, asking us to join them in responding to God's call in their lives. That's how our church became involved in sponsoring the Arlington Women's Shelter, in supporting the Arlington Night Shelter for the homeless, and in the founding of Mission Arlington, whose multifaceted ministries have had such phenomenal impact.

When spiritual sensitivities are sharpened, and ministry needs are perceived in the community, people have not been afraid to come before the church with their ideas and ask for help. If willing workers step forward, we want to affirm their vision and send them out with our blessing to make a difference in their world.

FACING DIFFICULT MINISTRY DECISIONS

Not every opportunity that comes knocking can be successfully answered. Sometimes we falter and fail. We faced that situation in 1986 when a family whose child had AIDS wanted to come to our church and have their little boy cared for in our preschool ministry. However, because of the widespread fear over the AIDS issue, they asked that knowledge of their child's condition be kept confidential and not shared with other parents.

I wanted to serve this family's needs, but I was fearful of the risks. We had conflicting information from doctors about ways the AIDS virus could be transmitted, and I could not find a way to include the little boy without making other parents aware of the situation. We were in a dilemma which devastated that family and was deeply, permanently painful to me. We failed to minister to them as we should.

As a result of that failure, God gave us a new vision. We researched the issue and obtained expert advice in order to be fully informed. We then put together a policy to deal with similar issues in the future. We now are able to confidently welcome any child or adult and minister to them in any area of our church. We will take care of every child so that all children are safe and all children are welcomed. When we were not able to do for that one child what his family needed us to do, it was a sad and tragic time.

The only redemptive thing we were able to retrieve out of the failure on my part was to develop a policy of care for all children that makes it possible for us to receive any child and to protect the privacy of the family as well. Since that time, over 300 churches have requested a copy of our policy so they might appropriately address this issue as well.

Our communities desperately need churches who have the courage to minister to the real needs of people. Where do we get such courage? We don't get courage by asking people to

> *We don't get courage by asking the people to vote on whether we should have courage.*

vote on whether we should have courage. We get courage by going to Christ in prayer, asking Him to think His thoughts through us. Then we have to put our lives out there where He wants us to be. If we mess up, we claim His forgiving grace, and then get up and go again.

A church does well to seek social involvement that will have a long-term impact on people. Ministering to people in the name of Christ not only changes the lives of those being served, it enriches the lives of the ones ministering. One day a city councilman, Methodist layman and physician, thanked me for the ministries our church has in the community by saying, *"Charles, the work your church is doing through Mission Arlington has done more to help the citizens of our city change their attitude about helping the poor than anything anybody else has been able to do."*

That affirmation of the work of our church meant a lot to me. It is not easy for the average church member to take that first step of personal involvement in the life of someone perceived to be different. Cultural, economic, and racial stereotypes create psychological barriers that often are difficult to overcome. But as we reach out to people in our city through various ministries, we know the best gift we have to give is Jesus. As people receive help from crisis ministries, we always invite them to participate in an ongoing Bible study group in their area. When Jesus becomes the bridge to relationships, fears quickly dissipate and problems become opportunities.

Within a time span of ten years, the three small apartment Bible study groups that represented the start of Mission Arlington grew to over 200 Bible study groups involving over 3000 people every Sunday. These groups form small congregations all across town—in apartments, motels, and mobile home communities. Hundreds of our church members head out each week to teach the Bible, lead worship, counsel, and be friends to those who would never enter our church building. These Mission Arlington Bible study groups have made a real difference in changing lives, in restoring families, in helping people get back on their feet economically, and in nurturing renewed spirituality. The police tell us that Mission Arlington has made a significant difference in the most crime-infested areas of our city.

For decades, my dream has been for church people to be as familiar with the words of Matthew 25:40 as they are with John 3:16. I really believe Jesus was serious in His vision of the judgment when He said we will stand before the King and He will know whether we "fed the hungry, gave water to the thirsty, invited the stranger in, clothed the naked, visited sick people and prisoners." James summed it up well when he wrote, *"Be doers of the word, and not hearers only" (James 1:22).* How can members of the Body of Christ take the words of Jesus seriously and not make time for social ministry?

Thoughtful ministry helps break the cycle of poverty in people's lives. Church people are more motivated to give of themselves and their resources when they can have a hands-on involvement in Christian ministry. Through Mission Arlington, many Christians in our community are finding ways to make a difference in breaking the cycle of poverty for disadvantaged families. People whose values have not been shaped by a biblical worldview are prime candidates for involuntary poverty. By leading Bible study groups and becoming personally involved with people who have special needs, they are able to apply biblical principles to everyday life choices.

> **People whose values have not been shaped by a Biblical worldview are prime candidates for involuntary poverty.**

When people discover God's love and begin to feel important as members of their small congregation, self-esteem goes straight up. When they are finally able to trust God to save them, everything begins to change—their family relationships, their job opportunities, their sense of belonging and their hope for the future.

Mission Arlington also supports homeless people by cooperating with churches and community groups to provide regular meals to the local Night Shelter, which operates from 6 p.m. to 7 a.m. Then Mission Arlington provides a Day Shelter where people can stay if they have no other place to go during the day. In the Day Shelter, people can get assistance in job hunting, resume development, job interview and interpersonal skills. A telephone is provided for job prospecting. Local employers frequently come by the Day Shelter to hire contract labor. Recently a new ministry was begun: haircuts for those who are ready for job interviews! New ministries grow out of discovered needs.

A licensed child development center is provided for homeless children, so their parents can seek jobs and handle their affairs during the day without worrying about their kids. Those children receive unconditional love in a beautiful environment from loving caregivers. God's blessing is poured on these children through this ministry.

A day care center for senior adults assists families who are not able to care for aged and infirm parents during the workday and can't afford to hire private caregivers.

COURAGEOUS SERVICE BUILT ON CONFIDENCE IN GOD'S PROVISION

Those who serve God with courageous commitment are not content with pathways that are easy, predictable, safe and secure. They risk to minister boldly to people in need, confident that God will guide, protect, and see them through to

> *God takes the side of the outcasts, the sick, the poor and the hungry.*

journey's end. Some people don't think of God as taking sides, believing that He is no respecter of persons. It's true that He is no respecter of persons, but it is also true that God stands with people who have no one else to stand with them. God takes the side of the outcast, the sick, the poor and the hungry.

If the church is to be true to its calling to reflect the character of Jesus, it must also take the side of people in need, ministering with courage and refusing to be turned back. It would be much easier to be a part of a church that takes care only of its own. But I can't get away from asking the question: *"What does Jesus want us to do?"* The Lord does not give His church the luxury of picking and choosing who to get involved with on the basis of our own desires. He calls us to His work!

Some churches have sought to justify their failure to help the people in the ditch by saying, *"We don't want to get so focused on feeding them bread that we forget to give them the bread of life."* Churches have turned that into an excuse for not caring about the physical and emotional needs of people, as well as their spiritual needs. It is true that we must give more than bread. We must give the gospel bread of life. But it is not true that we must choose one and neglect the other. We must do both!

Jesus said, *"Man shall not live by bread alone"(Matthew 4:4).* He refused to be a bread-and-butter kind of messiah—but He fed the multitudes when they were hungry. He didn't tell them to disregard their hunger pains and simply sit down and listen to His sermon. He fed them the kind of bread that fills empty stomachs. Jesus understood that the life of the spirit is more important than the life of the physical body, because He knew that spirit and body are connected. He preached the good news of salvation, but He also healed withered hands and made blind eyes to see.

> *Jesus clearly cared about both salvation and service. He saw people whole, and so must the church.*

My sense is that many church leaders are afraid that people will think they don't care about the salvation of the lost if they give serious attention to the immediate needs of people for food, shelter, medical care, education, friendship, and self-esteem. Jesus clearly cared about both salvation and service. He saw people whole, and so must the church.

⌘

COMMITMENT TO EVANGELISM AND MINISTRY AT THE SAME TIME

Evangelism and ministry go hand-in-hand. I cannot conceive how a church could legitimately separate the two and seek to do just one or the other. As Christians, we must behave in ways consistent with the beliefs we profess. Our lives, individually and corporately, must show evidences of the gospel's power—submission to the leadership of Christ, commitment to moral and ethical behavior, and dedication to act in love and justice toward our fellow man.

Our task is to allow Christ to live in us—to become servants ministering in His name, and then through our lives and testimony, witness to

> **The Kingdom of God is not just a future event; it starts in the here and now.**

what we know of God's saving grace. The Kingdom of God is not just a future event; it starts in the here and now.

As those who come to God through Jesus Christ begin to live new lives, they transform the world around them. The "great commission" of Jesus was to go to people everywhere, making them His disciples, and teaching them to obey everything He had commanded *(Matthew 28:19-20)*.

And what did He command? *Love God and love your neighbor as yourself (Matthew 22:36-40).* As Christians live out that vertical and horizontal pattern of the faith, they will give their lives in trust and love to God **and** they will minister to others.

Ministry is the evidence that our hearts have truly been evangelized, that we have received the gospel all the way down to our feet. As we do

> **Ministry is the evidence that our hearts have truly been evangelized.**

acts of ministry, evangelism often results. It is right for the church to encourage its members to register and vote, to enter the political arena in order to express a concern for all citizens, to speak up on issues that impact everyone. We should not shy away from issues of alcohol and drug abuse, justice, racism, violence, war and peace, public education, housing, gambling, sexual immorality, abortion, sanctity of marriage, children, family issues, and religious liberty.

Yet it is crucial for the church that none of the social issues takes precedence over the clear proclamation of the gospel of Jesus, the message of God's grace that calls for repentance and faith.

When the gospel is clearly and honestly preached and lived, every social issue of importance will receive biblical input. The light of God's wisdom will shine in that darkness and Christians will be compelled by the love of God to deal courageously and lovingly with all who need them.

⌘

⌘
JESUS PRINCIPLES
FOR SERVING COURAGEOUSLY
TO HEAL THE WOUNDED

⌘ The church is the Body of Christ, and is therefore a continuation of the incarnation of Christ.

⌘ Serving God and His people requires honesty and integrity. The members of the Body of Christ must live in harmony and integration with the head of the Body, Jesus Christ.

⌘ When evil, injustice or deceit is discovered in the church or in the world, a healthy church will speak out courageously.

⌘ A healthy church will be present in the community with the word of God, loving and nurturing people to life, interceding for the helpless, defending the oppressed, encouraging the broken-hearted, and healing the human spirit through the word of God which always creates faith, hope and love.

⌘ Decisions in the church must be reached by asking everyone to seek the mind of Christ, which leads to knowing the will of God.

⌘ We expect to be able to know the mind of Christ through a prayerful dependence upon the Holy Spirit for guidance, faithful study of Scripture, consideration of the convictions of other Christians, and thoughtful reflection based upon the wisdom God has promised to give.

⌘ When the mind of Christ is found, all in the Body will bring their prayers, gifts and energies to do God's work in the world, relying on the Holy Spirit to empower the Body for that task.

⌘ The Kingdom of God is present wherever and whenever Christ is present and the will of God is done. The Kingdom of God is both now and not yet.

⌘ The true work of Christians is to be partners with God in putting His good, but broken, world back together so that God's glory is served and believers begin to experience the unfolding of the Kingdom of God.

⌘ We seek to serve God faithfully and with courage in this life, knowing that Christ has promised to return and gather us into glory in His own time. In that hope, we live and persevere.

HEAVENLY FATHER:

WE MUST REMIND OURSELVES THAT WHILE WE WERE SINNERS, YOU GAVE YOUR SON TO DIE IN OUR PLACE. JESUS RESCUED US FROM SIN AND DEATH AND BROUGHT US INTO THE FREEDOM OF NEW LIFE IN YOUR KINGDOM. WE THANK YOU FOR SUCH LOVE, WHICH REACHES OUT TO ALL HUMANKIND.

IN RESPONSE TO YOUR LOVE AND MERCY, LORD, WE WANT TO SERVE YOU IN OBEDIENCE, FEEDING YOUR SHEEP AND BRINGING RECONCILIATION TO A BROKEN AND SUFFERING WORLD. WE ASK THAT YOU LAY AN AX TO THOSE BITTER ROOTS OF SELFISHNESS AND UNCONCERN THAT REMAIN WITHIN OUR UNREPENTANT HEARTS. FILL US WITH YOUR LOVE AND COMPASSION SO WE SEE WITH EMPATHY THE WOUNDINGS IN OUR BROTHERS AND SISTERS. MAKE US BLIND TO COLOR, CLASS AND IDEOLOGY SO WE REACH OTHERS WITH YOUR PURE LOVE. GIVE US WISDOM AND COURAGE TO MINISTER EFFECTIVELY IN THE NAME OF CHRIST.

MAKE US FAITHFUL TO YOUR CALLING. HELP US TO SEE AND UNDERSTAND THE NEEDS OF PEOPLE IN OUR COMMUNITY AND COURAGEOUSLY FOLLOW YOUR WILL AS WE MINISTER EACH DAY.

AMEN

Life Applications
⌘
MINISTER
Serving Courageously to Heal the Wounded

1. Do you agree that involvement in Christian ministry requires courage, both by individuals and the Body of Christ? Explain.

2. What are some of the greatest obstacles Christians must overcome in developing the courage to become involved in ministry activities? Make a parallel list of the obstacles you feel within yourself, and of those you perceive in the church as a corporate body.

3. How do you think these obstacles can best be overcome? What is the best way to motivate individuals and the church to action?

4. What ministry needs are crying out in your community? Specifically, how and where can your church act as Jesus in the following ways?
   ☐ Preaching good news to the poor.
      (Ministry of encouragement and evangelism)
   ☐ Proclaiming freedom for prisoners.
      (Ministry of intercession and aid)
   ☐ Promoting recovery of sight for the blind.
      (Ministry of healing, spiritual growth, education)
   ☐ Releasing the oppressed or victimized.
      (Ministry of comfort and justice)
   ☐ Making known the reality of God's love.
      (Ministry of presence and partnership)

5. Look up Matthew 25:31-46 in your Bible. Work on memorizing verse 40. What does Jesus say is required for us to receive His inheritance? How can you change the way you live as a Christian to live up to this requirement?

8

CREATE FELLOWSHIP
Strengthening the Body through Loving Relationships

> **Fel.low.ship -**
> Mutual love and ministering care expressed between
> Christians, based on their common experience of
> having been loved and cared for through the grace of
> Jesus Christ.

S ome Christians get starry-eyed when they think of how wonderful first century church life must have been—as though
being under the direct teaching of the Apostles quickly and
almost effortlessly brought those early Christians into perfect love,
generosity and unity of purpose. But one only has to read closely
the writings of the apostle Paul to understand how much disunity,
quarreling, and misunderstanding existed in the early church, and
how diligently Paul worked to mediate problems and create a fellowship where members loved and cared for one another.

Problems encountered within the early church were similar to
problems that have challenged congregations throughout Christian
history. Churches have fallen into periods of quarreling, sin and
disunity that have disgraced them before their Lord, but they have
also pulled together to achieve glorious victories. Much of our
New Testament Scriptures were written as circulating letters of
counsel to early Christian congregations. Those letters reveal a
"pastor's heart." They were written to encourage Christians to
rightly understand the gospel of Jesus Christ and to develop a loving fellowship so they could live out the reality of the Kingdom of
God and do the work of Christ in the world.

The earliest Christians had no stirring historical examples to
bolster their claim that the Christian way was the way to live. They
had no great scholars to which they could appeal for validation of
their claim to truth. They had no impressive numbers to give verac-
ity to their preaching. But what they did have was an ability to

function in a very hostile world with an amazingly sacrificial love. Despite their many problems, it was true of them that, as their Lord had hoped, they would be known as His disciples by their love *(John 13:35)*. They were a people who loved each other with boldness and a charity never before seen in their culture. Their love succeeded in turning the world upside-down *(Acts 17:6-7)*.

> **The key to power in the New Testament church, then and now, is the Holy Spirit who grounds us in the love and grace of the Lord Jesus Christ.**

Love builds fellowship, which produces unity. When love within a church begins to produce unity, the Holy Spirit of God gives power to overcome all obstacles. The key to power in the New Testament church, then and now, is the Holy Spirit who grounds us in the love and grace of the Lord Jesus Christ.

The remarkable witness of the early church is that so many of them took seriously the invitation of Jesus to deny themselves and to follow Him, no matter what. They went where He asked them to go, spreading the good news that in Christ there is life, abundant and free. They taught that men and women did not have to stay the way they were.

The early church worshipped, witnessed, taught and ministered like Jesus did. Those early Christians carefully taught their children and new converts how to live in Christ. Wherever they found people hurting, they applied the love of Jesus Christ. Through their love, the Spirit of God moved to bring comfort to those in need and the light of salvation and rebirth to those who were lost.

The word *covenant* is used throughout the Old Testament to describe the relationship of promise and obedience between men and women and Jehovah God. At the incarnation of Jesus Christ into human life, people were invited to come into a new covenant relationship with God, the Father. Through Jesus Christ, the Son of God, we experience a covenant and a *communion* that results in deep fellowship with God and with each other.

> *God, who has called you into fellowship with his Son Jesus Christ, is faithful. I appeal to you . . . in the name of our Lord Jesus Christ, that all of you agree with one another*

so that there may be no divisions among you and that you may be perfectly united in mind and thought.
(1 Corinthians 1:9-10)

At a pastor's luncheon, I sat at a table with a group of fellow ministers. Despite their mutual respect for one another, several had experienced wounds in the past caused by charges and counter-charges leveled against each other. And there had been differences of opinion concerning the direction our denomination was taking.

As we sang together the chorus *Jesus Is the Sweetest Name I Know*, I could hear my brother in Christ next to me singing the same words I was singing. In that moment, I came to the realization once again that my fellow pastor loves Jesus as I do. He wants his life to be an avenue of grace to others as I do. We still have our differences, and still would vote different agendas, but I felt love and genuine appreciation for him. I pray that good things will happen in his life and in his church.

I confess I am more at ease with those who see things as I do, but the brother who does not agree with me is important to me and I love him and wish him well. How does this happen? We both love Jesus. I am encouraged (yes, commanded) by my Savior to love and treasure those who love Him.

The word *fellowship* is the English translation of the Greek word *koinonia*. The concept of *koinonia* is to have communion, to share intimately with one another in common purpose. As Christians, we are bonded to one another by the realization that God has come near. He sent His Son to live with us. Through this relationship, we dare to believe that we can have personal fellowship or communion with the Father as Jesus did. We can look into the vast reaches of space, and confronted by the mystery of all that is there, still whisper "*Abba*, Father." We can look around us at people who are angry, discouraged and bitter in their relationships, and still call them brother and sister, because we are bound to them through the love of Christ flowing through us. Our fellowship with God and with each other centers in the relationship we have with Jesus.

⌘

HOW CHURCHES DEFINE THEIR FELLOWSHIP

Most churches understand that unity of purpose is essential to building Christian fellowship. Yet, the way in which that common purpose is defined will vary between congregations and will ultimately affect the quality of their fellowship.

Shared Values or Lifestyle

Some churches seek unity and fellowship based *on shared interests and common lifestyle.* Members may come from the same economic group, educational level, cultural, social or racial background and loyalties. The similarities of lifestyle provide comfort and enjoyment because the church is an extension of values inherent in their family, social and professional lives. They live, work and play together and their church fellowship is grounded in comfortable friendships.

Shared Social or Political Views

Some churches strive to define who they are and promote unity around particular political attitudes or stances, rallying behind *commonly held issues of Christian concern.* The common ground of the social or political issue builds support and agreement among the members. Their focus may be a defense of Christian heritage in the nation, promotion of either a "liberal" or "conservative" policy in government, support of the pro-life or pro-family movements, concern for peace and non-violence, or convictions related to the environment, world hunger, crime, drugs, the media, or education.

Commitment to a Crucial Spiritual Need

Other churches build themselves around *a shared spiritual emphasis.* Believing that certain needs in the church must be addressed, they commit themselves to the task at hand. The primary emphasis of the church may be interpreted as evangelism, ministry, discipleship, worship, or even fellowship. Whatever is viewed as the most crucial need becomes the central point of concern of the church. That great passion becomes the source of their unity and fellowship.

These emphases may be valid concerns that should be addressed. But if any one of them becomes the only focus, then the church will become misshapen—muscular and strong in one part of the body while withered and weak in other parts of the body. This approach to building a church is shortsighted and unhealthy.

Becoming More Like Jesus in Every Way
No other foundation is adequate or appropriate. All other agendas must become secondary.

> *No one can lay any foundation other than the one already laid, which is Jesus Christ.*   *(I Corinthians 3:11)*

It is no accident that in 1 Corinthians 1:1-10 Paul repeats the name "Lord Jesus Christ" nine times. He is reminding the church at Corinth that the harmony and unity of fellowship they seek is first based on their common relationship with Jesus, and secondly based on their relationship with each other. The church has an obligation to build its fellowship on the person of Jesus Christ our Lord.

As a pastor, I struggled with trying to be all that I needed to be for all the members of the church. There are, of course, limitations to the places I could be at one time. Healthy churches understand this about their leaders and believe that God raises up people throughout the church family to love others in personal ways, care for needs as they arise, carry each other's burdens, and pray for one another regularly. That is what it takes to be His people. No one in the church family should hurt alone or pray alone or cry out for Jesus alone. We all can call out to God on behalf of one another.

WITHOUT LOVE, THE CHURCH IS DEAD
When the people of God do not love one another with a deep, abiding and joyful love, the church is dying. It is possible to have a church without a great building or an educated preacher or a gifted choir and inspiring music. It is possible to have a church that has no great fiscal wealth. But it is never possible to have a church without the love of Jesus flowing through its members.

> **When the people of God do not love one another with a deep, abiding and joyful love, the church is dying.**

In most churches, we come to know and appreciate one another through small circles of friends. We give and receive encouragement, express love, and learn to carry one another's burdens through these small groups. Friendships are a vital factor in the functioning of the Body of Christ, but true fellowship in a church transcends the intimacy of those small circles of friends.

If we understand fellowship to include only those people who can fit within our comfort zone - the ones we would enjoy having over for dinner, or with whom we would enjoy going to a movie— then we will definitely limit the size and depth of our church. That's why many small churches stay small. When we view those people who normally would not be personally compatible with us as people with whom we share a Savior, then we can enjoy true fellowship. Christ has made us one and sends us all to serve. In spite of differences of opinion or disparity of lifestyle, Jesus Christ unites us to serve others in His name.

Coming into God's grace gives us places in the heart where other people can connect. We do this by carrying one another's burdens, by providing safe places for life stories to be shared, by confessing our sins and by revealing our brokenness. Out of this intimacy of trust, people are able to commit to a unity of purpose within the church.

> **Coming into grace gives us places in the heart where other people can connect.**

The fellowship of the Body of Christ is essential for those who serve. No one can care for others for very long unless that one also is being loved, receiving encouragement, and feeling significant in the Body of Christ. As people develop mutual trust and relationships in which they feel supported and cared for, they are then able to focus on their ministries in the world and encourage one another in service. The fellowship is strengthened and truly transcends issues of sociability, compatibility, and common interest. Members of the Body become focused on a common task in which each person feels a responsibility.

The strength of the fellowship within a church may never be fully appreciated until the church experiences a crisis and members discover whether their unity is precious enough for them to forgive and seek to understand one another. A church may not know how strong its fellowship is until members are willing to risk their fellowship for the cause of their mission. If the fellowship is something people idolize by saying, "We can't do that because it might offend someone," then their unity becomes the enemy of their mission. As important as unity is, true fellowship in the church is always tied to its purpose or mission. If the fellowship is centered in Christ and His work, then the fellowship will grow stronger.

True fellowship grows out of a common experience of grace through Christ by which we have been loved, forgiven, accepted as we are, and given a new sense of worth before God. Instead of building walls around ourselves in fear, we allow ourselves to be open and vulnerable. We become willing to care for others and to be cared for in return.

All of us are subject to certain mind-sets that grow out of the way we were nurtured and taught in our youth. We have ingrained tendencies of personality that we have picked up from family and associates throughout life. We are subject to cultural influences and

> **Christ-centered thoughts, attitudes and lifestyles are choices we make daily.**

prejudices that reflect the worldview and value systems of those with whom we live and are most comfortable. When we come into personal relationship with Christ and into fellowship with other Christians, these old patterns are often put to severe test. We recognize that our old clothing does not fit our new being in Christ, the garments of our past must be discarded and new ones chosen to take their place. That is part of what we call "born again."

Christ-centered thoughts, attitudes and lifestyles are choices we make daily. If we are to build fellowship and live in unity with Christian brothers and sisters, we have to be prepared to change.

> *Do not conform any longer to the patterns of this world, but be transformed by the renewing of your mind. Then you will be able to test and approve what God's will is—his good, pleasing and perfect will.* (Romans 12:2)

The Holy Spirit helps us in this transformation, but we are expected to be willing participants and faithful in our discipline to think and act in Christ-like ways. Our transforma-

> **Weeds whose roots choke out the good fruit of our salvation can overrun an untended garden.**

tion does not happen instantaneously because the weeds of sin in our garden must be recognized and uprooted one by one. Weeds whose roots choke out the good fruit of our salvation can overrun an untended garden. Leaders within the Body of Christ must be especially aware of attitudes and actions that either encourage unity of fellowship or discourage it. The proof of "Christ in us" is how we love one another. The apostle Paul warned that we must fully uproot those sins that would rob us of God's grace and bring defilement within the church.

> *See to it that no one comes short of the grace of God; and that no root of bitterness springing up causes trouble, and by it many be defiled.*   *(Hebrews 12:15)*

We all must seek the mind of Christ as we interact with one another and evaluate how we are living out the positive aspects of Christ-like character that build healthy fellowship. How effective are we in building unity within the Body of Christ? The following chart can be quite revealing as we apply the list of character traits to ourselves.

⌘

⌘ CHARACTER TRAITS CONTRIBUTING TO UNITY OR DISUNITY IN THE CHURCH

Unity is encouraged by Christians who are:	*Disunity is encouraged by Christians who are:*
Accepting	Judgmental, Critical
Accountable	Irresponsible, Accusing
Appreciative	Inconsiderate, Insensitive
Caring	Detached, Disinterested
Committed	Uncommitted, Tentative
Communicative	Evasive, Private
Consistent	Unpredictable, Changeable
Cooperative	Disruptive, Rigid
Courageous	Fearful, Timid
Encouraging	Critical, Unsupportive
Flexible, Adaptable	Unyielding, Rigid
Forgiving	Uncompassionate, Bitter
Fun-loving, Humorous	Dour, Intense, Humorless
Friendly	Exclusive, Unsociable
Generous	Selfish, Miserly
Honest	Dishonest, Manipulative
Kind, Compassionate	Uncaring, Mean
Loving	Hard-hearted, Hateful
Loyal, Supportive	Unfaithful, Disloyal
Moral	Immoral
Open, Transparent	Defensive, Guarded
Optimistic	Pessimistic
Patient	Pushy, Anxious, Irritable
Peace-loving	Combative, Divisive
Positive	Negative
Respectful	Impolite, Discourteous
Reverent	Profane, Crude
Stable	Unsteady, Wavering
Trustworthy, Reliable	Undependable, Deceitful
Truthful	Untruthful, Evasive

PRACTICAL STEPS TO UNITY
WITHIN THE CHURCH

1. Welcome new members to the fellowship and involve them in church activities.

If the people in the church love each other, and their love is genuine and deep, it's not hard to include newcomers in their love. If the love is fragile, shallow, and uncertain, then people tend to be jealous of their status because they are not sure what will happen to them if a new person comes in. They fear that perhaps the new person will displace them as part of the "in group." The best way I know to help nurture genuine and deep love in a church is for the pastor to love the people so sincerely and so visibly that people begin to know they are loved. Then they are able to love each other.

I'm not saying that it all depends on the pastor. A strong, mature, and healthy church whose members have a history of love and shared experiences may call a pastor who is not very warm and personal. That church can do fine, because there is enough love and acceptance circulating in the congregation. They can love their pastor even if he is not capable of showing a lot of love in personal relationships. But if a church is not healthy—if there is a broken and divided fellowship—the only way I know for the fellowship to come together is for someone of significance in the congregation to love everybody without reserve and without favoritism. Generally, that has to be the pastor.

> **People don't feel at home in a church unless they are made to feel at home.**

Sometimes church members take for granted that everybody knows they are welcome. That's not so. Even people who feel at home in church, who have attended church all their life, don't feel at home in a new church unless they are encouraged to feel that way. They have to be invited to go to dinner after the church service, or to come visit in homes or participate in recreational activities.

Occasionally a few rare kinds of people are so secure and confident that wherever they go they will make their own group. If people don't respond to them, they reach out to others and create their own circle of friends. Pastors love to have people like that join the church because they create a whole new core of folk who will find a place. But most people need someone there to sponsor them and nurture new relationships.

Many churches assign a deacon or other church member to be a friend to each newcomer. I've done that but I don't know if it's the most helpful way. It is best when friendships happen spontaneously, but it's very difficult to program spontaneity. (Most people can't, or won't, be a friend to someone on assignment.) The most effective way to increase genuine fellowship within a congregation is for Sunday school or small group leaders to create a variety of opportunities for members to invite newcomers into homes and to do things together in order to build relationships. A sensitive Sunday school teacher can deepen relationships by helping the class members to share and pray with one another. Mission activities and recreational experiences are other excellent ways to help people relate happily and genuinely with one another.

2. Show appreciation and give credit where credit is due.

I am a little amused at pastors who fuss at people for wanting recognition and suggest too piously, I feel, that we all ought to serve for God's approval and not for public applause. Yet that same pastor will almost always go to the back of the church house at the end of the service so the people can come by, shake hands and express how much the sermon meant to them. Almost all of us desire to be appreciated. No matter what we do, it feels good to have someone thank us and to express some awareness of what we did as special. Of course, desire for recognition can get out of hand. If we do good for the approval of others, we set ourselves up for frequent disappointment. It is better by far to do good because it is right, to shift the attention away from ourselves to God and to others, and relax in the knowledge we have been faithful to God's calling.

Showing appreciation is most effective when we are specific about what someone has done. For a pastor or anyone who is in a leadership role, the goal ought to be to pass appreciation around in every way possible and give people credit for the contributions they make.

3. Include each other in planning.

As a young pastor I had to learn many lessons the hard way. I was twenty years old and pastor of the Baptist church in Francis, Oklahoma. A dear lady in that church had responsibility for the 6-8 year olds in Vacation Bible School and took pride in her ownership of that role. I should have known better, but I made the mistake of sharing with the children where the Vacation Bible shool picnic was to take place before telling her. She took great offense at my oversight because it made her feel left out and unappreciated.

People naturally want to feel a part of what is going on and to share in having input and making decisions, particularly when they have been asked to help in leadership roles. Plans for church activities need to be developed as broadly as possible and disseminated as early as possible to as many people as possible. The more people who get their fingerprints on an idea or an event, the more enthusiastic participation you are likely to have. We need to share information early and broadly.

4. Treat each other with kindness and respect.

Jesus told us we are to love one another, and we can—but some people are, frankly, hard to love. When they reject us, treat us unkindly, and live in constant rebellion, we don't feel the same way about them as we do toward our spouse, children, or friends whom we deeply cherish. We can love the unlovely by being available to them in kindness and respect, but we who lead in the church are not required to pretend a deep friendship with those who consume us with constant conflict and struggle and drain us of our life energy.

We can respect people who oppose us, respect their humanity and respect their right to have a differing opinion—even respect their right to be wrong. We don't have to cut them down, criticize and attack them. We must not hold them in contempt. It is not our responsibility to control peoples' lives and their choices.

From time to time people were unhappy with me as pastor and with the way things were going in the church. I occasionally got a critical letter expressing concern or disapproval. In every case I can recall, I have attempted to sit down and discuss the issue with the person. Some friends have said I spend too much time with people who disagree with me. They think I should ignore criticism and go on. But I sense that if people understand what I am trying to do, they will accept the fact that I am doing my best even though they may not agree. If they can show me the wisdom of their views, I'm willing to change. When I discover that I'm wrong, it's not too difficult for me to admit it, or to say someone has a better idea than the one I have. I am willing to listen to their concerns and to express my own understanding. This helps build mutual respect.

Unfortunately, we can't always come to a meeting of minds and settle our differences to everyone's satisfaction. I remember saying to a chronically complaining church member after it seemed we were making very little headway in settling our differences: "I am not going to allow you to cast doubt on my life and ministry. Any time you say something that is not accurate, I will challenge you and I will not let you get by with half-truths. I am telling you in advance that I will not allow you to treat the office of pastor with disrespect. I respect and appreciate you, and I am thankful for all you have meant to this church, but if you choose to wound the pastor, you are choosing to wound the church."

It is not our responsibility to attempt to control other people's lives and choices. That is the kind of stand a church leader can take and still remain kind and respectful.

> **It is not our responsibility to attempt to control other people's lives and choices.**

5. Be there for each other in times of trouble and grief.

When church members live in fellowship with one another it becomes natural to respond in love and support when one of the Body suffers serious illness, life-crushing trouble, or the grief of death. When we are most weighted down with life's problems, we discover our real Christian friends. True friends come to share the burden and lighten the load, while others fade away. It is disappointing when, in bad times, we feel abandoned by those with whom we worked closely in good times. Many people are uncomfortable around those who are facing tragedy, illness or death. It's not so much that they don't want to help; they just don't know how to be there to support or to give comfort. Consequently, they retreat and hope others will come forward to fill the gap.

My experience has shown me that healthy churches, like healthy Christian people, don't withdraw when things get rough.

When fellow Christians hurt, they reach out with aid and comfort. They pray for one another, but they also show up to sit with grieving families, or they bring food and take care of needed chores.

> **Healthy churches, like healthy Christian people, don't withdraw when things get rough.**

Healthy Christians will stand by one who has trouble with the law, intercede for families needing psychiatric care and even put themselves at risk for the sake of doing what is right. Healthy Christians really care, and the impact of their caring makes all the difference in the world to those in need. I think of Nancy Pittman, a member of our church who was dying of cancer. I went to visit her and she was grateful to see me. But she said in our conversation, "Pastor, there are other people who need you worse than I do. I appreciate your coming, but my Sunday school class is taking good care of me. Pray for me, but you don't have to worry about me." That's bearing one another's burdens. That's knowing the church is doing what it should be doing, where genuine fellowship has penetrated deeply into the lives of the people.

People asked me, "How can you pastor such a large church?" Well, it can't be done unless you have a lot of people to help you. What happens when a church has strong fellowship is that the members help to "pastor" one another, and they become "pastors" to their pastor as well.

6. Be there for each other in times of joy and celebration.

Perhaps the finest examples of supporting each other in times of joy is the way people show up for each other's weddings, baby showers, and anniversaries. On an ongoing basis, those events have been a natural way to affirm the positive experiences happening among church family members.

First Baptist Church, Arlington, recognizes families with newborn babies by having a rose displayed at the morning worship service just following the birth. We then take the rose to the birth family with a congratulatory message from the church. Twice a year we have a special church service in which we dedicate our new babies and their parents to the Lord. We also give special recognition to graduating students for their important accomplishments. Those are meaningful times of celebration in which the church can participate.

Church members who love each other are quick to celebrate each other's successes and refuse to be jealous or begrudging in times of victory and joy. It is a healthy thing when Christians offer up as many prayers of thanks and praise as we do prayers of supplication.

7. Set the example: do the loving thing, and refuse to do the unloving thing.

The apostle Paul left us a real treasure of spiritual counsel when he described what true love is in 1 Corinthians 13. This passage explains what love promises to do and what love refuses to do.

> *Love is patient, love is kind. It does not envy, it does not boast, it is not proud. It is not rude, it is not self-seeking, it is not easily angered, it keeps no record of wrongs. Love does not delight in evil but rejoices with the truth. It always protects, always trusts, always hopes, always perseveres.*
> *(1 Corinthians 13:4-7)*

A good rule for us all to follow is to speak about people in their absence in the same way we would speak about them in their presence. Focus on building people up, not tearing them down.

8. Choose forgiveness and administer grace.

> *Therefore as God's chosen people, holy and dearly loved, clothe yourselves with compassion, kindness, humility, gentleness, and patience. Bear with each other and forgive whatever grievances you may have against one another. Forgive as the Lord forgave you.* *(Colossians 3:12-13)*

Jesus wants to bond His people together to create a corporate identity as the church, the Body of Christ. To help Him accomplish this, we must realize that we are not just separate individuals; we are in a marriage and a family, united to each other in such a way that whatever happens to one happens to all. What wounds one wounds all. What blesses one blesses all. As the church encourages blessing rather than criticism, forgiveness rather than judgment, people grow and change. The true test of the effectiveness of church is what kind of people are people after they have been around us five years. Are they, or are they not, full of grace?

9. Work to develop high levels of trust within the congregation.

Trust basically depends on trustworthiness. We trust people who are trustworthy and we don't trust people who prove not to be trustworthy. Therefore, the responsibility of developing a high level of trust in the congregation is on both the people who need to trust and those who want to be trusted. Trustworthiness is a process that demands a history of positive confirming experiences.

We can love people we don't trust and trust people we don't love, but we certainly would like to confidently trust those we love. Some people have been so wounded and their trust has been betrayed to such a depth that they can't give normal trust even when a person deserves it.

In a normal kind of relationship, we start out with a deposit of trust in the other person. As long as they keep depositing trustworthy actions into our account, they can draw from the reserve and be trusted. But if they withdraw from our account more than they put in, the account becomes bankrupt. The call to trust people is also a call to be worthy of trust. That's why it is so crucial to tell the truth even about little things. Fellowship in church demands that trust levels be developed, nurtured and protected.

> **The call to trust people is also a call to be worthy of trust.**

10. Mentor unselfishly.

One important method of building leadership in a church while also protecting the harmony of the church is to balance membership on committees between older members and younger members. In that way, the less experienced will learn from the more experienced and mentoring will take place in a natural way. It is a beautiful testimony to the fellowship within a church when older members recognize it is time for younger people to assume more responsibility and yield leadership to them with grace, encouragement and loyalty.

George Hawkes was chairman of the pulpit committee for First Baptist Church, Arlington when my predecessor, Dr. H. E. East was called. Twenty-five years later he chaired the committee that invited me to the church. No person has been more respected or given more solid leadership to our church then George Hawkes. But it has been the remarkable manner in which he has blessed the next generation of leaders in our congregation that has marked him as one of the greatest Christian laymen I have ever known. He continues to be involved, but he encourages other leaders to take up their responsibilities. George and Dr. East, our pastor emeritus for twenty-two years, have together modeled the way mentoring can take place and leadership transitions can be fruitfully accomplished.

In my years as pastor, our church has had great success bringing in young seminary students as part-time interns to work as assistants to staff ministers. We have employed many students in mutually beneficial service opportunities. These young men and women have contributed much to the life of the church and many of them have moved on to do creative and successful ministry. They have been mentored by gifted ministers who are committed to ministry, gladly sharing what they have learned. Every Timothy needs a Paul and every Paul needs a Barnabas as well as a Timothy.

11. Put the needs and interests of others before your own.

Do nothing out of selfish ambition or vain conceit, but in humility consider others better than yourselves. Each of you should look not only to your own interests, but also to the interests of others. Your attitude should be the same as that of Jesus Christ. *(Philippians 2:3-5)*

When a church learns to act on this counsel, it really begins to live in Christian fellowship. If we give Jesus the right place in our lives, our personal needs will be met. We can have a healthy appreciation for our own needs and those pleasures that give us joy, but we must not focus on ourselves to the detriment of others. We must be willing to put others before ourselves. When we are able to do that, we discover the true path to joy. Jesus said:

Whoever wants to save his life will lose it, but whoever loses his life for me and for the gospel will save it.

(Mark 8:35)

12. Encourage participation by all: listen to ideas, no matter what the source.

No job that is worth doing can be done alone. The work of the church demands partnership. We need one another. The task of the church is big enough to challenge us all to service. If we pay attention to what people are saying, we can always learn something new. I've never attended a committee meeting where I didn't come away with at least one better idea than I had going in.

I have learned over the years that it's not new ideas people don't like, it's *your* new idea they aren't sure about. Their new ideas they like just fine! When everyone is given an opportunity to contribute and to be heard, friction and controversy are greatly reduced. Open communication allows people to feel appreciated. They become more willing to trust what is being presented and more willing to be supportive of what is ultimately decided by the entire group.

⌘

Koinonia is What Motivates Us as Christians

When members of the family of faith are lonely, sick, depressed, in agony over unexpected tragic situations, or are experiencing the grief of loss, the church's job is to love them and care about them. A healthy church stands with its members no matter what it takes as they move toward God's healing. A healthy church gives meaningful opportunity to all its members to do God's work.

> **We cannot sacrifice any of the five functions of the church in order to emphasize one. Churches must emphasize all: worship, evangelism, discipleship, ministry, and fellowship.**

Wherever there is a need, we are there with hands that want to minister. Healthy church fellowship means we are willing to love one another as God has loved us, and we are always ready to welcome opportunities God places in our path or brings to our door.

The fellowship, the *koinonia,* is the basis of a church's life together. We cannot sacrifice any of the five functions of the church in order to emphasize one. Churches must emphasize them all: worship, evangelism, discipleship, ministry, and fellowship. There may be times when we focus on one function so the Body of Christ can grow and mature in that way. Then, at other times we will focus on other functions as the need is appropriate. But we want a balanced ministry, which will put the presence, power and heart of Christ up close to the needs of this world.

⌘

⌘

JESUS PRINCIPLES
FOR CREATING UNITY WITHIN THE CHURCH

⌘ Welcome new members to the fellowship and involve them in church activities.

⌘ Show appreciation and give credit where credit is due. Affirm the contributions people make and their value as persons.

⌘ Involve a broad base of people in planning and evaluating. People naturally want to feel a part of what is going on and to share in having input and making decisions.

⌘ Treat each other with kindness and respect. Respect people who oppose you—respect their humanity and their right to have a differing opinion. Don't hold others in contempt.

⌘ Be there for others in times of trouble and grief. Pray, share the burden, and lighten the load.

⌘ Be there for others in times of joy and celebration. Celebrate each other's successes. What blesses one blesses all.

⌘ Set the example—do the loving thing, and refuse to do the unloving thing. Focus on building people up, not tearing them down.

⌘ Choose to be forgiving and administer grace. The church must continually ask, "What kind of people are we becoming?"

⌘ Work to develop high levels of trust within the congregation.

⌘ Mentor unselfishly. Yield leadership with grace, encouragement and loyalty. Gladly train younger less experienced people.

⌘ Put needs and interests of others before your own. If we give Jesus the right place in our lives, our needs will be met.

⌘ Listen to ideas, no matter what the source. Open communication makes people more willing to trust what is being presented and more willing to be supportive of whatever is ultimately decided by the whole group.

FATHER, GOD:

PLANT IN EACH OF US A VISION OF HOW TO INVITE INTO THE FAMILY OF FAITH ALL THOSE WHO NEED TO BE A PART OF YOUR FELLOWSHIP. WE REPENT OF OUR PRIDE, SELFISHNESS AND JUDGMENT OF OTHERS AND ASK FORGIVENESS FOR THE WAY WE HAVE BEEN OBSTACLES TO THE UNITY YOU DESIRE WITHIN YOUR CHURCH.

HELP US TO BREATHE INTO THOSE SACRED PLACES OF CHRISTIAN INTIMACY AN HONEST OPENNESS WITH EACH OTHER. REMIND US WE ARE ALL NEEDED TO DO YOUR WORK IN THE WORLD.

TEACH US TO BE SENSITIVE TO PEOPLE WHO ARE QUIET ABOUT THEIR HURTING. TEACH US HOW TO DRAW CLOSE AND MINISTER WITH LOVING CARE WHEN IT WOULD BE EASIER FOR US TO WALK AWAY. BLESS US WITH YOUR MERCY AND GRACE AS WE SEEK TO GROW INTO THE HEALTHY CHURCH YOU WANT US TO BE.

AMEN

Life Application
⌘
CREATE FELLOWSHIP
Strengthening the Body through Loving Relationships

1. How does your church welcome and integrate new members into the fellowship? Talk to some new members about how their needs are being met as newcomers. Ask for suggestions about how this transition can be handled better and quicker for the new members and new families.

2. Look at the chart in this chapter listing those things that either encourage or discourage unity in the church. Scan the words. Be honest enough to notice which words from either column describe your character and behavior as a member of the Body of Christ. What areas of your life need some work so God can use you more effectively?

3. Where is the deepest level of fellowship evident in your church? Sunday school classes? Home study groups? Committees? Among choir members? In other program organizations within the church? Evaluate for yourself and discuss with others how and why the feelings of fellowship are strongest there?

4. Do you personally have a sense of close Christian fellowship in your church? What could you do to help create healthy church fellowship or to deepen the fellowship you already are experiencing? Discuss this idea with church friends.

SECTION
THREE

BUILDING
JESUS KIND OF CHURCHES

9

God's Vision for a Church

How does a church discover its vision? In a recent study by the Barna Research Group, several thousand pastors and church leaders were asked to identify the areas in which they would like more information and help. Their number one request: *How to discover God's vision for my church or ministry.*

That expressed need may surprise some because in the past, most pastors and church leaders have operated with the assumption, *"I already know what my church's vision is."* Unfortunately, many of us have been reluctant to admit our church is defined by the status quo, content to maintain tradition, and timid in its anticipation of the future.

Researcher George Barna says many churches who decide they want to move to a useful future often settle for describing a "mission" for the church and never get around to capturing their unique "vision." In studying the effectiveness and health of churches, he believes one of the best indicators of the condition of a church is the state of the vision.

Barna says, "In every one of the growing, healthy churches studied, a discernible link has been forged between the spiritual and numerical growth of those congregations and the existence, articulation and widespread ownership of God's vision for ministry for the leaders and participants of the church. Conversely, visionless congregations fail to experience spiritual and numerical growth. Rarely, in my research, do I find such overt, black-and-white relationships."[1]

I agree with that assessment. Over the years, I have observed that in churches where a sense of God's vision truly exists, the probability of growth and impact is high. In churches where vision is absent, growth is absent as well.

DIFFERENCE BETWEEN MISSION AND VISION

One of the confusions among church leaders is the difference between *mission* and *vision.* The terms need to be clarified. A church's *mission*, which is more philosophical and broad in scope, usually gets summarized to a *mission statement*—a slogan or brief phrase which everyone can memorize and which is printed on all the church publications. The mission statement is a hook on which a church can hang its identity, but it doesn't go into details of how the church accomplishes its mission. Putting too much emphasis on a shorthand slogan can be misleading, causing church members to think the slogan represents the full depth and breadth of God's call upon the church.

Churches within a community might share a very similar *mission*, but would not likely share the same *vision* about how they will achieve their mission. Mission statements generally are too vague to provide much direction or to motivate people to action.

A church's *vision* is a specific, unique, customized understanding of who God wants us to be and what He wants us to do in our community as a church. The *vision statement*, strategic in nature, puts feet under the mission, detailing how we as a church will influence the world in which we minister. No two churches in a community would have carbon copy visions because God wants churches, like individuals, to do their distinctive work in a community. A church's unique vision will express in detail how a particular church body will relate to a defined community of people and their needs.

Vision relates to specific actions, while *mission* relates to a general approach, the "raison d'être." The purpose of articulating a vision is to create the future. Risk, of course, is a natural and unavoidable outgrowth of vision. The absolute goal of any vision for ministry is to glorify God and that may call for some unsettling changes in priorities for a church.

Finding the Vision for our Church: Reflecting Back

While I was pastor, First Baptist Church, Arlington struggled with the vision-finding process. I naively assumed for years that everybody knew what the church was about and therefore did little to articulate what I assumed to be our vision. I was surprised to discover in early 1988 that some of the church leaders thought the average church member did not personally have a clear understanding of the church's vision. Many suggested the church was riding along on the vision of the pastor or staff ministers, not really seeing or sharing any kind of real vision themselves.

I was amazed at the degree of confusion among church members over what our local church was about. It seemed

> *Reaching and teaching people is the fundamental mission guiding any healthy church.*

obvious to me our purpose was to reach people and then to help those people mature in Christ. The very simple idea of reaching and teaching people is the fundamental mission for any healthy church. The often-quoted "great commission" in the gospel of Matthew sums it up:

> *Therefore, go and make disciples of all nations, baptizing them in the name of the Father and of the Son and of the Holy Spirit, and teaching them to obey everything I have commanded you.* *(Matthew 28:19-20)*

In an effort to make progress in this area of clarifying our vision out of the mission, the church held a series of group discussions in 1988 and later brought in an outside consultant to help us through the process. In these meetings, the leaders of our church all agreed on the basic reaching and teaching concepts, but that was not enough for them. They were seeking a more personal application of *how our church reaches and teaches* people in *our community, i.e.* the unique vision for our church. So we began to look deeper.

One of the first topics for discussion was the setting of a goal for the church's numerical growth. In the future, how many people would we like to have in Bible study each Sunday? How many people would we like to reach and what would be required to provide adequate facilities to accommodate them? We assumed we could *teach* people. The question was — could we *reach* them?

We collectively came up with a proposed goal to build buildings, prepare facilities and purchase property so 3000 people could attend Sunday morning Bible study and worship at First Baptist Church, Arlington by the year 2000. That decision certainly added specific detail to our vision.

As we began to develop a plan, it seemed simple enough to begin with our current attendance figures and decide what percentage of 3000 persons each teaching division of the church would need to have in the future. We worked out a table of projected growth for each year, through the year 2000.

Later, I sat down in a separate meeting with the church staff. They took a long look at the "vision chart" we had constructed with the outside consultant and the idea fell flat on the ground. The hard numbers listed were not what the church staff wanted to serve as the measurement of their success. They looked at those numbers listed for the next twelve years and felt overwhelmed and defeated before they began.

In my experience, church leaders don't like numerical goals to gauge their progress. Bottom-line, our vision-stating effort did not motivate our staff and it did not motivate our Sunday school directors. Devising a growth chart with lists of projected numbers for the next few years was not going to get us there. Quietly, we let that chart slide into oblivion.

Numbers for the sake of numbers motivate no one who is focused on developing people spiritually. Similarly, I'm not sure pushing for numerical growth motivates people in the business world over the long haul either. When organizations set goals, achieving the numbers alone is not enough. As a church, we can become satisfied with what we are doing and careless about what we need

> **As a church, we can become satisfied with what we are doing and careless about what we need to do.**

to do. For people to remain eager and productive over many years, there must be a sense of purpose, teamwork, personal growth and meaningful service to others. Most sales organizations find that money can motivate people only to a certain level and for a limited time. But if a person is "making a difference in people's lives" and receiving generous compensation, he or she will work creatively, energetically and faithfully for a long time.

After our initial effort to construct a vision fizzled, I began to think and pray daily about what it means to find *God's vision* for our church. I realized I did not want to be pastor of a church where the vision is only this: "We want to have x number of people in Sunday school in the month of March." With that realization, my journey toward discovering *God's vision* for our church continued.

Maturing the Process
The vision-finding process for me matured to ask this question:

"What kind of church makes a difference in people's lives, genuinely bringing them into a relationship with Jesus Christ, nurturing them so they become true disciples of Christ, and helping them to be more like Jesus?"

When I began to think like that, I felt much better about the possibility of us getting closer to a worthy vision for God's church. If churches do not accept the responsibility of reaching more people, it is easy for the staff or lay leaders to become simply custodians of the status quo. We can become satisfied with what we are doing and careless about what we need to do to reach new people. So we continued to ask, "What is our vision?" As we considered what we were doing through our on-campus Bible studies, Mission Arlington, and all the other ministries and activities of the church, it seemed to me we needed to go back to the baseline. Through re-examination of the fundamentals, we came up with these principles:

♦ **The Church is the Body of Christ; therefore, the vision for the Body has to come from the *head* of the Body, Jesus Christ.** If we are going to have a true vision for our church, it has to grow out of the life of Christ. One day a man asked Jesus, *"What is the greatest commandment?"* (That's the kind of question that gets to the baseline.) Jesus said, *"Love the Lord your God with all your heart, and with all your soul, and with all your mind."* Even Jesus couldn't put the answer into one sentence. So He added, *"...the second is like it: Love your neighbor as yourself" (Matthew 22:37-39).* That really puts it in focus.

♦ **The church is to do Jesus' work, guided by the Holy Spirit.** A description of the Lord's work is found in the gospel of Luke where Jesus is teaching in the synagogue. When they asked Jesus to read the Scripture, He turned to Isaiah 61. Obviously He could have turned to any part of the Scripture scroll. He chose a text which summarized what He understood Himself to be doing *(See Luke 4:18-19).*

> *The spirit of the Lord is upon me*
> (that is where God's vision must come from)
> *because He has anointed me to preach good news to the poor* (the people who have no advocate or voice).
> *He has sent me to proclaim freedom for the prisoners*
> (those in bondage)
> *and recovery of sight for the blind,*
> (those in darkness, without sight, lost and left out)
> *to release the oppressed,*
> (those who are treated unjustly)
> *and to proclaim the year of the Lord's favor*
> (the word of hope that now is the time God is doing a special thing).

♦ **People are changed by the grace of God, and as we live the character of Christ, we experience abundant life.** Jesus says in John 10:10, *"I have come that they may have life and have it abundantly."* This is about a gospel that fills us and changes us, as individuals and as the Body, giving life its depth and texture.

All of those things were working in my mind as we were proactively working on the mission and vision for our church, coming from the mind of Christ, the head of the Body. Focusing our growing understanding of that process into the everyday life of our own congregation became central. Out of the several-year journey of seeking, we began to say that the mission of First Baptist Church, Arlington is *"to change lives."* Our mission statement grew out of this revised view of our purpose:

First Baptist Church, Arlington lives to change lives by helping people love God through worship and love others through service.

As mentioned in earlier chapters, we conceived our mission statement to represent living life in the shape of the cross. It was to be the living out of Jesus' two great commands:

1. Love God with all our heart, soul, mind and strength
2. Love others as we love ourselves.

The mission statement above is about changing lives, about announcing good news to those who have none, about announcing freedom to those who are in bondage, and about being present with those who have no hope, communicating to them that God has heard their cry. That is our mission. He wants us to have life abundantly, with purpose, joy and fulfillment.

⌘

In February 1995 the quest for a *vision* statement for our church came into its fullest form with the development of seven areas to which our **family of faith** would commit itself. We had refocused our direction for the church on seeking the mind of Christ and began to ask ourselves consistently, *"What would Jesus do in our community?"*

Outreach ministries through Mission Arlington became an important part of the answer we heard from God. It became evident that many people in the community were reticent about coming to study and worship in a large, traditional church building, so we had begun in 1986 to take the church and the gospel of Christ to the people. Increasing numbers of our congregation began to get personally involved in ministry in the apartment complexes and resident motel units in our city. Many of our volunteer workers would attend worship in our early service on Sunday morning and then spread out all over the city to lead small-group Bible studies.

Interestingly enough, it wasn't long before our original numbers-oriented plan of having 3,000 in Sunday school by the year 2,000 proved totally inadequate in view of what God had in mind. By 1996 we were reaching 3,000 people in small-group Bible studies all over town through Mission Arlington, in addition to the almost 2,000 people attending the traditional on-campus Sunday school.

A *living vision* was born and began maturing in the hearts and minds of our staff and church members before we could ever formally define it and write it down. Christ led us so clearly in so

many ways that we were kept busy just keeping up with the opportunities as they came knocking at our door.

The closest we came to developing a formal vision statement
grew out of a series of sermons I preached entitled "A Theology

> **Christ led us, and we were
> busy just keeping up with the
> opportunities as they came
> knocking at our door.**

for Doing Church". In summary
form below are the basic tenets of
the vision of First Baptist Church,
Arlington, articulated in those sermons.

⌘

The First Baptist Church of Arlington, Texas believes the Gospel of God as revealed in Jesus Christ and the Holy Scriptures. We
are committed to live out its message in the world. Our Family of
Faith rejoices to be a people who are committed to:

♦ **Joyful Worship**

♦ **Intentional Outreach**

♦ **Spiritual Growth**

♦ **Strong Relationships**

♦ **Sensitive Hospitality**

♦ **Courageous Service**

♦ **Dependable Maturity**

Joyful Worship: God is great and good and worthy of our praise.

Worship emphasizes God's love for us and our love for Him, holiness *and* grace, command *and* invitation, warning *and* encouragement. Our lives are enriched and blessed when we regularly seek His thoughts, offer our prayers, acknowledge our sin, and praise Him for His holiness. Worship confronts, challenges, inspires and encourages us. It draws us closer to God, binds us to one another, and sends us into the world to make a difference. In confession, prayer, praise and music, we joyfully worship God and experience His grace as He removes our sin and guilt. Our whole lives are offerings we bring to God.

1 Chronicles 16:8-36   *Hebrews 10:19-25*
Psalm 8:1-2, 77, 100, 130, 150   *1 Peter 2:2-3*
Matthew 6:9-13, 22:37   *1 John 4:7-16*
Ephesians 1:3-6, 3:20-21

Intentional Outreach: People need God.

Contacting, visiting and encouraging people to join us for worship and Bible study is God's intention for the church. We have the privilege and responsibility to have a ministry of presence with people in our community who are not members of our church, to witness to the gospel of Jesus Christ and to minister to them in times of need.

We train and encourage church members to be effective witnesses in the community within their sphere of influence. We affirm and utilize the spiritual gifts of every member of the Body to enhance the Kingdom of God—men and women, boys and girls. We communicate our ministries to the city and welcome into our fellowship all who will participate. Through Mission Arlington we take the church and its gospel to the people where they live, providing opportunities for Bible study, worship, fellowship and evangelism in their neighborhood.

We are consistently open to the Spirit of God as He leads us to creative new ministries designed to meet the needs of people and grow the church.

Isaiah 60:1-3, 61:1-3   *Acts 1:8*
Matthew 28:18-20   *Romans 10:1-15*
John 3:16-17

Spiritual Growth: God calls us to be growing Christians.

Prayer is the greatest resource God gives us for accomplishing the goals of our church, families, and personal lives. Everything done in and through the church should reflect the reality of God and His care for every aspect of our lives. The church helps its members grow in knowledge and understanding of God and of Jesus Christ as Savior. It teaches growing Christians to be obedient to the teachings of Jesus and to understand that all we have is a gift from God. It encourages members to use their time, energies, abilities and money so that God's work can be done in the world and to view themselves as partners with God in building the Kingdom. The church helps members live productive and meaningful lives in the midst of stress, disappointment, temptation and fear. It helps its members enjoy God every day, prepare for godly service in the world, and face the end of life with joyful assurance and confident hope.

Luke 2:52   *Galatians 5:13-26*
John 14:15-19, 25-27   *2 Peter 3:18*
1 Corinthians 1:4-9

Strong Relationships: God calls us to love one another.

Creating a strong fellowship is essential to building a strong church where people know they matter to someone else, are missed when they are absent, and are not left alone through difficult times. The church helps people grow in their ability to love one another with kindness, sensitivity, wisdom and support. We protect our church from pettiness, careless criticism, and side issues which are not crucial to serving Christ faithfully. We safeguard our unity by respecting the diversity of gifts which the Holy Spirit gives to the members of the congregation, both women and men, for the building up of the Body of Christ. We take responsibility for restoring to active fellowship those who grow weary or disenchanted with the life of the congregation.

Genesis 4:9-12   *1 Corinthians 12:7-26,13:1-13*
Leviticus 19:18;   *Ephesians 4:1-3*
Matthew 22:37-39   *Philippians 2:1-4*
John 13:34-35, 15:17   *1 John 4:7-12*

Sensitive Hospitality: God's people deserve to be respected.

The way in which our church welcomes and receives people who come to us speaks of how we really love and respect them as people of worth whom God loves. Members and newcomers respond favorably to sincere caring and an atmosphere of love and acceptance. This church endeavors to meet people with sensitive hospitality expressed through courtesy, friendliness, helpfulness, and convenience, in clean, comfortable, and efficient surroundings.

Genesis 1:27-31   *Matthew 26:6-13*
Ecclesiastes 9:10   *Romans 12:9-16*
1 Corinthians 28:20; 29:1-19   *James 2:1-4*

Courageous Service: God takes the side of those in need.

The church is the Body of Christ, a continuation of the incarnation of God on earth, enabled through the Holy Spirit to do God's work in the world. The church will be present in the community with the word of God, acting to create faith, hope, and love in those who are poor, outcast, brokenhearted and have no one to intercede for them. When evil, injustice or deceit is discovered in the church or in the world, we are committed to speak out with truth and integrity to right the wrong. This church courageously bases its ministry decisions on the mind of Christ, sought through prayerful dependence on the Holy Spirit's guidance, faithful study of the Scripture, consideration of the convictions of other Christians, and thoughtful reflection based upon the wisdom God has promised to give.

Exodus 3:7-12   *Luke 4:16-30*
Isaiah 1:15-20   *Philippians 2:3-11; 3:17-4:1*
Micah 6:8   *1 Thessalonians 4:13-5:11*
Matthew 6:9-10; 25:31-46   *James 1:2-5, 5:1-6*

Dependable Maturity: God builds character into people.

It is important to be both a risk-taking church open to new challenges and a church that treasures stability, tradition and the confidence that people have in us. Accountability to the congregation and to the will and purpose of God as revealed in Scripture protects the church from the abuse of power by any one person or small group of persons.

The church is called of God to grow in its ability to handle crisis and change, to weather storms, and to stay faithful to God and one another. The church is committed to providing young families a place to raise their children where they will be lovingly taught and nurtured within our family of faith. We treasure the presence of young and old in the church and recognize that we must always ask ourselves, "What kind of people are we becoming?"

Galatians 5:22-26
Hebrews 5:12-6:3, 12:1-3, 13:1-9
Ephesians 4:1-3, 11-16, 25, 5:2

These seven ideas expressed the vision of First Baptist Church, Arlington.

⌘

Ideas for Finding the Vision

So what is the task of helping a church find its own vision? It is simply to encourage all members of the Body to take a close look at Jesus by reading the gospels with a special thought in mind. Ask yourself: *"If a church is the presence of Christ in the community, what would Jesus do if He were here?"* Don't be too hasty to answer that question. And don't assume you know the answer. (Study the charts in the first two chapters of this book exploring what Jesus did.) I've heard people attempt to answer with a knee-jerk response like, "He would go about doing good," or "He would love people." Those things are true enough. But finding the answer to what Jesus would do if He were in your church in your community is an ongoing process.

As you read the gospels, what words inspired by the Spirit of God become liquid fire? Where does the Scripture quicken your spirit and bring molten power to your heart? Where is that wonderful moment when you read the text and the text reads you in a marriage of God's purpose and your own sense of calling? Right there is where the pastor and church leaders begin to see what Jesus wants the church to do. When people experience the power of God's word, and the vision is inseparably tied to the life and ministry of Jesus, nothing can stop the church from embodying that vision in the community.

People in the church who oppose a developing vision may initially be confused. But if the vision stays focused around what Jesus would think and feel and do, many will eventually accept and understand the vision and its directives for the church. Others may need to move on to other churches where they can align with that church's vision and priorities. Again, it is a process, appreciating the past, being keenly aware of the here-and-now, and focusing on the future God intends for a church.

Vision Requires Leadership

Vision comes from leaders who want to see beyond the present moment to encompass the big picture—from leaders who care enough and are sensitive enough to move past crisis management to take the long view. Vision for a church ministry relates directly to the state of the heart of its leaders.

> *Vision for a church ministry relates directly to the state of the heart of its leaders.*

There are models of church leadership which suggest that the senior pastor is the one who goes off to a quiet place and gets the vision from God, then comes back to announce it to the membership. That process works if the pastor truly wants and is open to the response of the congregation to the vision he has articulated. Does the vision find a home in the hearts and minds of the members? When they hear the pastor articulate the vision, do they sense it is of God and feel drawn to rally to it? If they genuinely feel God's leadership, and not a spirit of coercive leadership, the church will confirm the pastor's vision as God's vision. However, if they rally because they are afraid to disagree and don't want to be put in an embarrassing position, tension and division can and will build up in the Body.

Another way to find the church's vision is for the pastor to mobilize elected and/or appointed men and women in the church who are people of prayer. They gather together and begin to pray:

"God, we are Your Body in this community. We want to do what You would do. Bring to our minds Your will and purpose for the life of this church."

An important part of this time is the "exegeting" of the community and culture. What needs are really here that Jesus would meet and wants us to meet? Meanwhile, the church at large is praying, studying the Bible, and thinking about their calling from God. God will give them a task, an idea, a project, an opportunity, a ministry. Out of that comes the vision, rooted in the character of Jesus.

The approach I personally preferred to take as the elected spiritual leader was to pray continually for God to give me guidance—to be granted a sense of direction and spiritual insight. I preferred not to suggest that I am the only one who could receive the vision from God. I tried to listen to the people and really hear what they sensed God was saying to them. Committees and staff members met together and shared where they believed God was leading us.

> **Pray that the Body will know the mind of Christ.**

Out of that grew a vision, an idea, a dream. We worked on it, studied it, shaped it. Eventually, the idea was taken to the council of deacons and then to the congregation who were asked to pray that the Body would know the mind of Christ—what He would do in this situation and how He would handle it.

Several years ago, First Baptist, Arlington, bought some nearby property that we knew we would eventually need for parking space. The property contained several duplexes. Some women from the community came to me looking for a place to put a shelter for women and children who had been abused and needed a safe place to go.

That kind of need was difficult for me to understand. I thought Arlington was such a great community, and nothing like that could possibly be needed in our town. But I asked some women in our church to check it out. They came back with the report that we definitely had such a problem in our town. Real abuse was happening in all kinds of families.

So we went to the deacon council with a report and a recommendation. Several deacons brought up some "what ifs" that came to mind—liability insurance, risk of violence from an angry husband looking for his wife, confrontation for church members who might be accused of harboring runaways.

Then one deacon stood up to say that all those ideas were worth thinking about, but we had a smart group of people who could figure how to deal with those problems. Then he said, *"I've been sitting here thinking about what Jesus would do. I believe He would care about those women and their children. I move we do it!"*

There was no further discussion. Our deacon council unanimously passed the recommendation.

That was one of the events that helped change the church. Change doesn't come all at once. But bit by bit, every time we try to decide what we really need to be doing, we ask ourselves, *"What would Jesus do?"*

As we follow this process of discovery, the mind of Christ begins to grow in the minds and spirits of the members of the Body. When the congregation gets a sense of the direction it should go, individuals with specific convictions are encouraged to respond in an appropriate way, offering their support, suggestions or objections to the idea being discussed.

⌘

ONE CHURCH CAN'T BORROW ANOTHER'S VISION

In a pastors' conference in South Carolina, I listened intently to the messages of the preachers. Every speaker was talking about how a church must discover its vision. The leaders at the meeting were struggling with clarifying their *vision* and their *mission*.

All the ideas were good. But I became increasingly convinced that no one pastor or church leader can tell another what the vision for a particular church should be. No one church can simply give their vision to another church. The only vision with the power to call people forward is God's vision growing out of the life of a particular church in a particular place.

The vision for a church cannot be something we get out of someone's book (including this one), or borrow from another church and its vision statement. The only vision worth the name grows uniquely for a church out of the mind of Christ applied to that church's specific situation. Barna says, "The leader who takes a me-too approach in defining vision is neither operating on the power of God's leading nor demonstrating a capacity for authentic leadership."[2]

After spending years refocusing on God's vision for First Baptist Church, Arlington, I was increasingly convinced that our unique vision is very much tied into the church's history. It provides Arlington a kind of anchor at the historical and geographical center of the city. Even though the church has been in downtown Arlington since 1871, there is no guarantee it will continue to thrive. The church must stay alive and vital, willing to adapt and change to the needs of the community, moving forward, never satisfied with standing still.

> *A vision from God will not allow any church to pick out only a few people for whom the church chooses to care.*

Unfortunately, a church can have a stunted vision. Look around; examples abound. A vision from God will not allow any church to pick out only a few people for whom the church chooses to care. I see a lot of churches focusing on one type of people to the exclusion of others. I see churches that look more like social organizations than ministries. Churches must continue to ask the tough questions about who they are and who they should be.

When a church has a vision, the people will know it. When a church doesn't have a vision, the people aren't sure what it would be like to have one. When a church as a whole sees the vision, they understand how all the pieces fit into the puzzle. When individuals in the church do not see the bigger picture, they can develop tunnel-vision, become critical of others, and jealous of activities or ministries that don't center around their personal needs and preferences.

When a church is secure in the vision God has given them, they are more confident, focused, and energized. They also are more able to say "no" graciously to possibilities that present themselves, which they may agree are good ideas but are not focused on the vision they share or would deplete resources targeted for other priority ministries.   ⌘

GOD'S VISION FOR A CHURCH AND
GOD'S VISION FOR AN INDIVIDUAL

If God has a prophetic vision for each church, does He also have a prophetic vision for each individual Christian? Does seeking God's will individually relate to God's vision for the church we "belong" to? Can we listen to God on two levels—as individual disciples seeking His voice, and as members of the Body seeking His voice?

One of the big challenges of the church is to teach and equip individuals to listen for God and to really hear Him as He speaks to our hearts. As a child of the Father, we should expect to communicate with our Father daily. As we listen to God, we must also be accountable for discerning what is and is not God's will. Satan is an expert in counterfeiting. Scripture always supports God's will.

Self-limiting thinking can be a big roadblock for people. We all have practices that can keep us from risking. Fear, tradition, status quo, and life scripts lock us down and leave little or no areas for change or growth. Think about what may be the roadblocks for you. If the church had to wait for you, how well would it be fulfilling its God-given vision? (For further discussion, Chapter 11.)

Can God's vision for an individual change?

I know several people who moved to the Dallas-Fort Worth metroplex to do what they believed God was asking them to do at that time—attend theological seminary to prepare for the pastoral ministry. God got them here, which is better than where they were, but the path of opportunity didn't turn out the way they expected. With time, changed circumstances in their lives and further insight into God's guidance and call, some have changed career directions and are now involved in lay vocations.

There are many wonderful members within the First Baptist, Arlington congregation who are theologically educated, experienced in church leadership roles, and committed to continuing service in Christian ministry. Yet their new "calling" has taken them into areas of work such as counseling, teaching, music, journalism, business, and other endeavors through which God has channeled their abilities and creative energies. They are a great blessing to the church and actively contribute to the vision of broad-based ministries in our community. They continue to seek God's call as He opens doors of opportunity for them to serve.

⌘

TEN THINGS THAT STOP GOD'S VISION FROM TAKING HOLD

1. The vision captured is for the pastor, not for the church.

When an individual pastor or church leader spearheads a vision, the vision may last only as long as the leader lasts. If a pastor's vision for the church is actually a vision for career success, recognition, or private pride, God will not trust the pastor with His inspired vision. The channels become too clogged with noise and static. The vision a pastor must seek is for the church currently being served, not for the purpose of positioning him for another church. When a church genuinely captures God's vision, the vision is not the pastor's vision or the vision of any other individual. The vision is God's. In that case, the vision will outlast the leader.

2. The vision being sought by the pastor is not for this church.

If God has given a pastor a vision that cannot be affirmed by the church served, then the pastor needs to reflect on these questions:

♦ Have I thoughtfully and creatively involved the church in understanding the vision God has given me? (See the ten ideas to help a pastor discover God's vision for a church later in this chapter.)

♦ Do I need to ask God for another vision that this church can understand and to which it can rally?

♦ Do I need to go to a place where God has prepared a people to be open to the vision He has given for the ministry I have been called to do?

It is not a legitimate option for a pastor to arrogantly assume that because the church called him to be their pastor, he has a right to lay on them the vision he never communicated to the church before coming. If he must resort to intimidation and isolation of those who oppose his vision in order to get control of the church, then the vision will never inspire the people to do great things for

Christ. He may have been given a vision for his ministry from God, but his vision may not be for that church.

By the same token, sometimes God brings a pastor with a vision to a church that needs a new vision—and there will be opposition. At this point, the most creative spiritual sensitivity needs to be in place on the part of the pastor and the lay leaders of the church.

- ♦ Do enough of the lay people feel this is God's new vision the church has needed?
- ♦ Are they willing to support the direction articulated to them from the pastor's heart for the good of the whole church?
- ♦ Are opposition and blockage coming from a very small but influential segment of the membership?
- ♦ Can there be a sharing of the vision, enlarging it to include as many of the church members as possible?
- ♦ If not, can there be a harmonious way to go separate ways with a blessing given and received?

3. The pastor is not actively involved in the vision-seeking process.

If the pastor doesn't have a vision, is not seeking a vision, or does not share the vision, the lay people in the church in my opinion cannot succeed in a vision quest on their own. God's vision for a particular church will always involve the pastor.

I'm reluctant to say a church can't be effective doing God's will without the pastor because I don't ever want a church to be pastor- centered rather than Christ-centered. The pastor is important as a member of the Body, but so is every other member. The reason the pastor is unique in the congregation is that he or she is the person the church has invited to be their spiritual leader. Other men and women in the congregation may have also been called of God to preach or teach, but the pastor has a special role as shepherd.

> *God's vision for a particular church will always involve its pastor.*

First Baptist, Arlington, has many ordained persons in the congregation, but none of them has been called to be the pastor. The person a church has called to serve as the pastor must provide the leadership. If not, a mixed signal is sounded. Different lay leaders and staff ministers will seek to fill the leadership vacuum when a pastor does not lead. People want to know where the pastor thinks God is leading the church to go because they want the pastor to be there when they get there. They know intuitively that if the one asked to lead does not lead, the church will grow confused, and disappointment and hurt will rise in the hearts of the people.

The story in Numbers 12 and 13 where Moses sends the twelve spies into the land of Canaan to see what needs to be done to enter the Promised Land illustrates this problem of weak leadership. They returned with a divided report. Ten of the spies said they could not succeed. The challenge was too great. Caleb and Joshua said they were well able and must go forward. But those who gave the majority report shared their fears with the people and spread a bad report among the Israelites. Moses should have stepped forward and said clearly what he believed God wanted the people to do, but he didn't. *"That night all the people of the community raised their voices and wept aloud. . . and they said to each other, we should choose a leader and go back to Egypt."*

When God's leader does not lead, disappointment and hurt fill the hearts of His people.

4. The pastor dictates vision from a position of authority.

When a pastor makes articulating the vision an authority issue, he may not be giving God the opportunity to develop or confirm the vision in the hearts of individual church members. He could be taking over God's job of forming and shaping the vision. Some in denominational leadership take it upon themselves to prescribe a theological creed and define what they perceive to be an appropriate vision for local churches. And some pastors believe their role is to be the absolute ruler of the church.

The pastor's role must be one of leadership—servant leadership *(Matthew 20:25-28)*. Pastors should not get their cue from what is expedient, or what even a majority of the people want to do. The majority is not always right. God's servants must get their cue from the mind of Christ.

To say that the majority is not always right is obviously true, but the will of the majority must be respected. Patiently a pastor can help the majority, and eventually almost everyone, come to a good decision if they can be led to pray for the mind of Christ to be the standard by which they make decisions. Wise pastors work hard to help their church members pray until they too are asking God to show them His will. Then when the congregation votes, they vote not simply their own opinion, but what they perceive to be the will of God, the mind of Christ, for the congregation.

5. The pastor or committee tells the congregation what they are supposed to do.

A pastor or church leader who announces that he or she knows what the church has to do creates defensiveness in the listeners. The deacons in a church are offended when a committee chairperson presents an idea, glibly announces that it has been prayed over, and expects them to support it without question.

What church members want to hear is that a committee of the church, or a minister, has studied a situation prayerfully, carefully thought it through, has found what seems to be a Godly and wise solution, and now offers it to them for their counsel, insight, and support if the idea shows merit.

Church members do not want to re-do the work of the committee, but they want some information about how the committee did its work and the rationale for the recommendation. They want

> *Members of the Body want to know that they have been included as decisions are made.*

to know they have been included as decisions are made. They want to listen prayerfully, and if they feel the direction is consistent with the church's vision and has been carefully prepared, they will gladly support the recommendation.

6. The pastor is unwilling to pay the price of seeking God's will and sensitively communicating it to the people.

The pastor must be willing to ask God diligently and humbly to provide a clear vision for the church and to help impart that vision to the congregation. Depending on the pastor's leadership style and God's gifts, the pastor either finds the vision and draws people to it, or discovers the vision alongside the people. At some point, however, the pastor must step forward to articulate the vision with clarity and confidence in order for the church to join fully in the vision. The vision must be held before the people. In sermon, in teaching, and in conversation the vision flows out of the pastor's heart as he embraces the congregation. If it is not the deepest thing in his soul, if it has to be programmed and planned each time he speaks about it, then it is not God's vision.

7. Church leaders take something that worked at one church and package it for another church.

There are many "packaged" programs that can help churches implement their visions in practical ways. But the programs cannot substitute for the vision itself. Publishers who create, package and sell resources to churches must do their work with an understanding of the limitation of their role. Denominational offices and church growth experts must see themselves as a resource to assist the church, not as the arbiter of standards and procedures by which a church must do its ministry. Formulas represented as a guaranteed way to accomplish something are usually a disappointment.

8. Church leaders attempt to build a vision on the contemporary American business model of vision.

Church leaders cannot blindly follow the path charted by people who operate on the basis of a different worldview. Many authors underscore the importance of capturing and living the vision in the business world, but they fail to include the mind of Christ in the equation. Corporations emphasize profits. Churches and Christians emphasize people. When churches create a vision that is not God-centered, it may result in temporary progress but unlikely will provide sustained, positive, long-lasting impact.

An interesting turn of events has happened in the business world in recent years. The current literature of management, business and leadership development has become very principle-centered. In fact, the best corporations seem to be led now by men and women who are committed to people values and not just to the financial bottom line. They have discovered that if they don't take care of people, their customers and their employees, no one will be successful in the long run. Businesses have come to understand that their personnel are their greatest resource for the continued success of the company.

Paradoxically, sometimes leaders in churches emphasize performance so much that both the vocational and lay people who work for the church are pushed into burn-out and become used up rather than developed. Effective pastors work hard to encourage growth and excitement in their staff and lay leaders.

9. Church leaders limit the vision to what the human mind can conceive.

When it is our vision, it is limited by what our minds can conceive. When it is God's vision, it is an unlimited vision. When we work to filter the vision through man's societal and cultural boundaries and expectations, organizational restrictions and obstacles, the vision loses its power. It becomes limited and flattened by our massaging it through human fear and inertia. Only the Holy Spirit can keep God's vision alive.

One of the greatest moments in the life of First Baptist, Arlington, came when the finance committee came to the end of their resources. They realized that the needs were too great to address in the ways we had been doing and out of the normal giving anticipated through our projected growth. We needed to increase our giving by 25% within two years. Past giving trends showed an annual increase of only 3 to 4% per year.

We were willing to do whatever we needed to do, but we felt we couldn't challenge the people enough or convince them enough to accomplish that kind of increase. We knew that God had to do a work in our hearts. The finance committee and other leaders in the church began to pray and admit that we had to have a God-sized vision. It was not a vision that we could achieve on our own. We asked God to accomplish it through us and we promised that we would give Him the glory when it was successful. God made it happen. Our financial need was met and we continue to give God the glory for it.

Don't be afraid of doing something bigger than you have ever done before as long as it is not something that you have just dreamed up. Lofty goals are appropriate if they grow out

> **People will respond when they see their challenges as a God-sized and God-ordained vision.**

of your sense of the spiritual lostness and need of your community, and a deep conviction that God has placed your church in this particular place in order to make an eternal difference in people's lives for Christ's sake. People will respond when they see their challenge as a God-sized and God-ordained vision.

10. Church leaders attempt to narrow the vision, for convenience and clarity, to one thing.

As pastor, when I began attempting to articulate the vision for our church, I kept getting pressure from people to put forward one primary goal. They kept saying our church had to have one clear vision. They kept telling me, "The main thing is the main thing is the main thing."

When asked what the single purpose of a church is, many church people respond with "evangelism." A liturgical church or a praise and worship church would probably say "worship." A Bible church would think that means "discipleship." Some street-focused churches would say "ministry." A lot of churches would let the pastor say whatever comes to mind but they all know that the main purpose of the church is "fellowship." Their friends are there—the people who make a difference in their lives and in whom they have confidence are all in the church. As you can see, by these stereotypical examples, any of the five main functions of a church can inappropriately become a tunnel vision for a church, to the minimizing of the other functions. (See Chapters 4-8.)

⌘

> *The mind of Christ pulls people from where they are to where they really want to be as Christians.*

The power of discovering and living in God's will is this: *A church can be motivated to want to do the will of God. The mind of Christ pulls people from where they are to where they really want to be as Christians.*

No formula, campaign, or leader can sustain spiritual energy as Christ can. Churches change and grow or they die. The vision in the mind of Christ is always greater than we can conceive. He draws us to attempt ever-greater things for His Kingdom. God's will is deeper than our imagination can fathom. He calls us to seek His mystery in faith and obedience. If we limit God's will to the boundaries of our common sense and logic, we put God in a box and wonder why our church has no energy and no expectations.

I think of God's vision for the church as the way He matures us to know His purpose and live out the character of Christ. He wants us to function within the parameters of that vision with confidence and ease, while watching and appreciating other churches whose vision may be different but still is as valid and important as our own.

In First Baptist, Arlington, I saw the vision of individual Christians blending into and complementing our church's vision. It's fun to watch God at work in a church where He has made His vision known. One never knows what God will do, but there is a spirit of expectation that energizes the Body.

After some trial balloons, some personal detours and then a fizzled official attempt, I spent a decade and a half as pastor focusing on God's vision for the church. My personal reward is that I now see the Body using their God-given gifts, becoming equipped to do whatever they need to do to evangelize and serve our community. For me, God's Kingdom on earth is finding expression in our own city. We will always have a long way to go to see that vision fulfilled, but we are moving in the right direction.

Jesus followed God's vision with the cross in view knowing what it would cost. He did God's will in the temple and in the streets, where all the people could be touched. He listened to people, and took them seriously. He discovered what people needed, and responded to their needs. Jesus went home with all kinds of people. That's the way Jesus was, that's the way His churches must be. That's the way His vision will be fulfilled.

⌘

⌘

IDEAS TO HELP A PASTOR DISCOVER
GOD'S VISION FOR A CHURCH

⌘ Ask God to reveal His vision for your church.

Focus on the reality that the church is the presence of Christ in your community. Ask church leaders to study and pray as you seek God's vision. Make the investment required to capture God's vision.

- Study the Bible to seek guidance in Scripture.
- Begin to pray that the Holy Spirit will take what is written and make it come alive in the hearts of His people so the Scripture is not just an historical document but a lively witness to the Spirit and Mind of Christ.
- Focus on the character of Jesus. Seek to understand His passion and discernment. Notice what decisions Jesus made and what admonitions He gave. Pay attention to what He said and did not say.
- Listen to what the disciples said about what Jesus taught them and what He meant to them.
- Take the whole witness of Scripture as a basis to understand the mind of Christ.

⌘ Check your heart.

Is God's vision what you are truly seeking? What pieces of your own prideful vision must you lay down in order to capture God's vision for the church? Vision involves integrating personal abilities and limitations within God's plan to accomplish what needs to be done through His people. God's servant leaders blend their vision for personal ministry with the vision imparted by God for the church they lead.

⌘ Don't think you must have the entire vision yourself before you discuss it with the members of the church.

Share your sense of direction and get counsel from others. Seek confirmation of what you believe God is saying to you. Gain energy not only from ideas that are affirmed by members of the church but also from the quality of the challenge to some of your ideas.

- Provide adequate Scriptural basis for every idea presented.

- ♦ Discuss and do everything in the context of seeking the mind of Christ *(Philippians 2:5).*
- ♦ Encourage members to recognize that an idea can accurately express the will of God, even though they are not yet ready to embrace it.

⌘ Don't think you have to "sell" the vision to the church.

You must communicate the vision clearly and passionately, but it is God's vision, not yours. God is perfectly capable of making it "come alive" to those who have the ears to hear.

⌘ Challenge the church's leadership to think about what God's church really is.

Get them talking about what it means to be church. Doing flows out of being. Vision entails change; it focuses on the future. Vision is never about maintaining things the way they are. When the idea takes hold that the church is the continuation of the incarnation, there is no stopping the people.

⌘ Diligently study the New Testament yourself to see what the earliest church of Jesus looked like, acted like, and what He expected of it.

Seek to capture an understanding of His will for your church based upon His point of view. (See Chapters 1 and 2 for insights into what Jesus said and did as He modeled the church.)

⌘ Teach a series on the images of the church in the New Testament.

Talk about the church being the Bride of Christ *(Ephesians 5:25-27),* the Army of God *(Ephesians 6:10-20),* and the Family of Faith *(Ephesians 2:19).* Continuously refer to the image of the Body of Christ *(Ephesians 1:22-23; Romans 12; 1 Corinthians 12).* (This was the Apostle Paul's favorite comparison.) Vision has no force unless it spreads from the visionary to the visionless. You will know you are making headway when people begin to say, "I never thought about the church that way before!" (See Chapter 3 for more on this point.)

> *Vision has no force unless it spreads from the visionary to the visionless.*

⌘ **Discuss what it means for the body to be in harmony with the mind.**

What happens when our physical body does not respond to the commands of the brain? *Paralysis!* What happens when the Body of Christ does not respond to the mind of Christ? *Paralysis!* Talk about how knowing the mind of Christ is authenticated by the actions of the Body *(1 John 2:3-11)*.

⌘ **Challenge church members to study the gospels themselves.**

Perhaps they could do this in small group Bible studies or individually. Encourage them to focus on what Jesus said and did —what He taught and how He acted. How can you as a church involve yourselves in your community to do what Jesus would do?

Pay close attention to the balance in Jesus' life. Look at judgment and discernment. Look at evangelism, ministry and teaching. For instance, Jesus was not just a nice man. He offended people. He got into hot water. He cared about people no one else cared for. He loved God and wanted more than anything to do the will of God. Jesus prayed deeply. He both healed and taught people. He created a fellowship of people who loved each other. He wanted the good news to be heard by all people. Jesus ultimately became a ransom for others. What does this teach you as you consider what it means to be the presence of Christ in your community?

⌘ **Sit down with a representative group of the congregation and begin doing what you have decided is important.**

Take a long look at your community and its needs. Ask what the church can do and how you can do it. How do you become Christ's presence in the community? All kinds of possibilities will arise. No two churches will come up with exactly the same ideas, though in the community several churches may see the same needs.

Now it's time for a unique church to put feet to its unique vision. Mobilize people to the task. There may or may not be a need to form new task forces, committees, or ministry teams. Pay attention to the energy already in place in the Bible study groups and committees that exist in your church. Empower the groups to go forward. Go and do!

⌘

[1.] George Barna, *The Power of Vision*, (Ventura, Calif.:Regal Books, 1992), p.12.
[2.] George Barna, ibid., p.53.

GRACIOUS FATHER IN HEAVEN:

ALL KNOWLEDGE, ALL WISDOM, AND ALL PURPOSE IN LIFE COME FROM YOU. IN THE BEST OF TIMES WHEN WE DEPEND ON THE WONDER OF YOUR FORGIVENESS, GRACE, AND PROVISION, WE KNOW THAT TO BE TRUE. IN THE TROUBLESOME TIMES, WE TRY TO RUN AHEAD OF YOU TO MAKE OUR OWN WAY IN THIS WORLD. WE ACKNOWLEDGE OUR SELFISH PRIDE WHEN WE ATTEMPT TO DO YOUR WORK FOR OUR GLORY, OR COME TO YOU WITH OUR OWN AGENDA, SEEKING YOUR BLESSING FOR OUR PRESUMPTUOUS DECISIONS AND PLANS.

HELP US, FATHER, TO SO LIVE IN YOUR PRESENCE THAT EVERY THOUGHT WE THINK IS GUIDED BY YOUR HOLY SPIRIT. GIVE US THE PASSION TO SEEK A VISION FOR OUR CHURCH AND FOR OURSELVES. YET, MAKE THAT VISION YOUR VISION, NOT OURS.

THANK YOU FOR JESUS WHO IS OUR SAVIOR AND MODEL FOR ALL THINGS GOOD AND TRUE.

AMEN

Life Applications

⌘

GOD'S VISION FOR A CHURCH

1. Where is your congregation in regard to clarifying God's vision for your church in your community?

2. What formal vision-seeking process has been attempted? Has a formal statement of vision ever been constructed? If so, study it. If not, why not?

3. To what degree do you feel the people in the congregation really understand the vision for your church?

4. Look around in your community. Identify ministry needs God may be calling your church to address?

5. What personal action will you take to become involved in a vision quest for your church? Discuss these ideas with your other church leaders.

10

GOD'S CALLING
How We Make Up Our Minds

One day when I was in high school, the question of careers came up in a classroom discussion and I told the class that I felt called to ministry. The teacher looked at me with a curious smile and asked, *"Charles, what exactly is a call to ministry?"* Everyone who has ever tried to answer that question understands the difficulty of putting it into words. I can't remember what I said to the teacher, but I do remember how difficult it was for me to answer. Now after having years to think about what it means to be called to ministry, let me try to state what I believe.

There are always choices to be made about what to do or not do with the life entrusted to us by God. If we are faithful in our commitment to follow God's lead, we will lay our hearts open to Him in prayer. We will be sensitive to the ways in which God communicates to us and trust that He will give us direction and peace, an inner confidence that we are going the right way.

Many have experienced a deep sense of inner direction to go a certain way. This is a "calling" so strong that it is almost like being *compelled* to follow Christ. For some, the feeling builds over a long period of time. For others, it comes suddenly. But the common characteristic is that when the calling comes, it has a clarity that can't be denied and a depth that surpasses any ordinary personal desire. As one begins to walk in the direction of the call, there is confirmation, affirmation, and joy—a sense of rightness about what one is doing with one's life.

Learning to Follow One Step at a Time

My father taught me this about knowing and doing God's will: *"God gives us light to go as far as we can see, but He does not light the path all the way to the end of the journey."* Think about that. If you and your family want to take a trip after dark, you load up your car, start the engine and turn on the headlights. But what would happen if you decided you were unwilling to pull out of the driveway and head down the road unless your headlights could reach all the way to your destination? You would never start the trip.

In our faith journey, we begin with our lights on, and we go down the road as far as it is lighted for us. As we move, the lights will be out in front of us, directing our way. God lights the way as we travel in faith. We may not be able to see where the journey will end. There are times we may not even know the direction we are heading. But if we move forward into the light, He equips and guides us as we go. It is much easier to adjust the direction of a moving object than to get an inert object moving!

> **God equips and guides us as we go.**

How does God give us His light?

How does God make Himself known? How does He communicate what His will is for us in this world, personally and corporately? Most Christians agree that it is possible to know and understand where God is directing an individual or a church. Yet many of those same people are skeptical that they personally could experience any direct communication from God.

The Bible speaks of God communicating in a variety of ways. In Numbers 12, God reveals to Aaron and Miriam that He speaks to His prophets in dreams, visions, and riddles; to Moses, He speaks face to face. From Abraham to Joseph to David to Jesus to the Apostles, we have many accounts in the Bible of how God has made Himself known through dreams, visions, angelic messengers, miracles and personal communication. These are not phenomena limited to ancient history. God still speaks today and those who seek Him can develop an increased ability to understand, however He chooses to reveal Himself.

We may be puzzled by dreams, confused by the images God places in our minds, or struggle to decipher the messages for us within Scripture. But as we seek to act on our sense of God's calling, we are not without help in clarifying the substance of that call. We have the Scripture as a guide to God's character and will. And we have the Body of Christ to help us listen, interpret, and understand. In our attempt to discern what decisions to make, it is helpful to seek the wise counsel of mature Christian friends in whom we see good judgment and faithful service to Christ and the church.

It is easy for people to do something or plan to do something that is rather difficult, and baptize it with the quick blessing, *"I believe this is God's will."* Many Christians as well as almost all non-Christians hear that kind of talk as a too-easy justification for whatever we want to do and dismiss it as being simply "clutter" or "fluff" language. It is scarcely better than a vocal pause. It is what some people say when they don't want to admit the truth of how decisions were really made. It can even be a form of blasphemy—carelessly using God's name in vain.

How do we experience a sense of vocational calling in which we become aware of God directing us to leave whatever we are doing in order to take hold of what He has for us to do? It helps to be the Son of God. But even Jesus spent time in prayer and fasting as the will of the Father was tested in His soul *(Matthew 4:1-11).* And like Jesus, the deep sense of God's presence comes to us in the spiritual disciplines of prayer and waiting upon God. When this happens, God gives an inner certainty, a harmony or peace, as many describe it, which is a confirmation of His will.

It is clear that when Jesus was tempted after forty days of fasting and prayer, He answered Satan's temptation through Scripture. We can do the same. We can turn to God's Word to guide us in making decisions about God's will for us.

We know God does not want us to be hateful, deceitful, dishonest, or immoral. These are contrary to the character of Jesus as revealed in Scripture. The Scripture becomes a mine in which we

> **Scripture becomes a mine in which we work the mother lode in order to live in the rich deposits of God's truth and wisdom.**

work the mother lode in order to live in the rich deposits of God's truth and wisdom. Surrounded by God's purpose, we live in a context and environment where the will of God can be made clear. Then as we pray, listen and wait, God reveals Himself. He shapes our consciousness. As we allow ourselves to be pliable, He bends us to His will.

God's speaking to me has always been a deep and profound conviction that rises up in my life. I have never audibly heard the voice of God, although some people apparently have. Neither can I claim significant God-sent dreams or visions like other people have described. I can best define God's speaking to me through a growing feeling that matures into insight and conviction. I can feel it like I feel love for someone. The reality of God's presence and His will is there. Through prayer, study, meditation and the confirming counsel of trusted Christian friends, God's will becomes clearer to me.

Many within the church are aware that God can and does give guidance and insight to everyday issues of life through impressions, insights or what other Christians might say to us. That is a wonderful awareness and spiritual sensitivity that all of us should seek. However, we must beware of presumptuous thinking that may mistake our own desires and imaginings for God's voice and will. We cannot give in mindlessly or carelessly to a prideful subjectivism.

> **Beware of presumptuous thinking that may mistake our own desires for God's voice and will.**

Anytime someone tells me that God has personally told him or her to do a certain thing, I listen attentively. But that does not guarantee my automatic agreement. God certainly has the power and ability to tell people different things in unique and personal ways. But I have observed people often attempt to manipulate the truth in order to get *their* will done. They represent their own desires as being the voice and will of God. I often remind myself and others that true prayer is not seeking to get God ready to do my will, but to get me ready to do God's will. Remember how Jesus prayed the night before He died? *"Yet not as I will, but as you will"* *(Matthew 26:39).*

THREE WAYS GOD CALLS US INTO HIS SERVICE

God calls us into His service in three ways—first to salvation and discipleship, then perhaps to vocational ministry and possibly to a specific task or place of service.

1. The Call to Salvation and Christian Discipleship

The first call of God is to every person to be saved. We are all sinners, hopelessly lost in separation from our Creator. Our lives manifest a host of wrongs against God and our fellow man— greed, pride, lust, hatred, rebellion, unbelief, apathy and/or envy. Yet because of God's love for us, He has compassion. He seeks us out by His Holy Spirit, moving here and there, calling us to follow Him.

Through the prompting of God's Holy Spirit, we come under an awareness and conviction of our sin. We see the result of sin— our condemnation and death. We want to be different. We confess our sin and repent. We open ourselves before a holy and loving God for cleansing and blessing. We trust God to save us through the work of Jesus Christ on the cross who died in our place.

We cannot save ourselves. Jesus had to die—the righteous for the unrighteous. He had to rise up in power from the grave so we could live on the other side of sin. And He had to make the message clear and compelling. That is exactly what God does when He calls us to salvation. Every person who is called by God into salvation is called into discipleship and ministry. Baptism is every Christian's ordination for service.

> **Every person called into salvation is called into discipleship and ministry.**

The calling to every Christian is to serve God. The German reformer Martin Luther hallowed the role of the layperson by his reflections on the priesthood of the believer. He taught that a woman who cares for her children and manages the household is doing God's work as much as any priest—that a man working over the blacksmith's fire and anvil can be doing God's work as surely as any bishop of the church. Luther glorified the ordinary tasks of living as service to God and others.

We are all called, whether into vocational, bivocational or volunteer ministry. How that plays out for some people can be very specific. I have known people who were called by God to be teachers and touch the lives of young people. I have friends who feel called to conduct businesses based on Christian principles. Others who do not have a sense of a specific role or career focus still feel God's call on their life in their day-to-day activities.

> **God asks us to watch for, and to act upon, opportunities where we can make a difference in people's lives.**

If God has not impressed His specific call upon your heart at a deep enough level that you cannot ignore it, He is essentially giving you the freedom, as a servant and disciple, to look at life and the world around you and do whatever interests you and will be useful to God's Kingdom. He is asking you to watch for and act upon opportunities where you can make a difference for others. If you see a need, that is an invitation to Christian ministry. So get with it!

Some of the finest Christian lay persons I know are ones who are called to serve God, but don't feel God's call for them to a particular career. I know a deacon who is a real estate appraiser, but that career position would not be his description of what God has called him to do with his life. He finds deep joy in working with a group of mentally handicapped young people on Sunday morning. God probably has no great concern about whether we sell used or new cars, Fords or Chevrolets, pick-up trucks or vans—but no matter where we work, He does care if we are first and foremost His disciples!

2. The Call to Vocational Christian Ministry

> **The responsibility for convincing people to do the will of God is God's.**

There is a specific calling to vocational Christian ministry. I have observed over the years that those men and women who are the most effective ministers over the long haul are the ones who fully believe that God has tapped them on the shoulder and said, *"This is your task. I call you to a life of service and I will go with you."* The task of serving a church or a Christian institution or ministry is too daunting, too demanding, too complicated to attempt without a deep sense that God has issued a call to the task. If God has something specific for us to do, He is able to let us know. The responsibility for convincing people to do the will of God is God's. He is certainly able to make a clear and compelling case.

It is possible to know what God wants us to do and reject His calling. Some people, out of fear, worldly ambition, or rebellion, decline to do what God clearly calls them to do. In a sense they stare God down and say, "I won't do what you want me to do." The story of Jonah from the Bible is a good example. Jonah knew what God wanted him to do, and resisted mightily. During Jonah's resistance, God kept pressing him, turning up the heat, churning up the storm, making clear the cost of his rebellion until Jonah acted on God's calling and went on to Ninevah.

Obedience breeds confidence. People who have had a history of following the will of God in their life have more confidence that they will recognize the will of God when it is set before them. When I was six years old, and the Lord prompted me to give my life to Him, I responded that very evening. I struggled to find the courage to step forward before the congregation, but God heard my cry and helped me to put one foot in front of the other, and I went forward to confess my allegiance to Jesus Christ. I didn't put it off or run away. By the grace of God, I just did it.

When I was eleven, I sensed a distinct call of God for me to be a pastor. I quickly stepped forward to that calling too. When I was fifteen, I struggled with what I thought was a call from God to become a missionary. I wrestled with that because I did not want to be a missionary in another part of the world. I was in North Carolina at a retreat. After several days and nights of pondering my response, I finally said, "Lord, I don't know what I need to do. I don't really understand it all. But I do know that whatever it is You want me to do, I will do it."

Later, I learned that most missionaries work as administrators of local mission efforts or as enablers of native pastors. It would be unusual for a missionary to become the pastor of a mission church. Since my clear life calling was to be a pastor, it seemed evident that I needed to be pursuing that calling in my own country, speaking the language I already knew. Until the call came to work with Texas Baptists as their Executive Director, I had never wanted to do anything in my life other than to be a pastor and preach the Gospel of Christ.

As the later calling began to grip my heart, I began to sense God was leading Rosemary and me to take up a different challenge, but of the same cloth. Rosemary and I both loved the pastorate, but we began to wonder, "Could God use us to help the churches of Texas be the presence of Jesus in every community and put their arms around our state and hug it up close to God?" It has been a huge learning curve for me. But I have wonderful help from staff and the pastors and people of Texas Baptist churches.

Early on I asked Baptists in Texas to pray for me that I would have the necessary wisdom. James 1:5 becomes very encouraging to me. I later asked them to add courage to the prayer requests on my behalf, noting Joshua 1:9. It became clear to me I needed both wisdom and courage. Courage without wisdom can be dangerous and wisdom without courage is useless. I need prayers that petition the Father on my behalf for these two great qualities of Christian character.

This denominational leadership experience has taught me that the passion for missions planted in my heart by God could be fulfilled by helping churches have both a world-wide missions agenda and a strategy for doing missions right where we are. For me, the calls to preach, to be a pastor, and to be involved in missions are finally all tied together.

Persons diligently focused on discovering God's will in their life, but who have never had previous experience in following the will of God, need to be cautious about jumping into situations they know little about. Wise counsel and discussion should precede action. But if God is calling us to service, He won't let us loose.

> **If God is calling us to service, He won't let us loose.**

My best counsel for Christians is to pray to be willing to do whatever God asks and work on being obedient each step of the way as God reveals His will. Here are some helpful checkpoints for understanding God's will.

God's call is always consistent with His word and His revelation. God has spoken to people in many ways. We should be open to every possible way He may speak to us, but carefully test what we think we hear. We can apply these principles to evaluate what we feel to be God's call:

- God is able to communicate, and He can make His will known.
- God will never direct us to do something that is contrary to His word as revealed in Scripture.
- God will never ask us to do something inconsistent with the character of Jesus.
- The specific task God gives us to do will always be consistent with the deeper calling He has placed on our life when He saved us and called us to follow Jesus.

Guarantees aren't available. It is only natural for us to want some control over our lives and not have to live with the unknown. So the temptation we face is to hold out for absolute certainty before we are willing to commit. Unfortunately, guarantees aren't available when we respond to God's call. We have to live with a certain amount of uncertainty and trust God to guide us along the way and faithfully provide for our needs. It is important to consider the demands of our journey of faith as we stand at the beginning, but we don't have to know all the steps and all the answers before we begin.

Don't just stand there, do something! When trying to make a decision about what to do, I depend on the grace of God in the midst of my uncertainty. I would rather do something and not do it quite right, or maybe even do it wrong, than not to do anything at all. With my intention being right, I would rather be found wrong than lazy.

During the American Civil War there was a general named G. B. McClellan. He was a marvelous horseman who trained his troops and cavalry to march about Washington D.C. with an impressive flair. But he could not be cajoled into going on the offensive. The time was never right. On one occasion, McClellan wrote to President Lincoln that he could not attack the Confederate troops because his horse was tired. The president retorted, *"Will you pardon me for asking what the horses of your army have done . . . that fatigues anything?"* [1] It was not until Lincoln found General U. S. Grant to command his armies that action replaced excuses.

Proactively doing God's will is very different from hesitatingly waiting around talking about doing God's will. Throughout history, God has mightily used men and women of action. We have to guard against the paralysis of analysis.

> Proactively doing God's will is very different from hesitatingly waiting around talking about doing God's will.

. . . faith by itself, if it is not accompanied by action, is dead. (James 2:17)

In order to live boldly, one has to have a healthy confidence in the mercy and grace of God. If I felt God would judge me harshly for my mistakes, that the punishment would be so severe that I would be safer doing nothing, then I would not step out and risk. But I know I can count on God's understanding and forgiveness, so I am willing to push ahead and take action.

This is not justification for doing things I know are wrong and trusting God will overlook my deliberate misdeeds. Anyone who takes that presumptuous approach drums himself out of service.

Matthew 25:14-30 tells the classic story about the servants who were entrusted with the assets of their master. One was so afraid of failure that he buried his and did nothing. The others invested theirs and received a remarkable return. Jesus believes in taking risks.

The great church reformer, Martin Luther, once wrote to his friend, Melancthon, *"Be a sinner and sin strongly, but more strongly have faith and rejoice in Christ."* Luther wasn't encouraging his friend to sin deliberately. He was trying to get at the idea that as Christians, what we should be about is so important and so significant that we have to put our life on the line. In the process, we may make mistakes, and our mistakes may be colossal errors. But, if in trying to do the bold and courageous thing, we fail, God's grace is sufficient.

A woman believed God called her as a girl to be a missionary to Africa, but for some reason she didn't pursue it. Many years later she felt her life had been wasted because she had not responded to that call. However, throughout her life, she had innumerable opportunities to be on mission for Christ in her own community, including ministry to many people in similar circumstances she would have found if she had gone to Africa. But over the years her regrets blinded her from seeing what God could do with her life where she was. As wonderful a foreign missionary as she might have been, the greatest tragedy is not that she didn't go to Africa, but that she failed to serve God and the people God loves right where she lived.

People who have a sense that God has called them to vocational Christian ministry, yet haven't been offered a place to serve, might do well to look around them to see where God is already at work, and cooperatively join Him wherever they can. Those who learn to see needs and respond in faithful service are likely to discover that God rewards the faithful with greater and even more fulfilling opportunities to minister.

> **Look around to see where God is already at work, and cooperatively join Him there.**

3. The Call to a Specific Task or Place of Service

The third calling of God is to a specific place to do God's work, whether in a church-related vocation or elsewhere in the world. It is focused service to God and others.

Years ago, when Rosemary and I were called to an English-speaking Baptist church in Germany, her parents were totally opposed to our going overseas. They didn't seem to mind if I went. It was the idea of taking their daughter and two grandchildren that upset them! My folks weren't very excited about it, either. Going to Germany meant dropping out of seminary for two years. Some of my friends at the seminary also were very concerned that I might be making a mistake to interrupt my education.

I could have told them that God had clearly called us to go and there was no need for them to try to persuade me otherwise. But I didn't want to say it that way, for several reasons. Rosemary's father was a Christian, but he was impatient with "religious" language. I didn't want to excuse myself from the responsibility I had in the decision by piously (as he would have interpreted it) suggesting that it was God's plan for us. I felt a responsibility for my portion of the decision. Neither did I want to escape my responsibility to explain by hiding behind God-talk.

What I did say was, "As best I can tell, this is what God wants us to do. I have prayed about it. I have thought it through. I have evaluated it in terms of what I believe God's larger call to be in my life, and I believe God has provided us with this opportunity to serve."

I was aware that I could be wrong. But God had given me enough of a sense of direction that I was willing to risk acting on what I believed to be His call. I didn't believe God had to convince our parents or my friends at the seminary. His call was for Rosemary and me.

I had asked the Lord that when He called me out to do something specific, He would give my wife, Rosemary, the confidence that it was what God wanted us to do. I had prayed that she would find an agreement in her own spirit that matched mine.

How did I know going to Germany was what I was supposed to do? I felt God confirmed our move in several ways.

- ♦ The call to go to Germany fit into my sense of God's life calling for me. It was not inconsistent with the core calling to preach which I had recognized at eleven years of age.

- ♦ The invitation to Germany gave me an opportunity to demonstrate to God and to myself that I was ready to go wherever He might lead. I previously had made a commitment to international missions. Yet, I did not have a passion for being a missionary. This assignment in Germany was a golden opportunity to go to a foreign country and serve for a couple of years and experience what being a missionary in an unfamiliar place might be. Somewhere inside, I knew it would clarify my sense of calling to missions.

- ♦ Rosemary had a deep sense of rightness about the direction we were taking, although it was very difficult in light of her parents' objections. She was as steady as a rock. I saw God give her courage to match the challenge. God confirmed the decision by the sense of release I felt from the current commitments I had. For the previous four years, I had served as pastor of a church in Oklahoma and was about at the end of my vision for that ministry. I also was attending seminary and was not pleased with my performance. I was commuting by train between the church field in Oklahoma and the seminary in Fort Worth, Texas. I did not have enough time to devote to my studies. As I reflect on that situation now, I was in many ways burned out on school and needed a change. My sense of release from my church and my educational effort came with a confident sense that I would return with a fresh commitment to continue my education.

♦ My feeling about the rightness of moving to a new assignment was very different from those times in my life when I had been frustrated and attempted to conjure up some way of escaping current anxieties by legitimizing a re-direction of my focus. I asked myself, "Am I running away from situations I am not happy with, or am I running toward something God has asked me to do?" The decision to go to Germany was definitely a move "toward" rather than "from."

Our two years in Germany significantly deepened my sense of what church is about. God blessed our efforts in wonderful ways as people found the Lord, families were strengthened and lives were healed. We saw the amazing power of a church fellowship to bless and encourage people. In the lives of these American soldiers and their families we confirmed the desperate necessity of church life.

When we returned to the United States two years later, I had discovered what I really needed to learn at the seminary. I was more focused, more experienced, and more able to move through school purposefully and confidently.

The Church Also Needs to Discern God's Calling

A church may pursue a vision of ministry that turns out to be something they can't do or, in fear, they simply give up and quit. It is better to have gone for the vision and adjust the vision later if necessary, than to sit idly, frightened to try. Doing nothing is a *choice* to do nothing, and that is the sin of omission. What is the sin of the third servant in the Matthew 25 parable? He was afraid. He knew his lord was a hard taskmaster, so he sat on the asset instead of taking the risk. How many churches sit in indecision while their community waits for them in desperate need? What do those churches have to show as a result of their unwillingness to invest their gifts and abilities in the lives of others?

⌘

TRUTHS ABOUT DISCOVERING AND DOING THE WILL OF GOD

You Will Know When God is Calling You.

How do you know if you have been called of God? It's similar to knowing you are in love. Did you ever ask your parents how you would know when you were in love? My parents told me they couldn't describe it but that I would just know. It's like that with God's calling. If you don't yet sense a calling from God, don't worry about it. It's God's business to call you. God is quite capable of getting through to you to be sure you know what He wants.

Don't conjure up the call. Don't yearn for the call. If you have a desire for a call from God, ask, and then be patient. In the meantime, God is trusting you to be doing what you know is in line with Scripture and with the character of Jesus. He is mindful of your life as it is. So invest it in His Kingdom. Celebrate your freedom to put your hand to the task nearest you.

Joy Will Be an Evidence of God's Calling.

Many people are afraid God will call them to do something they don't want to do or believe they cannot do. They think the will of God being made known is like draping a funeral shroud over them. They speak of "surrendering" to God's will. It is only surrender when we are reluctant recruits. And some people are very reluctant. Perhaps they feel unworthy, or they have other ambitions. But if God persistently continues to make clear His call in their heart, they will discover joy on the other side of surrender. My encouragement to any man or woman is, *"If God graces you with a life call, celebrate it! You can trust God to lead you to your greatest joy."* Joy follows obedience. If joy seems absent, then you may not be hearing God's true call in your life *(John 15:10-12; 16:21-22).*

Whatever is within you, God wants to release it. If you have the faith to believe God knows and wants what is best for you, you will gladly volunteer. When God calls you, go with Him. He will call you into service where everything you are and have can be released. That is the meaning of the gifts of the Spirit. Spiritual gifts are given so you can serve God with an inner joy and with confidence you are doing what God has called and gifted you to do. Look around and you will see people joyously doing things you would never want to do. They are called to those tasks and are responding enthusiastically. You can too.

Initially, God's Call Will be a Call to Prepare.

If you feel called of God to do something, you will take it so seriously you will do whatever it takes to get ready. You won't be careless about it. You won't take shortcuts. If you are not willing to prepare, then God may not have really called you to do the task you think He has. When God calls you, it makes you humble, not proud. You see how much you need to know rather than how much you already know.

So what if you try to follow God's call and then you begin to feel you are making a mistake? Let's imagine you are a musician, and you feel God is calling you to the ministry as a musician. You start to prepare and, a year into the schooling, you discover that you have the musical performance gifts but you don't have the people skills or the administrative abilities to be a competent and successful minister of music. So now what?

Probably what happened is that music was the only area you could have imagined God calling you toward, since that was already what you did so well. It was the only thing He could have called you to do that you would have believed you could do. He essentially got you off dead center, and as you trusted Him to begin preparing, then He could guide you into another ministry area. Let Him call you however He will. Begin to prepare and if your aim is off, He will give you a course correction along the way.

I remember a missionary telling me as a teenager, "You will never learn anything God can't use sometime in your life." That exhortation influenced me to take bookkeeping in high school. I was the only boy in the class. Nobody understood why I was taking that class. But since I knew I was called to be a pastor, I knew I would benefit from an understanding of money management. Although I was never good in advanced mathematics, God has used that basic bookkeeping knowledge to help me give credible leadership in the financial workings of local churches.

> *You will never learn anything that God can't use sometime in your life.*

When I was a boy, I went every year to visit my grandfather who lived north of Austin, Texas in the cedar brakes. We cut cedar posts each year, and later when I heard this story I could identify.

A grandfather and grandson went out in the forest to chop wood. They picked a spot and the boy began chopping immediately. The grandfather sat down on a log and spent half an hour sharpening his ax. As the boy examined his pile of wood, he thought his grandfather had wasted a lot of time. But when Grandfather stood, with sharpened tool in hand, it took only one blow to do what it was taking the boy twenty blows to accomplish. Within ten minutes, he had caught up with the boy's production. The older man understood the importance of serious thoughtful preparation.

God's Call is Always a Call to Service Now.

I've known people who feel called to be missionaries to other parts of the world, but they won't get acquainted with the people in their immediate community who are different from them. They love people far away but they don't seem to love people who live next door. I have observed many people who go to seminary, presumably called into God's service, but who seldom attend church while they are preparing to be a minister. They plan to serve a church after they get a degree, but right now they believe their service to God is studying. Studying is important—more important, I fear, than many ministers appreciate. But studying can be no excuse for failing to worship and serve in your church.

I remember a man who came to Arlington to attend seminary after retiring from the military. He felt God's calling to serve as a pastor and was a member of our church. As he was nearing completion of his seminary training, he began looking for a place to serve. He was a quiet, laid-back kind of person who had not taken any responsibility for service in the church while he attended seminary. He came to me to discuss recommending him. I was happy to be a personal reference for him, but I made a suggestion. I told him that if a church did not extend an invitation to him right away, he could "pastor" one of the adult Sunday school departments in our church by becoming a director. He could develop relationships, encourage growth, enlist new members, recruit other leaders, and organize activities — just the thing he would be doing in his first church!

God Will Give You Courage Needed to Respond to His Call.

When God really has called you, you will find a personal willingness to risk everything to respond. If you don't have the courage to do something, your hesitancy may very well be the protection keeping you from getting into a place where you couldn't do well. If God really is calling you to a particular task, I believe along with the call He will give you the courage you need to take the necessary risks. If God gives you the courage to respond, go for it. If you don't respond, choose not to spend the rest of your life regretting that you did not act. Accept what happened.

It saddens me to hear a person say, *"When I was a child, the Lord called me to be a _____* (fill in the blank), *and I didn't do it, so I have wasted my life"*. If someone fails to respond to their perceived call to international missions, to be a minister to youth, to become a pastor, or to work in inner-city ministries, that doesn't mean life has been wasted. God is quite capable of working with us using Plan B, C or D. If the original calling didn't materialize, for whatever reason, do what you can do and do it with gladness. Don't spend the remainder of your life regretting some past failure to make the right decision. God can forgive and use us anyway.

As I look back on my life, I believe that as God has given me jobs to do, He also has given me the courage to do them. The beautiful part of discovering how God's will works in a

> *Discovering God's will is a life-long process, not a single point in time.*

person's life is that once we make a decision to act on His call, the fruit will become evident. With each obedient response to God, we gain more confidence to act. Confidence builds on confidence. When things don't seem to be working out, we learn to adjust our course and get on track with God. Over time, those responses to God and related adjustments necessary for our growth and learning become the way we live our life. Discovering God's will is a life-long process, not a single point in time. Whatever it takes to get our attention, God is willing to do to get us moving. We can live each day joyfully and with thanksgiving as His light shows us the way, confident that we are important to God, and that the task He has for us to do is important.

Trust God to Provide You with Increasing Opportunities.

I believe in the open door concept. When God opens a door, walk through it. How are you supposed to know which church to serve? I believe when you are without a place to serve, the first church to invite you is the place where you should go. When I first started and did not have a church to pastor, the first church that asked me to preach is the one I went to. When God originally called me to preach He did not call me to First Baptist Church in Arlington. When I responded to God's calling, it was His calling to which I was devoted, not to where He would place me to fulfill His calling. When I became the pastor of Fairview Church out in the open country of western Oklahoma, I thought it was the greatest church I had ever seen. I was willing to stay there as long as I was needed. I was as happy then in that small country church as I was later serving a large city church in Arlington, Texas.

> *When God opens a door, walk through it.*

I've seen young people who are willing to give themselves in ministry, but only if it can be done in a certain way or in a certain place. If God doesn't provide the situation they have in mind, then they consider their commitment no longer to be valid. In my experience, doing God's will has much to do with what you do and little to do with where you do it.

> *Doing God's will has much to do with what you do and little to do with where you do it.*

For people who believe God has called them to ministry, there is a way to check the validity of the call. If a church believes in a person's call, the church will affirm that call with an opportunity to serve. If a church invites you to visit them in view of an opportunity to serve and never invites you back, either the church is out of God's will or you are. And so you go to the next church that asks you. After visiting several churches and none asks you to come serve with them, you may have misinterpreted the will of God, or you may need a lot more preparation to become adequately equipped to serve.

What do you do when the evidence of call seems elusive? You pray, *"God, I'm willing to do whatever You want me to do, go wherever You want me to go. If this isn't it, I'm open to whatever You suggest."* In your willingness, God will guide you.

God Expects You to Do Your Best, Wherever You are Serving.

As you grow in wisdom about how to minister within the Body of Christ, you begin to take on certain convictions and principles about what is wrong and what is right for the church you are called to serve. A minister's relationship with the congregation is a lot like a marriage. Sensitivity and open communication are very important in building good relationships. Unfortunately, sometimes a minister will be called to a church and the match turns out not to have been made in heaven. The minister needs to evaluate this situation with some hard questions.

"Is my vision of church compatible with the church's vision, or will those visions be at odds?"

"Do I see a church that needs to reach out to the community when they seem to want to focus on taking care of themselves?"

Even when the initial match seems to be questionable, you can help sharpen a church's vision if you are willing to pray, love the people, and work consistently and patiently with them over a period of time.

Several young preachers have asked my advice over the years about how to know whether to accept a church's call. My statement to them has always been,

♦ *First, pray that God's will become clear. If you don't have a church to serve, and a church asks you to come, treat that call as an opportunity provided by God. The church is showing confidence in your ability to fulfill God's will for their congregation.*

♦ *Second, if you accept the call, love the people where they are and lead them where they can go.*

♦ *Third, be prepared to learn as much as you teach.*

God Calls Churches to Specific Ministries.

God expects every church to be the Body of Christ and to do what Jesus would do. We don't have to pray about what is the baseline purpose of the church. As we live in Christ and He lives in us, that basic task is clear.

With that understanding, we can pray, *"Lord, here we are trying to be the presence of Jesus in this community. We don't have eyes as clear or ears as sensitive as Yours. But we want to be Your people at work in this community. Show us and we will follow."*

The Missions Committee of our church came to me years ago and said, "Pastor, we have mission activities going on in a lot of places and we give money for people to do missions in other parts of the world. We need to keep doing that, but we are praying that God will give us missions to do right here in Arlington."

Several church members, along with myself, began to pray. Before the month was over, Patrick So came to ask if he could organize a Chinese congregation and meet in our building. The next month John Lee came to ask if he could start a Korean congregation. Prayer was our way of getting ready for what God wanted done.

We had a Spanish-speaking congregation meeting in our building already. Where would we put a Korean and a Chinese-speaking congregation? We were short on meeting space but we worked out an adjusted schedule and now, by the grace of God, all three of those congregations are now strong churches meeting in their own buildings. For a few years it was like a United Nations meeting in our church. And it was great for all of us.

A Church Can Offer Encouragement to Individual Members Who Sense a Call to a Specific Ministry.

Sometimes a person feels drawn to a ministry that only a few others in the church may want to do. Hopefully, the church will encourage and pray for the new venture. Some guidelines are appropriate:

- ♦ Does the ministry advance the vision of the church?
- ♦ Will it negatively impact other ministries?
- ♦ Will it require money from the church budget?

If the answers are yes, no, and no to those questions, then without a lot of discussion the Body can affirm and bless the new effort. Only a few may be called to help, but that's perfectly all right. Count the "yes" votes and go forward. The "no" votes can be encouraged to see that not every ministry needs everyone's help. Give permission and set people free to serve God in unique and sensitive ways. I like to say, *"As a pastor, I'll clear off a little space for you to get some traction . . . and the rest of us will cheer you on as you take on the challenge God has given you."*

In summary, these last words about God's call in your life:

♦ **You can trust God! He will lead you to joy.**

♦ **That you serve God is more important than where you serve.**

⌘

[1] T. Harry Williams, *The Life History of the United States*, Vol. 5: 1849-1865, *The Union Standard*, 1963, pp. 104-105.

⌘
JESUS PRINCIPLES
FOR RESPONDING TO GOD'S CALL

⌘ You will know when God is calling you. Wait in confident patience for His timing.

⌘ Joy will be an evidence of God's calling.

⌘ Initially, God's call will be a call to prepare. Equip yourself through study, spiritual discipline, and experience.

⌘ God's call is always a call to service now, even while you prepare.

⌘ God will give you the courage needed to respond to His call.

⌘ God will provide ever-increasing opportunities to those who serve faithfully.

⌘ God expects you to do your best, wherever you are serving.

⌘ God calls people and churches to unique ministries.

⌘ A healthy church offers encouragement to individual members who sense a call to a specific ministry.

⌘ It's more important *that* you serve, than *where* you serve!

LORD OF OUR LIFE:

HERE WE ARE TRYING TO BE THE PRESENCE OF JESUS IN OUR WORLD. WE DON'T HAVE EYES AS CLEAR OR EARS AS SENSITIVE AS YOURS. BUT WE PASSIONATELY WANT TO BE YOUR PEOPLE AT WORK IN THIS COMMUNITY. SHOW US WHAT YOU WOULD HAVE US DO, AND WE WILL FOLLOW.

PROTECT US, WE PRAY, FROM THE TEMPTATION TO FOLLOW OUR OWN WILL RATHER THAN YOURS. WHEN WE ARE CONFUSED ABOUT WHAT TO DO, GIVE US THE CLARITY OF YOUR VISION. WHEN WE ARE FEARFUL, FILL US WITH COURAGE. LET US SEE THE NEEDS OF OUR WORLD THROUGH THE COMPASSIONATE EYES OF JESUS. EQUIP US TO BE YOUR SPIRITUAL WARRIORS THROUGH THE UNMATCHABLE POWER OF YOUR GRACE.

AMEN

Life Application

⌘

GOD'S CALLING
How We Make Up Our Minds

1. In what ways do you believe God communicates His will to Christians?

2. What could you do to sharpen your ability to hear God and to more clearly understand His will for your life?

3. Describe your true feelings about being willing to do whatever God asks. What is the basis of your fear of trusting God to do only good for you?

4. Consider your immediate sphere of influence among family, friends, and associates. What needs do you see where you could become involved to make a difference in a person's life, in the name of Jesus?

5. Do you feel God is at work right now, calling you into a ministry? If so, describe that call by writing your feelings on paper. Then share those feelings with a friend and explore the ways in which God is speaking to you.

11

FUNDAMENTALS
OF CHURCH LEADERSHIP

Much can be said about leadership in the church. I don't pretend in this book to give a comprehensive analysis of what good church leadership should be. There is ample literature in both Christian and secular bookstores to address the broader issues. What I have to say about church leadership rises out of my personal experience as a church leader for over forty years.

I am a Baptist minister. My church leadership experience has been in the context of the polity and practice of Baptist churches born out of distinctive beliefs concerning the priesthood of the believer and the autonomy of the local congregation. Baptists do not function under a hierarchy of authority beyond the local church. They choose voluntarily to cooperate with other churches in "associations," "fellowships" and "conventions." Baptists look only to Jesus Christ as the head of the church and the source of authority. The Holy Scriptures provide context, parameters, examples and instructions for knowing the "mind of Christ" and thereby the will of God for the church.

My lifetime focus and experience have been on pastoral leadership. It is from that perspective that I write. However, the principles of leadership in the church are universal enough that what I say here can be adapted to apply to any church staff or laity position. Over the years I have condensed my thinking down to four fundamental church leadership principles. In order to make these more memorable, the principles are divided into the familiar acrostic **VIPS,** generally known to stand for "Very Important Persons." In my framework of church leadership fundamentals, VIPS stands for:

```
V      I      P      S
Vision  Integrity  Passion  Synergy
```

V = VISION

Strong and consistent leadership is essential to produce a healthy and growing church. Early in my ministry I gave a great deal of thought to what it would take to be an effective leader over a long period of time. In talking with other pastors who had long tenure in their churches, I was able to develop and refine some important ideas. I knew from the very beginning that I couldn't be an effective leader for any length of time if I didn't have some sense of where I wanted to go. Knowing where you want to go is called "vision." (Chapter 9 of this book thoroughly addresses the importance of personal and church vision.)

> *If you know where you're going, it's easier to get there.*

Abraham Lincoln said, "If you know where you're going, it's a lot easier to get there." No leader wants to be like the man who shoots arrows against the barn and then walks up and draws bull's eyes around the point where the arrows hit. That kind of haphazard vision or goal setting allows people to be blown about by every wind of doctrine or every trendy fashion that comes along. Without a solid sense of direction, aspiring leaders simply scatter-shoot and hit nothing.

Early in my ministry I began to understand that leadership is not asking people where they want to go and then jumping out in front to lead them. It is not wetting a finger and holding it up to determine which way the wind of popular opinion is blowing. That kind of leadership is for sale. That's the kind of expertise that political candidates buy from consultants and campaign advisors. Whatever the popular idea, they can package and sell it. There is no real place for that kind of leadership, especially not in the church.

Church leaders must have a deep sense of God's calling and know what it is God is calling them to do. For example, when a church calls a pastor, they expect to get spiritual leadership. They want maturity and sensitivity in their pastor—not someone with an arrogant, domineering, my-way-or-the-highway attitude. They want someone who has spent enough time in prayer, Bible study and service that God's gifts have become evident. A church wants their pastor to lead the congregation sensitively by utilizing those gifts.

From the earliest days of my calling I felt God wanted me both to lead people to Christ and to grow them up in their faith and Christian life. I never felt called to be a vocational evangelist who preaches, sees people make professions of faith, and then leaves them for others to disciple. On the other hand, I didn't want to be a pastor who was content to minister just to those who were already in the fold of the church. My personal calling has been to evangelize and to disciple.

The church has a mission to reach out, include, and bring people to Christ. God has called Christians to have passionate concern for people without Christ, to have a heart for pastoral care, and to lead those who know Christ to grow in wisdom and service and to be on call for the Lord.

Many years ago I found a description of preaching that has been unforgettable. *"The preacher's job is to comfort the afflicted* (the pastoral task) *and to afflict the comfortable* (the prophetic task)."* I have tried to blend both of those into my ministry. Being both pastor and prophet has helped me develop a sense of vision. I don't ask first, *"What is it this church wants to do?"* I ask, *"What is it God wants every church to do?"*

This essential question is answered by leading people in Bible study and biblically-centered sermons to discover what tasks Jesus expects of the church. As the Bible is studied, people discuss those Christ-ordained challenges and begin shaping ideas. The insight of the people, and the priesthood of their response to God become part of the mix that defines what the vision is for a particular congregation.

Vision is crucial to leadership. If contentment with past accomplishments is more important than enthusiasm for what can happen in the future, a church is dead in the water. The past should provide building blocks for the future. In the words of Sir Isaac Newton, *"If I have been able to see further than other men, it is because I have had the shoulders of giants to stand upon."* That shows an appropriate appreciation for the history and the contributions of those who have gone before while clearly stating the intention of the leader to move forward.

Every Christian leader builds the future out of the materials on hand from the past. That is the hope of the Kingdom of God. That is the eschatological pull of the Christian faith. The Kingdom is now, but it is not yet. It is present, but it is on its way.

When a vision is verbalized, it becomes real to the people. There is an *ah-hah* moment when they "get it." The vision becomes expressible. People share in its motivating power. A pastor preaches, teaches, and talks about the developing vision in many ways, and then listens for what comes back from the congregation. When people pray, what phrases do they use? When they talk about the church, how do they describe it? As they catch the vision, their words begin to reflect their commitment to the idea and the vision is shared.

When church members begin to share insights with church leaders, the vision concept becomes theirs as well. Ideas spin off and multiply. Sunday school teachers will not be content to maintain the status quo. They will want their class members to press forward and grow to become all that God wants them to be. They will want to challenge people for the sake of the Kingdom. Committee members will want to do more than tread water. They will want to find creative new ways to tend to the needs of the church and extend its arms to embrace the people who need God.

A church's vision is never frozen in time. It is a growing, expanding, challenging force that drives a church always to seek ways to do better the task Jesus has given them. For example, I remember asking several staff members to imagine how we could improve our work with senior adults and establish a stellar ministry. We focused on what we could do in four major issues that relate to senior adults.

    1. *Need-based ministry* - Senior adults have personal needs. How can we help them stay connected? How can we ade-

quately serve their needs for physical and emotional health, transportation, overcoming loneliness, etc?

2. *Service-based ministry* - Senior adults want to serve. How can we organize them into volunteer ministries so they can find fulfillment through service?

3. *Mission-based ministry* - Many seniors are wonderful evangelists. How can we encourage them to be involved with others inside and beyond their own congregation, impacting others who need to know Jesus?

4. *Activities-based ministry* - Seniors want to stay active. What social, educational, and travel activities need to be created so that strong senior adult networks can encourage fulfilling relationships with others?

Church leaders should do their best to surround themselves with people who also dream big dreams and are full of energy. New and creative ideas will be sparked and the vision will be expanded when creative people are enthusiastically enlisted to share their input. Nothing will kill a vision quicker than people who are weary and don't want anything else to do, or who seem intent on finding reasons why new ideas won't work.

Christian leaders are not free to let the church be satisfied with itself. The church has to have a sense that it is on mission to touch and change the lives of people. Leaders must teach that, preach that, and get the people to think outside the church walls. Leaders must involve the congregation to help shape the specific vision and plan what it is their church will do in the community.

A PROVEN PLAN OF ACTION FOR CHURCH LEADERS

I would follow a simple three-step plan of action to lead any church to where God wants it to be:

1. Talk to the people about what the church is—its nature and its functions. Functions grow out of nature. Talk and teach about the Body of Christ. What does it mean to be the Body of Christ and to do His work in the world? As you continue to preach and teach, look around and listen carefully to see what those ideas stimulate in the minds of the church members. People will begin to talk about the church as a living organism. They will begin to connect with the idea of doing what Jesus would do. Spend time listening to the heartbeat of the church and the community, discovering where God is already at work and where He wants His church to become involved.

2. Gather together the established leaders in the church: deacons, committee members, Sunday school teachers and staff. Take a look at where the church is strong and where it's not so strong. Take a look at the five functions of the church (to worship, to evangelize, to disciple, to minister, to create fellowship) and decide what most needs to be worked on.

3. Seek the mind of Christ in prayer and ask that His vision for the church be revealed. If people start praying, God will provide ministries for the church to perform. When people pray, God shows up at their door. He is already out there loving people and working in their lives. He's looking for somebody to see what He sees. When the church begins to think of itself as the Body of Christ, it begins to see people as Jesus saw them. The church's agenda is set not by the newspaper and not by the latest religious fad or trend. It is set by knowing what Jesus would do if He walked into town today. Who would He care about? Where would He go? What would He say?

Remember the stories in Luke 18:35-19:10? As Jesus approached Jericho, He had an encounter with a blind beggar who cried out to Him for mercy. Although the crowd rebuked the beggar, Jesus stopped to talk with him and restored his sight. Then, while in Jericho, Jesus called Zacchaeus, the tax collector, down out of a tree and invited Himself to dinner. The people despised both the beggar and Zacchaeus. One was poor, the other rich. Both were blind—one physically, the other spiritually. Jesus healed them both to see. That paradigm can teach us. Jesus wouldn't come to our town just to deal with the homeless, and He wouldn't come just to hob-nob with the wealthy. He would try to open the eyes of everybody to the needs of everyone else.

⌘

PRINCIPLES OF
VISIONARY CHURCH LEADERSHIP

Lead proactively to avoid a vacuum of decision-making that others must fill. One thing is worse than having a dictator for a pastor, and that's having a pastor who won't lead. Leadership is so essential that it is better to have heavy-handed leadership than none at all. What happens when a pastor won't lead? Deacons and other lay leaders haphazardly try to fill the cracks, resulting in chaos and stress.

> *One thing is worse than having a dictator for a pastor, and that's having a pastor who won't lead.*

A pastor friend who was new to a church complained to me about his deacons whom he described as "control freaks." Usually there are reasons why people attempt to control. I encouraged him to check the history of the church. Almost always a church is the way it is because of the way it has been led. When a pastor abuses the leadership role and takes advantage of his position to manipulate and exploit the people, a church has a hard time trusting the next pastor. A new pastor has to earn back the confidence of the people. But with faithful and patient care, an abused church eventually can trust again.

> *A church is the way it is because of the way it has been led.*

Become a servant leader. Cultivate an attitude of servant leadership which focuses on drawing forth the best from others and serving the interests of others rather than your own.

The issues of leadership in the church have been on my mind every day for decades. While attending seminary in the late 1960s and serving as pastor of the Central Baptist Church in Italy, Texas, I remember going to various conferences and hearing pastors present their ideas on church leadership. I got the distinct impression in those days that most preachers preferred a unilateral approach to church leadership. As pastors, they wanted to be in control. They grasped for ultimate authority.

I heard one prominent pastor use the word "ruler." I heard other pastors say that deacons are a necessary evil and the more you could ignore them, the better. They talked about going off into the wilderness and praying to receive God's guidance, then coming back to announce God's vision to the church.

Many of my seminary contemporaries listened to these authoritarian ideas of what church leadership should be, and I watched them begin to emulate the model as young pastors. I also observed how many of them were asked to leave their first churches within eighteen months to three years after assuming the pastorate.

I can remember disagreeing with a young pastor one day about the necessity of church committees. He had heard, and subsequently believed, that church members need to be involved only in Christian witnessing. They should leave the running of the church to the pastor and staff. That might sound good in theory, but a church that has a pastoral turnover every two years knows better than to leave the administration of the church to the pastor. Many pastors get in deep trouble over this issue and have to learn some tough lessons the hard way.

I have never believed that total pastoral authority would work; although, in my early years in the ministry, I didn't know how to counter that position. If men who were the shepherds of huge churches believed that was the way to lead, who was I to question it? But I kept thinking and evaluating the issue. I have come to understand that church leadership patterned after the example of Jesus is not autocratic rule. By teaching and example, Jesus demonstrated leadership based on love, respect, humility, and service.

> **By teaching and example, Jesus demonstrated leadership based on love, respect, humility, and service.**

Jesus said that people would recognize His disciples by the way we love each other. He did not say we would be recognized as His disciples by our academic achievements, the power of our influence, the prestige of our church, or our apparent success. Love is demonstrated through our deeds—by the way we treat people. Loving God with all our heart, soul, mind and strength is more than a statement; it is a lifestyle expressed by loving our neighbors as we love ourselves. Jesus identified loving commitment to God and to neighbors as the greatest commandments. Consequently, these commandments must become our constant goal in personal behavior and in church life.

⌘

I = INTEGRITY

Integrity always is a pivotal issue for any church leader. It entails being faithful to God, the church, one's family, oneself, and living up to the high calling of Jesus Christ. Integrity requires courage, transparency and commitment. It demands that we work hard at knowing what we believe and why we believe it.

I am reminded of that wise saying attributed to Samuel Smiles: *"Sow a thought, reap an action; sow an action, reap a habit; sow a habit, reap a character; sow a character, reap a destiny."* The time for us to check ourselves is before we make that first unwise choice! We bring our wills under the authority of Christ because character is built on the choices we make. Fred Smith is a Christian layman with a keen sense of what is important in life. In a presentation to a group of ministers and lay leaders, he counseled, "In middle life you don't want to make a junk yard out of your old age."[1]

PRINCIPLES OF INTEGRITY IN CHURCH LEADERSHIP

Be willing to be accountable for your time. Many people are not willing to do this. It's okay to be alone, enjoying quiet solitude. But if being alone means hiding out, something's wrong. If people have a need in their life for private islands of time when they are not accountable, they are headed for failure. One way I hold myself accountable for my time is to schedule everything through my administrative assistant. There isn't an hour of the day that my wife or my associate doesn't know where I am.

Admit vulnerability to temptation. As Christians, we need to take meaningful precautions to keep from setting ourselves up for a fall. It is no accident that Jesus taught us to pray, *"Lead us not into temptation."* Jesus is not naive about how we are tempted. We are not perfect. We have not been delivered from vulnerability to sin. Christian leaders should never assume that their calling will protect them from doing wrong. Greed and power can easily corrupt those who are not wary. Lust can chip a crack in our character that will weaken us to the core.

Always tell the truth. The root meaning of the word "integrity" is "to be whole." Wholeness is based on truth. A leader new to a church or a position is offered a beginning measure of trust from the staff and congregation. Church leaders build on that trust by always telling the truth, doing what they say they will do and honestly acknowledging the contributions of others.

When trust is broken, cooperation ceases. Telling the truth is a two-way street. Church leaders and church members must tell each other the truth. I don't believe the old adage, "What you don't know won't hurt you." Integrity demands speaking clearly about the way we see things. Clear and honest information breeds trust and cooperation. It takes a courageous person to be transparent, to allow ourselves to be known. But transparency and truth help keep us pure, and they are among the most precious gifts we can bring to others. Tell the truth. Handle relationships with all people with truthfulness.

> *Clear and honest information breeds trust and cooperation.*

Keep your hands off the church's money. My preacher daddy didn't give me a lot of advice about being a pastor, but he did say, "Son, keep your hands off the money." One cannot succeed as a church leader without total integrity about handling one's own money and the church's money. As a church leader, do not give anyone a reason to question what you have done with the church's money, an expense account, or an income tax return.

Keep your hands off the women (or men, as the case may be). The church has been particularly scandalized in recent years by the illicit sexual activity of Christians in places of leadership. Sin is sin, whether committed by lay persons or by those called into vocational gospel ministry. Leaders should recognize there is an extra measure of expectation that must be upheld by those who stand before the congregation as ordained shepherds of God's people. Those to whom much is given, much is expected.

Human sexuality is one of God's greatest gifts but it is a complex issue both physically and psychologically. Sex can bring the

Christian great joy and fulfillment, yet it also can tempt us to perversion and sin if not properly channeled. For the sake of Jesus Christ and His Church, leaders must avoid any suggestion of immoral behavior. We can enjoy and celebrate our sexuality without acting on it inappropriately. People are on the right track if they cherish God's gift of sex to such a degree that they do not want to do anything to cheapen or defile it.

I am a touching person. I like to shake hands, pat arms and hug people. There is nothing wrong with expressing affection and giving people encouragement through this kind of touching if it is done appropriately. Whatever we do, we must be careful to guard against inappropriate attitudes and actions. Christ compels us to deal with others in love and respect and to cherish the well-being of others in a manner that reflects Christ living in us and us living in Him.

I know male ministers who are uncomfortable having a pastoral relationship with single women, widows, or married women whose husbands are not actively involved in the church. As a result, they avoid personal conversation with women and withdraw from anything other than very casual contact. This is unfortunate because these women need a pastor too.

A pastor or church leader can minister effectively to people of the opposite sex if the following principles are in place:

- Don't be afraid of others. Don't make people feel uncomfortable by your apparent anxiety.
- Show genuine interest but be modest and appropriate in the way you look at and touch others.
- Do not make visits alone to the homes of parishioners and do not see individuals behind closed doors when no one else is present or close by.
- Admit the limitations of your professional ability. Don't become involved in long-term counseling or therapy.

Get to know people and call them by name. Names are symbols of who we are. Everyone wants to feel significant. It is one of the basic needs of life. People want their pastor and their church leaders to recognize them, know them by name, know something about them, and express love and care. Names are so important that a leader can't escape behind the facade of saying, "There are so many people, I can't remember the names of anybody." Although that may certainly be true, it is wrong to use it as an excuse for carelessly treating people as nonentities.

I decided long ago I would rather be embarrassed than to be uncaring—therefore, I have often been embarrassed. There have even been times while praying with a family that I have gone blank on their names. I have prayed, "Lord, you know their names but I can't remember right now." Then I would stop and ask them to help me. It always is a light moment. People understand and respond well. We all have been there.

I put myself under the pressure of wanting to learn names but I have not used any particular memory device such as word associations as some people do. I find that when I really want to know who that person is, and I listen to the name and repeat it back to be sure I got it, I can usually remember. I tend not to remember names when I am really more interested in what people are thinking about me. The key for me is to focus on that person, his or her needs, hopes and dreams. When I do this, I connect with that person because I am listening and I remember their uniqueness.

Be available to people. When the disciples said Jesus was too busy to pay attention to the children, Jesus made time for them. That's an important leadership lesson. Everyone is important in Jesus' eyes—children, teenagers, single adults, married adults, senior adults. I don't believe a person can be a pastor or a church leader if he or she is not willing to take time for one-on-one attention to people—people of all ages and all groups within the church. One of the ways that is done is through visiting people in times of need in their homes and in hospitals and nursing homes. Pastors and staff members set the standard. Lay people in the church will do what leaders think is important. In many churches, hospital visitation may be almost completely handled by lay people. But that won't often happen in churches where the leadership acts as though hospital visitation is beneath them. The act of hospital visitation is an unspoken sign of love among the church body. Good leaders know that.

Honor disagreement. It is a matter of integrity to encourage everyone's opinion to be heard. I believe all church members should have an opportunity to express their concern in some fashion. We should never isolate or brand people as "opposition" because they disagree with us. I try to live that out daily in my walk. I may ask to discuss the issues privately with a person so I can better understand his or her position. Or I may just wait a while to bring it up again when an opportunity presents itself.

When it is time to vote on something in the church, preface the discussion with some statements about the process. Remind the members that *they probably will not all agree* and that *the vote seldom will be unanimous*. I don't know many pastors who begin a church conference expecting unanimous opinions. But I do know some who do all the talking at church meetings where decisions are to be made. When it is time to come to a decision, they will ask all in favor to say "aye" and seem to forget to ask for the "no" vote.

At First Baptist, Arlington, we used ballot voting on each major issue and many church decisions were made on an 80% / 20% secret ballot vote. A clear majority opinion should be established, but I don't believe in waiting until every deacon or every church member agrees. That expectation puts terrible pressure on people to vote to go along with majority opinion. As pastor, I was content with a split vote as long as the issue had been carefully explained and questions had been honored and answered.

Encourage church members to vote the mind of Christ. As the church approaches a vote on a major church issues, remind the congregation that *we are all priests* in the church, and we all can personally ask God for guidance in our decisions as individuals and as a corporate body. Ask them, regardless of the issue, *to seek the mind of Christ* and vote what each believes Jesus would ask us to do *(see Philippians 2:5).* Ask each person to refrain from publicly communicating only his or her personal opinion. Instead, ask them to think about each issue, pray about it and as best as each person can, at whatever level of spiritual maturity each one is, vote the mind of Christ.

That means a choir member might vote to support something she would never intend to become involved in personally. Or a deacon might vote against something he is interested in because the recommendation presented has not been developed adequately, leaving holes in the proposal. Even if we know we aren't where Jesus is in His position on whatever issue is at hand, we do at least know where He stands and can vote His mind. That kind of thinking pulls us forward to a place we can't see yet.

People may ask, "If we all vote the will of God, why doesn't everyone agree?" It's because we are not all at the same place in our spiritual pilgrimage. Jesus may not be asking you to do what He's asking me to do. His plan is to take us where we are, as a church and as individuals, and grow us into His likeness. That is definitely not a cookie-cutter process. None of us is at the same place at the same time, spiritually.

> **Pay more attention to the "yes" votes than to the "no" votes.**

Pay more attention to the "yes" votes than the "no" votes. That means noticing what issues or programs or ministries have support in the congregation, even though many are not interested and some may even oppose. Let those who will, do! I don't believe a unanimous vote of the congregation is necessary to encourage people to begin doing what they think Jesus is asking them to do.

Learn through successes and failures to make the best of circumstances. I try to learn from my successes and my failures. I have had some big failures to learn from. One was a building campaign in the early nineties. We came up very short on the money commitments. We had one of the big fundraising organizations come in to assist us. (They don't list us as a reference today.) We were going to build a new sanctuary. Looking back, I think we failed at explaining and sharing the vision behind our building campaign.

I was sick about the situation as I went to the pulpit to tell the church we would not be able to do what we said we wanted to do. How I handled the failure would be a critically important model of church leadership. I was clear with the church about where we stood. We put a group of people together and did some wonderful things with the money that had been given, including the complete remodeling of our existing sanctuary. The church is a better church because of that experience.

In another critical time of my pastorate, I went through a serious conflict between two staff members. In the midst of the situation, my leadership was called into question. I was angry because I had done everything I knew to help these men do what they needed to do. One of them really tried to take me down with him. I have always trusted staff. This experience was very painful. Several families left our church because of the hurt. Through the entire experience, I prayed, *"Dear God, don't let me waste this pain."* Romans 8:28 gave me the strength to know that God would salvage the wreckage and allow good to come from the bad.

> *And we know that in all things God works for the good of those who love him, who have been called according to his purpose.* *(Romans 8:28)*

⌘

P = PASSION

Effective Christian leadership requires a passion that springs from three basic sources: loving God, loving people, and loving the task to which we are called by God. Without passion, we are desperately vulnerable to disappointment, disillusionment, mental and physical fatigue and spiritual burnout. In large part, passion is a gift from God, a spiritual gift that comes with our calling. But it is

> *Passion is a gift from God, a spiritual gift that comes with our calling.*

important that we work with God both to cultivate and to protect that wonderful passion that compels us to do God's work in the world.

PRINCIPLES FOR PRESERVING PASSION FOR GOD'S WORK

Actively pursue personal devotions and prayer life. There is refreshment in prayer and in reading God's word. Leaders must never underestimate the importance of time spent with God. The most fundamental temptation of fallen man is to turn away from God and try to live life in our own strength and understanding. We need prayer and Scripture to nurture our souls and to renew our minds and spirits. Our passion must be fed with a regular diet of spiritual intimacy with God.

Define personal availability for counseling or other time-dominating tasks. One-on-one counseling should be an important part of every pastoral ministry. Some pastors and other church staff members enjoy counseling and have a special gift for it. However, when counseling becomes a primary emphasis that claims an inordinate portion of time, it can be a detriment to other essential duties and drain off energies that are needed elsewhere.

As a pastor, people would often come to me for counseling. I was willing to meet with anyone at least one time. Usually, that's all he or she needed. If there was a need for a second counseling session, I confessed that I was a general practitioner and would refer the person to a specialist who could help better than I could. I could counsel, comfort, and help people to make good decisions, but if long-term therapy was needed, it was best that they be referred to someone who was a trained professional. That worked for me over the years and it kept my counseling involvement in proper balance with other responsibilities.

Pastors or other church staff members must keep personal counseling on a professional level. Sessions should be conducted in the church office rather than in a home or some other private location, and for everyone's protection should be conducted in close proximity to a third party such as another church staff member or leader.

Don't overanalyze personal motives. Just do the right thing. In my opinion, motives often are overemphasized and over-analyzed. I hear a lot of people doubting the good that someone does because "they have the wrong motive." I can't tell you how many times I have driven to the hospital or nursing home wishing I could be doing something else. In those situations I pray, *"Lord, my heart is not right about this. These people need me and they need to know the church cares. Help me to care—not pretend to care, but really care."* Then as I arrive, I am almost ready. I visit with people and I pray. Usually by the time I finish praying, my heart is at rest. If I had waited to go to the hospital until my motives were right, I might not have gone for days.

Take time to be well prepared. In the heavy workload of typical ministries, it is difficult to find the time to stay adequately prepared to preach or teach effectively week after week. As a pastor, my most effective preaching came out of a planned outline, carefully thought through and prayed over, some key sentences written down and then delivered extemporaneously, with minimum notes to refer to in the pulpit.

After over forty-five years of preaching, I still work hard to improve my sermons. I struggle to prepare thoroughly and to stay sensitive to the clock while delivering a sermon. I would love to be able to deliver a succinct, twenty-minute start-to-finish sermon, but I don't seem to be able to do that on a regular basis. As a pastor, in an effort to clearly define and structure a sermon, I sometimes wrote it out in manuscript format. Unfortunately, when I did that, I fell in love with the words. Then I edited and edited to improve the sound and expression. By the time I got to the pulpit, after all the work done, I usually read the manuscript word for word and I was seldom happy with the spirit of its delivery. There is no substitute for writing out a sermon to help yourself clarify and focus the message. The key is in the balance of the written word and the spirit of the delivery, with the Holy Spirit guiding.

Like many speakers, I am comfortable in extemporaneous moments. Give me a few moments to collect myself, pray over the matter, and I can speak cogently—and people sometimes say, compellingly—from Scripture. I have been speaking in public since I was thirteen. My ability to speak in the moment can become a temptation to carelessness. I monitor myself to be certain I am doing adequate study, reading and praying for God's guidance. I never come out of the pulpit thinking, "I couldn't have done better." A sermon is always in process. The privilege to speak a word from and for God never ceases to amaze, humble and challenge me.

Cherish and protect your personal family life. Schedule adequate recreational time to avoid burnout. The best way to protect your family time is to have a spouse who won't let you neglect it. That can be frustrating and upsetting at times, but I have known that I can check whether I'm doing what I need to do by the way my wife is behaving. If she begins to get a little short or testy with me, I know she is feeling neglected. I have learned to pay attention to her. She is almost always exactly right in her counsel to me. She, better than anyone, knows when I have pushed the boundaries of my schedule too far and need to be paying more attention to responsibilities at home.

I haven't been in many crises in ministry, but in the bad times I have experienced, it was clear that the people who meant the most to me were my family. They love me through whatever happens. When I'm feeling vulnerable, they are the ones I can depend on. A leader who cherishes and nurtures family builds a deep reservoir from which to draw

> *A leader who cherishes and nurtures family builds a deep reservoir from which to draw.*

when times of frustration, discouragement, disappointment and hurt come along. Families can be a great source of comfort, encouragement and recreation. But the family as a resource of supportive love and spiritual revitalization must be nurtured with sensitive care and presence. That often will call for making concessions in a heavy workload in order to make time for the family.

I love to snow ski, golf and play racquetball. I recognize how important it is to get regular exercise in order to stay fit both emotionally and physically. The challenge of games and competition is invigorating. Recreational time is crucial to keeping alive the passion in life.

One of the most exciting and rewarding moments of my life came on a Friday night in October of my son Mark's senior year at Arlington High School. I was supposed to be in Oklahoma City that night for a meeting, but I decided to delay my departure until the next morning so I could see Mark play football. That night Mark caught the winning touchdown against archrival Lamar High School. Arlington High hadn't beaten Lamar in many years. I was in the stands yelling and stomping and carrying on. I was amazed at how excited and proud I was. I realized that if I had made that touchdown myself, I wouldn't have been as happy as I was for him. God taught me a lesson. I have always been glad I was there for Mark and myself that night instead of away on church business. Don't let family moments be consistently put aside in favor of other obligations. Our families need our attention every day.

When you pray and care for yourself, you won't be getting up to preach because it is 11:00 am on a Sunday morning, but because God has put a passion for His Word and for people in your heart. You are there with a message that cries out to be delivered.

⌘

S = SYNERGY

I've always wondered about people who say that if you want a job to be done right, you have to do it yourself. That position seems awfully pretentious and doesn't give people credit for the wonderful talents they can bring to a task if properly motivated. I think most jobs worth doing are bigger than any one person can handle alone. Jesus enlisted help to carry out His mission and ministry. The truth is, when people work together, one plus one often equals three or even five. That's synergy. When the creative energy of several come together, the production is greater than the sum of all its parts. Good church leaders will find a way to effectively tap into the power of people willing to work in tandem.

PRINCIPLES IN DEVELOPING SYNERGY IN MINISTRY

Enlist and cultivate staff members and volunteers who are positive thinkers. I hope I have worked with the last staff person with a negative attitude. People who look for the negative and don't see the positive block the work of Jesus. As pastor, I spent many years trying to change the core attitude of one of my staff, thinking I could somehow make him different. I was wrong. I learned a lesson about the kind of people who make effective staff members. The best minister or professional staff member or lay leader is not necessarily the most gifted person or the most experienced; it is the one whose life reflects the life of Jesus in the simple things. Recruiting the right people for church staff and church leadership is a real art, requiring wise sensitivity to people, their character and personality. Pray much over personnel decisions.

> The best leader is not necessarily the most gifted or experienced, but the one whose life reflects Jesus in the simple things.

Encourage creative new ideas among church members. Part of the work of church leadership is to help people come up with new ideas for themselves. Success is always easier when the people involved believe they have part ownership in the idea or project. Church members often are tied to comfortable traditions; so many people have never been encouraged to be creative or innovative thinkers. They need to be encouraged to see new possibilities, to spread their wings and fly. A mature leader will not be threatened by creative ideas that come from other sources. People need to be appreciated and affirmed for their creativity.

> A mature leader will not be threatened by creative ideas that come from other sources.

Sometimes a leader may come up with a good proposal that church members are not yet ready to embrace. In that situation it makes sense to plant the seeds and give those seeds time to germinate among the people. When the same idea springs forth later from someone else, be ready to affirm it as a new creation and encourage people to bring it into reality.

Appreciate the value of organization. Utilize groups within the church to broaden personal involvement and accountability. I don't think people can be effective church leaders if they care a lot about people yet seem critical of the church as an institution. There are people who think they can have a church without having an organization. They want to play it by ear and be aloof to organization.

In 1976, when I moved to First Baptist Arlington, there was a group of young adults who felt the church had gotten too big, too structured and too impersonal. They bought out of the organized Sunday morning Bible study and worship service. They met in homes for small group study and fellowship but they did come to church on Sunday evenings. One Sunday night, I observed two of the women talking together and making a list. I greeted them and asked what they were doing. They said they were planning childcare for their small group Bible study. I jokingly responded, "Uh oh, you better be careful, you're beginning to get organized!"

Utilize other church leaders for their counsel and support. The role of deacons or elders will vary from church to church, but in First Baptist Church, Arlington, the deacon's job has been to counsel and serve others. The church constitution does not give deacons the authority to deny to a committee permission to take recommendations before the church. Therefore, final church decisions are made by the church and not by the deacons unless the church has specifically authorized them to make certain commitments.

All committees take their recommendations to the deacons first, for review and questions. This allows a maturing and refining of the committee's ideas in a broader context. It provides an opportunity for committees to improve their proposals before they are presented to the church body for a vote. It allows for hard questions to be asked plainly without fear of confusing a novice Christian. It provides the best of both worlds—committees that feel accountable to make their recommendations good enough that the Deacon Council will pledge their support, and deacons who see their role more as consultants than gatekeepers.

Deacons can express their support or opposition in a setting where openness and mutual respect are practiced. If the Deacon Council endorses a committee recommendation, even the individual deacons who oppose the recommendation have had their chance to speak. Then when the recommendation is brought before the church, those opposing deacons usually remain silent, in support of the Deacon Council's position. With this balanced approach to decision-making, the committees work harder and the deacons listen better.

As a pastor, I always took time in Deacon Council meetings to share whatever was on my mind. I presented new ideas for their consideration. I freely expressed my gratitude for their support, their prayers and their leadership in the church. I asked for their counsel, I listened and I paid attention to the process. Then I attempted to find ways to act on and include their ideas with mine. I have avoided using a small group of confidants with whom to seek clearance on issues. I have always had a sense that if I picked a preferential group, it would create jealousy within the congregation. My active deacons were my sounding board. Because deacons rotated off the Council every three years, I had a new "group" each year to work with and learn from.

The chairpersons of church committees have been my consultants. When a person was the chair of the Finance Committee, I communicated openly and often about the finances of the church.

When that person no longer served on the Finance Committee, I did not continue to go to him or her for counsel on finances. When the church elected a person to an office of church leadership, I expected church members, myself included, to honor that office for the good of the church.

Leadership of any kind is difficult and often lonely. Leadership in the church has its own set of personal challenges because of the nature of being set apart to live in balance between two kingdoms —being at peace with this world while waging spiritual warfare against the powers and principalities that would destroy us. Church leadership requires a special combination of spiritual vision, human sensitivity, loving kindness, firmness of conviction, moral boundaries, patience and tenacity. Above all, effective church leaders will have a personal passion to fulfill the task to which God has called them.

⌘

---

1. Fred Smith, "Making Your Message Memorable," *Leadership* magazine, Vol. 19, No. 2, Spring 1998, p.94.

⌘

JESUS PRINCIPLES
FOR CHURCH LEADERSHIP

⌘ Actively study, pray and work at developing a **shared vision.**

⌘ In all things, act with complete **integrity** and honesty.

⌘ Protect and preserve your **passion** for God's work.

⌘ Seek help from others and be receptive to their creative ability. Create **synergy** through cooperative and collaborative efforts.

DEAR GOD:

GIVE ME THE WISDOM TO FOLLOW THE EX-
AMPLE OF JESUS TO BECOME A SERVANT
LEADER. HELP ME TO BE CREATIVE, BOLD,
AND DECISIVE, BUT TEACH ME ALWAYS TO
SEEK BENEFITS FOR OTHERS RATHER THAN
SELFISH GAIN FOR MYSELF. LORD, I CON-
FESS MY VULNERABILITY TO SIN AND SEEK
YOUR PROTECTION FROM EVIL. FILL ME, I
PRAY, WITH YOUR HOLY SPIRIT THAT I MAY
HAVE THE POWER TO OVERCOME EACH
TEMPTATION AND EACH TRIAL THAT MAY
COME MY WAY.

MOST OF ALL, LORD, SUSTAIN IN ME THE
PASSION TO DO YOUR WORK IN THE WORLD.
LET ME DAILY LIVE IN JESUS AND HE IN ME.
AS I LEAD OTHERS, HELP ME ALWAYS TO BE
AWARE OF THE HIGH CALLING OF JESUS
CHRIST, MY SAVIOR AND LORD.

AMEN

Life Application

⌘

FUNDAMENTALS OF CHURCH LEADERSHIP

1. This chapter makes the point that quality of church leadership is linked to a clear sense of God's vision. Do you have a sense that your church has a clearly defined vision for what God has called it to do as the Body of Christ in your community?

   If so, what do you perceive to be the main thrust of that vision? Write out your response. Then share your perceptions with others. How are they similar? How do they differ?

2. What has been the history of your church? Research it. Talk about it. Write it down. What fundamental resources or materials exist as a foundation from which you can begin fashioning a plan for the future for your church?

3. Consider the changing character of the community your church serves. What are some of the ways your church must adapt to address effectively those changing conditions and circumstances?

4. Evaluate your personal leadership style. What are some specific actions you could take to become more of a servant leader based on the example of Jesus?

12

CARE AND FEEDING
OF THE BODY

The human body requires food, exercise and intellectual stimulation to maintain its health. The Body of Christ has similar requirements. It needs spiritual nourishment and the exercise of intimate personal relationships to flourish. The church is a unique organism. It grows out of its lively relationship with Jesus Christ. People come to salvation through repentance of sin and faith in Jesus as their Savior. This spiritual rebirth brings the Christian into unity with others who are members of the church—the Body of Christ. The church finds its character in Jesus and is guided and equipped with power through God's Holy Spirit.

People reborn in Christ go through a transformation process. As they allow the Spirit of God to live in them, they begin to think and act differently. They put off the old sinful nature and take on a new nature, patterned after Christ. The virtues demonstrated in a Christian's changed life are described by the apostle Paul as *fruit of the Spirit.*

> *But the fruit of the Spirit is love, joy, peace, patience, kindness, goodness, faithfulness, gentleness and self-control.*
> *(Galatians 5:22-23)*

The health of a church can be measured by the degree to which this fruit is present among its members. We can hold these virtues up as evidence of the Spirit-filled life, both as individuals and as a body.

The health of a church can be measured by the degree to which the fruit of the Spirit is present among its members.

Care and Feeding that Produces a Healthy Body of Christ

Galatians 5:6 provides a scriptural mirror to hold up before ourselves so we can see what it is God expects of us. In Galatians 5:22-23, the fruit of the Spirit, marking the life of the Christian, is identified in nine expressions. As the Apostle Paul says, the entire law of God addressing our relationships with each other can be summed up in a single command: *Love your neighbor as yourself (Galatians 5:14).*

Paul writes as a pastor dealing with issues that divide the Church and create problems in the lives of its members. Guided by the Holy Spirit, he draws on his experience and pours out his heart. Paul describes the qualities he sees demonstrated in the lives of people who are being used and blessed by God. The Spirit of God is visibly active when these virtues are present.

In Galatians 5:19-21, Paul's observation of those living a Spirit-filled life contrasts sharply with the behaviors of those who live according to mankind's sinful nature.

As God's Holy Spirit works in our lives, the fruit of the Spirit grows naturally within us. Instead of relating to others with criticism, ridicule and disrespect, we seek to love, understand and patiently draw others to deeper faith and commitment to live in Christ.

UNDERSTANDING THE FRUIT OF THE SPIRIT

⌘ LOVE - People who live in the Spirit are people of love. They care about others and want the best for everyone. They look for ways to support and encourage others to help them succeed. They unselfishly put the needs of other people ahead of their own.

> *The only thing that counts is faith expressing itself through love.* (Galatians 5:6)

> *Serve one another in love.* (Galatians 5:13)

> *Carry each other's burdens, and in this way you will fulfill the law of Christ.* (Galatians 6:2)

⌘ JOY - The Spirit of God breathes joy into the lives of Christians. As the Spirit equips us to overcome trials and persecution, we respond with thankful hearts. Our hearts, filled with joy, soar as though they had wings. Those who walk with the Lord have reason to rejoice. Their faith is secure. Their foundation is in God. Their future is open. They can face difficulty with a sense of humor and confidence that God will bring them through. That kind of joy gives birth to courage and sustains the Christian in the midst of seemingly impossible situations.

> *Those who belong to Christ Jesus have crucified the sinful nature with its passions and desires.* (Galatians 5:24)

God grants resurrection joy to those who die to self in order to live for God. Nowhere is this more beautifully worked out than in Philippians.

> *But our citizenship is in heaven. And we eagerly wait a Savior from there, the Lord Jesus Christ, who, by the power that enables him to bring everything under his control, will transform our lowly bodies so that they will be like his glorious body.* (Philippians 3:20-21)

⌘ PEACE - People who are filled with God's Spirit have a sense of peace about them. Peace is inner tranquility that comes from a conscience at ease with God. When sins are confessed in true repentance, and God's forgiveness is received, the sinner is freed to rest in God's grace. Those who belong to God have a better understanding of who they are, a greater sense of their own worth, and a comfort with their place in life. They can be at peace within themselves.

> *It is for freedom that Christ has set us free. Stand firm, then, and do not let yourselves be burdened again by a yoke of slavery.* (Galatians 5:1)

> *Each one should test his own actions. Then he can take pride in himself, without comparing himself to somebody else, for each one should carry his own load.* (Galatians 6:4)

⌘ PATIENCE - A Christian filled with the Spirit of God is patient, slow to anger and careful not to speak unkindly to others. Why are people impatient? Because they feel offended when others do not do what they want them to do. The opposite of patience is selfishness. Patience is a willingness to allow other people to learn at their own pace and not judge them for making different choices. Patience is a willingness to let others discover the truth for themselves or to make their own mistakes in order to learn. Patience is respect shown to others. Waiting on the timing of God is wisdom demonstrated as patience.

> *Let us not become weary in doing good, for at the proper time, we will reap a harvest if we do not give up.*
> *(Galatians 6:9)*

⌘ KINDNESS - We see kindness demonstrated through the caring attitudes and actions of Christians. Tenderness, compassion and a forgiving spirit are demonstrations of kindness. Kindness and tolerance do not necessarily approve and endorse another person's choices. But kind people don't speak harshly. Kindness is a willingness to be involved, to help, to feel what others feel, to be gracious. The opposite of kindness is in Galatians 5:15: *If you keep on biting and devouring each other, watch out or you will be destroyed by each other.* The world is too small for us to be unkind. As Christians, we gladly accept the admonition:

> *Be kind and compassionate one to another, forgiving each other, just as in Christ God forgave you.*   *(Ephesians 4:32)*

⌘ GOODNESS - Goodness is a virtue through which one makes the most loving choice. Goodness recognizes the necessity of establishing boundaries. Goodness is willing to rebuke and to discipline when needed to establish righteousness and justice. To be good is to be pure in heart, not self-righteous or arrogant. Simple goodness is refusing to do what we know is wrong. It is through our acquaintance with goodness that we sense most clearly the essence of sin (anything we do or say that hurts someone God loves.) Goodness is a commitment to live by God's law. The opposite of goodness is debauchery, letting go of values and giving in to vice. Living in debauchery means there are no boundaries (if it feels good, do it). Without goodness, life becomes a matter of unbridled imagination feeding on itself without care for the well-being of another person.

Therefore, as we have opportunity, let us do good to all people, especially to those who belong to the family of believers. (Galatians 6:10)

⌘ FAITHFULNESS - People filled with God's Spirit are people of integrity. They are reliable, committed, focused, and trustworthy. In short, they demonstrate faithfulness to God and the building of His Kingdom. A faithful person is unwilling to break promises, to use and abuse people who have been promised one's love and care. There is a standard set by God that must be fulfilled. At the heart of faithfulness is a commitment to give God first place in our lives. Life tempts us with many false idols—materialism, power, sex, drugs, even religion. If we give our life to such things, we betray our Savior and seek after other gods.

Live by the Spirit, and you will not gratify the desires of the sinful nature. For the sinful nature desires what is contrary to the Spirit, and the Spirit desires what is contrary to the sinful nature. They are in conflict with each other, so that you do not do what you want. But if you are led by the Spirit, you are not under the law. (Galatians 5:16-18)

⌘ GENTLENESS - For the Christian, gentleness means being teachable, open and submissive to the will of God rather than rebellious or stubborn. In relationships with others, gentleness means being sensitive, considerate, conciliatory, and kind. It does not rule out showing anger at immorality or injustice, but it never displays anger maliciously or indiscriminately. Gentleness does not make harsh demands but gives counsel and correction through love.

If someone is caught in a sin, you who are spiritual should restore him gently. But watch yourself, or you also may be tempted. (Galatians 6:1)

⌘ SELF-CONTROL - A Spirit-filled Christian is disciplined, slow to anger, unselfish, morally aware and does not walk carelessly or blindly into situations that present obvious as well as subtle moral temptations. Self-control develops in stages as we grow in experience and self-understanding. It is a victory that must be won and re-won daily. It is a virtue that must be continually rein-forced in order to stay strong and true. We learn that evil cannot be resisted entirely out of our own will. We must rely on the power of the Holy Spirit to guide us as we live in Christ and He lives in us.

A man reaps what he sows. The one who sows to please his sinful nature, from that nature will reap destruction; the one who sows to please the Spirit, from the Spirit will reap eternal life.   *(Galatians 6:7-8)*

⌘

APPLYING THE FRUIT OF THE SPIRIT IN A HEALTHY CHURCH

A church filled with God's Spirit is a place where love dwells, where joy is palpable. It is a place where there is deep peace because of the confidence in the grace and mercy of God. A church filled with God's Spirit is a place where people are treated with kindness and respect. It is a place where people are good, dependable, faithful and reliable.

> **A church filled with God's Spirit is a place where people are treated with kindness and respect.**

People showing the fruit of the Spirit are confident about God's ways. There is a real expectation that God is actively at work in them and through the Body of Christ. They cherish their role as a member of the Body doing Christ's work in the world. There is gentleness and sensitivity for others and for self, an openness to learn. There is a disciplined determination to work obediently before God and to *"keep in step with the Spirit" (Galatians 5:25)*.

Presence - Being there for friends and fellow church members is an essential part of creating fellowship and feeding the Body. I remember the day I heard that the newly-built travel agency in Arlington owned by Dan Dipert was on fire. Dan is a friend and church member. I drove quickly to the building and stayed there with Dan while the fire fighters fought the blaze. There was nothing we could do but watch the destruction. Later, after the trauma was over, Dan expressed how significant it was to him for me to be there while the building was burning. The ministry of presence is powerfully encouraging.

There is no substitute for "being there" when fellow church members walk through dark valleys of loss and grief. The presence, the embraces, the food and assistance speak deep messages of love to grieving souls.

Prayer - When people experience tragedy, trauma, or death in their life, comfort happens at the deepest level when church members reach out to them in prayer. It is emotionally transforming to receive a note in the mail telling of others who are remembering us in their prayers, or to know that a Sunday school class has us on their daily prayer list.

Prayer support doesn't need to be related just to trauma. It is wonderfully productive when people join together to navigate the everyday events of life through prayer. I love to hear how young mothers pray over the phone about their children and their families; how men meet for breakfast or lunch to share and pray about mutual concerns; how teenagers meet at school to pray and lift each other up through fellowship and Christian love. Those times of shared prayer provide daily food for the soul.

Mentoring - When older or more experienced Christians take the less experienced under wing, it is a lasting gift of love. I fondly remember Florelle Wilson from Central Baptist Church in Italy, Texas, who took a special interest in my wife, Rosemary, when she was a young mother and inexperienced as a pastor's wife. Florelle gave her tips on how to entertain and encouraged her to be a gracious hostess in a modest home. She helped Rosemary learn about special table cloths and nice china and how useful and economical a good sheet cake could be. She was a wise older friend and helpful teacher.

Mentoring is an important part of how the Body of Christ nurtures maturity into young Christians. Experienced Bible teachers can train class members through example and by giving individuals opportunities to substitute or team-teach. This mentoring develops the teaching skills of those less experienced and builds their confidence until they are ready to take over leadership of a class of their own. Likewise, older deacons or committee members can work side-by-side with those less experienced and give them the benefit of their counsel and experience.

Granting Grace - People grow into Christian maturity at differing rates. A healthy church will be patient and encouraging toward those beginning their spiritual journey, not impatient and critical.

> *A healthy church will be patient and encouraging toward those beginning their spiritual journey.*

Church people are sometimes criticized for being narrow-minded, judgmental, and quick to place their fellow Christians under restrictive roles and expectations. This is not characteristic behavior for a healthy church. A healthy church will want the best for the children of each church family, including the pastor and staff. They will rejoice with them in their accomplishments and refuse to be caught up in jealousy or a critical spirit. In a healthy church, all children and young people are loved. A church after Christ's own heart will pray for one another's children and always seek to encourage and bless rather than demean or criticize.

Similarly, a healthy church will encourage the spouse and adult family members of staff ministers and lay leaders to be themselves. The church will be comfortable with family members having their own opinions, their own outside interests, and their own personalities. Healthy churches will respect the family privacy of their ministers and grant them freedom to be a family when they are at home or on vacation. Staff members recognize the need volunteer leaders have to balance church responsibilities with business and family activities. Lay leaders also need time for their family to be together for vacations and recreation. There are countless opportunities for granting grace within the church body. We must all be ready to be regular grace-grantors.

Taking Care of Business - Christians who care about one another will not shy away from doing what is right to care for other persons. A caring church will provide adequately for its ministerial staff, in salary, in medical and insurance benefits, and in preparing for retirement. Those called to do God's work through the church should be given respect and support worthy of God's call *(I Timothy 5:17-19)*.

Caring Christians will respond to other needs within the church as well, individually or in the strength of small group support. I am aware of many incidents when Christian friends have responded to tide over families financially when the breadwinners were temporarily out of work, to "network" with others to seek employment opportunities, and to go out of their way just to be friends.

I remember when several members of our church acted to intercede on behalf of a fellow member whose untreated psychiatric condition posed a threat to her life. Abandoned and being divorced by her husband, out of control from refusing to take her prescribed medication, and suffering from malnutrition, she was in severe jeopardy both emotionally and physically. Christian friends were willing to take the bold move of having her committed to hospital care. They sought out social services, paid her rent and insurance, monitored her activity upon release from the hospital, loaned her money and worked with her lawyer to negotiate a fair divorce settlement. It was not easy or pleasant to become involved. But they felt compelled by Christ's love and their love for a Christian friend to take care of business over the long haul.

Celebrating Life - Joy will be evident when the Holy Spirit is present in a fellowship of believers. Christian joy is expressed freely and enthusiastically when the happy and the proud times of life are celebrated. Birthdays, graduations, engagements, marriages, the birth of children, new jobs, new homes, reunions—all are times when Christians join with other Christians to give thanks and be glad for each other's success and happiness. Christians delight in rejoicing with each other. They come to church eagerly each week to study together, worship together, minister to each other, and to share in mutual affirmation.

Joy is found in relationships that help others become successful and achieve personal victories. Joy is found as one boldly and confidently sets out for new horizons because of what Christ has done to make us whole and because we belong to a family of faith, which will not forget to pray for us and will gladly rejoice with us along the way.

⌘

KEEPING OUR EGOS IN CHECK AND OUR EYES ON JESUS

It's good when members of the Body of Christ sincerely believe that God can do anything. But a healthy church understands they cannot run ahead of God or expect God to endorse their agenda. We must understand that we are men and women, children of God, who can do amazing things in the Spirit's power, but we can't afford to become presumptuous. If our boldness and joy are in our flesh instead of in God's Spirit, we will *strive* to make things happen. In our power and cleverness, we will fail. In a healthy church, members will not strut around bragging about what God has done as though they have caused it. There will be a deep sense of humility about where power comes from and whose love it is that binds Christians together.

We don't really understand what happens when individuals and churches are filled with God's Spirit. It is perhaps enough to say that it is a mystery and to give God the glory. We must keep our egos in

> **God's Kingdom is not a destination; it is a journey.**

check, for about the time we think we have arrived, we discover we haven't. The Church must maintain a healthy skepticism about how it is doing. God's Kingdom is not a destination; it is a journey. It is the journey that shapes us and blesses us.

Church members will care for each other in direct proportion to the degree in which they live in character with Jesus. Fruit of the Spirit grows naturally from the soil of our relationship with Christ. Individuals who think they can defy God's standards, seek their own will, and treat a church as a social club eventually will discover there is a natural consequence to pay—a reaping of what we have sown. That is God's natural law.

Parents who love and nurture their children understand how God must feel about His Church. God loves each of us too much to let us continue in our rebellious ways. He loves us as we are, but He grieves if we chose not to grow into what He wants us to become. In our old nature, we were caught up in sin and deceit, yearning for things to be different. God has set before us the way that leads to life and He invites us to follow Him.

If you hold to my teaching, you are really my disciples.
Then you will know the truth and the truth will set you free.
(John 8:32)

⌘

⌘ WHAT FRUIT ARE YOU BEARING?

Traits of those who demonstrate fruit of God's Spirit	Traits of those who live according to their sinful nature
LOVE Caring, encouraging, supportive, accepting, unselfish	SELF-CENTEREDNESS Uncaring, hateful, critical, unsupportive, greedy
JOY Confidence in God's provision, hopeful, enthusiastic, affirming, fun-loving, courageous	SADNESS Negative, envious, suspicious, ungrateful, deep discomfort with life
PEACE Serenity of heart, tranquility, inner courage, quiet confidence	DISCONTENTMENT Insecure, restless, afraid, discordant, unfocused
PATIENCE Slow to anger, tolerant, empathetic, understanding, developmental, respectful of others needs	INTOLERANCE Selfish, irritable, rude, easily angered, impatient
KINDNESS Helpful, gracious, forgiving, blessing	MEANNESS Envious, callous, unforgiving
GOODNESS Pure in heart, honest, just, able to set reasonable limits, corrects and disciplines with love, healthy at the center, generous	IMMORALITY Uncaring, unfair, manipulative, dishonest, unjust, mean, unprincipled
FAITHFULNESS Reliable, truthful, trustworthy, single-minded, bold, having integrity	UNFAITHFULNESS Unreliable, untruthful, impure, puts things or people ahead of God, involvement in the occult, untrustworthy
GENTLENESS Submissive to the will of God, tender, teachable, considerate, conciliatory, able to show anger rightly	BITTERNESS Abrasive, demanding, harsh, rebellious, showing lack of empathy, holding on to old hurts
SELF-CONTROL Wise, disciplined, slow to anger, unselfish, morally sure, resists common vices	LICENTIOUSNESS Undisciplined, selfish, erratic, subject to moral ambiguity, submits to common vices

Living truth found in Jesus Christ is crucial to our health as individuals and as a church. We cannot accept every person's idea of
truth to be as good as every other person's. Truth is not relative to
the topic, the temper of the moment or the spirit of the age. We
cannot enjoy the fullness of life in the Spirit or function
successfully as Christ's Church
without faithfulness to discern the
will of God. The spirit of truth is
found by seeking the mind of Jesus
Christ and allowing His truth to live
in us.

> **The spirit of truth is found
> by seeking the mind of
> Jesus Christ and allowing
> His truth to live in us.**

When we attempt to produce good fruit on our own by striving
through will power alone to obey God's law, we shut out the Holy
Spirit, sent by Jesus to be our guide and enabler. Jesus did not
leave us as orphans to fend for ourselves. If we open our hearts and
minds to the Holy Spirit's presence, we will be transformed
through the grace and love of Jesus Christ. Fruit of the Spirit will
abound. Christians need each other to provide encouragement and
sensitive help in this wonderful journey of faith.

⌘

⌘

JESUS PRINCIPLES FOR CARING FOR AND FEEDING THE BODY OF CHRIST

⌘ Look to Jesus as teacher and example, staying mindful of how bad fruit results from rejecting God.

⌘ Recognize and celebrate the fruit of the Spirit in the church as the living presence of Christ in our lives.

⌘ Love and support one another with constant encouragement to be led by the Spirit of God in every relationship of life.

⌘ Keep modeling the fruit of the Spirit. Don't reward manipulators and intimidators or people who dwell in half-truths and delight in fear-mongering.

GRACIOUS GOD:

FORGIVE ME, LORD, FOR THOSE TIMES WHEN I BEHAVE AS THOUGH I AM AN ISLAND UNTO MYSELF. YOU GAVE ME THE GIFT OF MEMBERSHIP IN THE BODY OF CHRIST AND WITH IT COMES THE RESPONSIBILITY TO LIVE IN THE UNITY OF THE FAMILY OF FAITH.

GRANT ME THE VISION TO RECOGNIZE WHEN I PULL AWAY FROM INTIMACY AND ATTEMPT TO GO MY OWN WAY. BIND ME IN UNITY AND PEACE TO MY BROTHERS AND SISTERS IN CHRIST. MAKE ME A BRIDGE BUILDER AND ENCOURAGER. HELP ME TO BE PATIENT, KIND, GENTLE, GOOD, AND SELF-CONTROLLED. GIVE ME A HEART OF FAITHFULNESS AND COMPASSION FOR THE LOST AND HURTING WORLD AROUND ME. MAY YOUR HOLY SPIRIT SO PERMEATE MY HEART THAT I WILL RADIATE NOTHING BUT THE FRUIT OF YOUR LOVE. TRANSFORM ME TO BECOME MORE LIKE JESUS EVERY DAY.

AMEN

Life Application

⌘

CARE AND FEEDING OF THE BODY

1. Review the description of fruits of the Spirit outlined in this chapter. From these nine Christian character virtues, select the three you consider to be the most difficult to demonstrate personally in your life. What commitment will you make to growth in these areas?

2. Share your concerns about expressing these virtues with members of your group, or with a close Christian friend. From this discussion, write down key ideas describing the blockages you personally have that would prevent the Holy Spirit from accomplishing a transformation of your life in these areas. Be honest and be specific! Join in prayer with your group or a close Christian friend, asking the Holy Spirit to guide and equip you to be transformed in these areas to reflect the image of Christ.

3. Review the section in this chapter on "Applying the Fruit of the Spirit in a Healthy Church". For each of these six areas of application, write down one specific action you will take to become more involved in the care and feeding of your brothers and sisters in Christ.

4. Schedule those ideas on your calendar and commit yourself to follow through with action. Share these ideas and your commitment with a friend who will hold you accountable to do what you say you want to do.

5. Examine the chart in this chapter "What Fruit Are You Bearing?" listing traits that describe the fruit of God's Spirit and the fruit of sinful nature. Circle the words that jump off the page at you. Why do these words connect with your spirit at this time in your life? How do these words describe your church?

13

CHURCHES
LIVING THE JESUS PRINCIPLE
Daily Seeking the Mind of Christ

When a church is healthy, it is able to foster the growth and development of its members and reach out with a positive influence into the community it serves and into all the world. When a church is unhealthy, the members tend to look inward. They emphasize self-centered rather than other-centered concerns. A fundamental principle of the Christian life is that we are bound together in unity as fellow members of the Body of Christ. Our purpose is not just to enjoy the nurturing fellowship of our family of faith, but also to be God's dynamic people reaching out to bring others to Christ and to heal the wounds of a hurting world.

In a newsletter from the Metro Baptist Church in lower Manhattan Island, I read a wonderful statement from one of their members. *"Metro stares the worst of New York in the eye and responds with a hug."* The principle is simple. We must daily seek the mind of Christ, look around us, and as we see the needs of people, respond to them as Jesus would do.

TEN SIGNS OF CHURCHES
LIVING THE JESUS PRINCIPLE

1. Jesus Principle Churches depend on prayer as the greatest resource for discerning and accomplishing God's will. In response to prayer, God works to change our lives and our world. As church members encourage one another to pray and to undergird everything the church does by prayer, they open their lives and the life of the church to the transforming power of

> *In response to prayer, God works to change our lives and our world.*

Jesus Christ. God reveals Himself to those who seek Him, and He equips those who are ready to do His will. He unites those who come to Him together in prayer.

But many church people experience frustration over their apparent inability to pray as they think they should. Some feel awkward or intimidated about personally talking to God. Some have difficulty in clearly identifying their feelings or in organizing their thoughts into a prayer they believe will adequately express themselves to God. I have heard people say they are embarrassed by their lack of faith and don't feel worthy to ask anything of God. Some may pray desperately in times of crisis but give no thought to God when the time comes for praise and thanksgiving.

People often report to me that they have a hard time focusing on the process of prayer for any length of time. They become distracted. They want to pray, but when they try to stay focused, their mind wanders. I even had one man tell me that he feels so blessed by God that he doesn't want to call attention to himself through prayer for fear God will notice his unworthiness and stop being so good to him! If any of those descriptions sounds familiar, take comfort in the fact that you are not alone. But also take heart and do not become discouraged.

Prayer need not cause us fear or frustration. God invites us to pray. Jesus gave us an example of how to pray. Prayer is two-way communication. It is an expression of our mind and spirit toward God. It is the quiet, insistent direction and encouragement we feel from God. God is able to see beyond our poor ability to express ourselves and truly interpret what is in our hearts. Most encouraging of all, we can be confident that God desires only the best for us.

We do not know what we ought to pray for, but the Spirit himself intercedes for us with groans that words cannot express. And he who searches our hearts knows the mind of the Spirit, because the Spirit intercedes for the saints in accordance with God's will. *(Romans 8:26-27)*

A healthy church will teach that there is nothing about us that God does not already know. He knows our thoughts and deeds. He knows our darkest sins and our most holy aspirations. God is fair and compassionate. He is willing to forgive us when we are repentant and He wants to bless us as we seek His will.

> **There is nothing about us that God does not already know.**

Like the most loving parent we could ever imagine, God earnestly desires an intimate and open relationship with us, marked by prayerful communication. He wants us to be real, honest, open, and genuine. He can handle our doubts, impatience, anguish, and anger as well as our confidence, praise, joy and thanksgiving. God doesn't need to be impressed by lofty words structured in poetic imagery.

Wherever we are and whatever we're doing, we can offer up "flash prayers" that serve to keep us plugged in to our relationship with God:

♦ *"Thank you, Lord, for such a beautiful day."*
♦ *"Lord, watch over my children today."*
♦ *"I'm angry, Lord. Please give me the patience to hold my temper and to have wisdom in dealing with these people."*
♦ *"God, please give me the insight to discern the truth in this confusing situation."*
♦ *"Lord, forgive me for that lustful thought. I don't want to see other people as sex objects."*

It is natural to pray at mealtime, for what is more appropriate than to give thanks for food when it is set before us? It is powerfully nurturing to pray with our children at bedtime and to pray for and bless them as we send them off to school each day. It enriches our lives when we pray with and for our friends.

We can fill our entire day with prayer—while driving on the freeway, while caught in traffic, while walking to work, while cleaning house, while relaxing at break time or at lunch. We don't have to close our eyes to pray. And we don't have to be alone or on our knees. We can pray quietly, wherever we are. God will hear.

2. Jesus Principle Churches turn to the Bible and the character of Jesus as the basis for all guidance and decision-making. Thoughtful Christians understand that those things we focus on in our daily life shape our attitudes, behavior and character. For example, if we focus on how we have been wronged in the past, rehearse our pain, and seek to justify our unforgiving attitude, we inevitably will grow bitter toward those who have wounded us and our own vindictive spirit will hold us captive.

On the other hand, if we choose to forgive those who have wounded us, take responsibility for our own attitudes and actions, and move on positively into the future, we are free to learn and to grow and be happy.

With Jesus as our example and Scripture as our guide, we can enjoy healthy exercise for our minds and nourishment for our souls.

. . . whatever is true, whatever is noble, whatever is right, whatever is pure, whatever is lovely, whatever is admirable—think about such things.   *(Philippians 4:8)*

How profitable it would be for us to partake of the Word of God as regularly as we partake of food to nourish our bodies. A healthy church teaches its members from childhood to incorporate Bible study into daily devotions for personal and spiritual growth.

Your word is a lamp for my feet and a light for my path.
(Psalm 119:105)

For those who have not developed Bible study as a regular discipline, it is wise to begin with Scripture that will capture the imagination with exciting stories of people of faith and sections of the gospel that address common issues of greatest personal need.

I recommend that a new Christian, or a person desiring to learn what it would mean to be a Christian, read from contemporary translations of the Bible. Translations such as the *New International Version* or the *New Revised Standard Version* make the Scripture more understandable in modern language. Excellent paraphrases such as *The Message* and the *New Living Bible* are available to aid in understanding and applying the Scripture.

Begin by reading a chapter from the *Gospel of John* and from *Proverbs* every day. Then I recommend a chapter from the *Gospel of Luke* and from *Psalms* each day. The gospels help us understand the mind and heart of Jesus and the psalms help us learn how to pray and praise. After reading Luke, go to *Acts* and continue reading from Psalms. Then read *Philippians, Ephesians,* and *First John,* all the while continuing with Psalms.

In the reading of the New Testament epistles, a new Christian discovers the struggles of other new Christians and the strains as well as the blessings of church life. After these readings, a person is ready to read the New Testament straight through, from *Matthew* to *The Revelation.* Then read the *Old Testament.*

When a reader returns to the New Testament after reading the Old Testament, the radical newness of the life and message of Christ becomes evident in light of the fulfillment of Old Testament prophecies.

Growth will be steady and satisfying for those able to discipline themselves to write in a daily journal. Record insights, experiences, prayers offered and special verses to memorize from Scripture readings. When the journal is re-read months or years later, growth in spiritual discernment will be evident. The goal is to allow the Bible to become our friend—a comfort, help, and guide throughout each day.

> **Allow the Bible to become your friend—a comfort, help, and guide throughout each day.**

3. Jesus Principle Churches affirm that God notices us and cares about everything that happens in the lives of individuals and within the Body of Christ. Mature Christians walk in confidence that they cannot be separated from the love of God.

> *Who shall separate us from the love of Christ? Shall trouble or hardship or persecution or famine or nakedness or danger or sword? . . . In all these things we are more than conquerors through Him who loved us. For I am convinced that neither death nor life, neither angels nor demons, neither the present nor the future, nor any power, neither height nor depth, nor anything else in all creation, will be able to separate us from the love of God that is in Christ Jesus our Lord.* (Romans 8:35-39)

A healthy church teaches this and lives what it teaches. The Body of Christ surrounds and supports families. It helps them give their children the spiritual nurture and moral instruction to grow strong in the Lord. The Body of Christ provides an environment that promotes good health habits and healthy recreational opportunities. It encourages high ethical standards in vocational pursuits and the development of Christ-centered lifestyles.

The Jesus Principle church cares about and ministers to the sick, the aged, and those with physical and mental disabilities. The Body of Christ encourages its members to face the end of life with joyful assurance and confident hope. When we come to the end of the journey, we can face death with assurance that God is there in our dying and He carries us all the way home.

Jimmie Wilkinson was a member of our church who died after a long illness. Jimmie was a great witness to what being a member of the Body is about. For over a half century, she loved and cared for children in our church as one of our teachers. She never married and had no children of her own. But her nieces and nephews and all the children she cared for in our church were precious to her. Her sister told me that for several weeks before her death, Jimmie communicated personally with her nieces and nephews, "Don't worry about me. I am going home. God has everything taken care of. I have lived for Him and I am ready to go to meet Him."

Jimmie Wilkinson grew spiritually as she served in her church. She came to die with a joyful assurance that gave great comfort to her loved ones. Children she taught shared in the confident hope that sustained her all the way to the end of her journey. Although we may experience circumstances that cause us to feel distant from or abandoned by God, He is faithful.

4. Jesus Principle Churches enthusiastically worship God and teach members to become knowledgeable and committed citizens of God's Kingdom. Christians grow spiritually through a vital personal relationship with Jesus Christ and through a thoughtful understanding of God's Word communicated in Scripture. Worship is the first function of the Church. It breathes life and soul into the Body because it is communion with God the Father and Jesus the Son through the presence of the Holy Spirit. We focus on the one *"who is able to do immeasurably more than we ask or imagine, according to his power that is at work within us" (Ephesians 3:20).*

However, a healthy church will do more than ride the crest of praise and worship. Members will immerse themselves in the study of the Bible, Christian doctrine, and church history. They will seek a depth of knowledge about the Christian life to equip themselves to be effective servants of God in evangelism and ministry. We will seek the breadth of life which marked the earthly life of Jesus who *"grew in wisdom and stature, and in favor with God and men" (Luke 2:52).*

5. Jesus Principle Churches recognize that change is an inevitable and necessary part of life. Evangelical Christian theology and the fundamentals of our faith may remain constant, but the changing circumstances of life will continually confront individuals and churches with new challenges to face and new problems to solve. Christian confidence to overcome all obstacles is grounded in the unflinching belief that God's Holy Spirit will equip us to accomplish whatever task God calls us to do.

A healthy church stays flexible to apply the changing resources available within the Body of Christ and to creatively meet new challenges presented by a changing community. Dependable maturity will keep a church from chasing after every contemporary fad in hopes of staying relevant. It will balance the best of tradition and gospel foundations with creative new techniques to faithfully fulfill God's revealed vision for the church and community.

A healthy church will remain resilient in the face of changing leadership, changing financial needs and resources, and changing demographics in the congregation. A healthy church will see change coming, seek feedback from those who can give wise counsel and take the initiative

> *A healthy church will remain resilient in the face of changing leadership, changing financial needs and resources, and changing demographics in the congregation.*

to meet change head on. A healthy church will see itself as an alive and dynamic organism that relies on a faithful God who will provide.

> *I know what it is to be in need, and I know what it is to have plenty. I have learned the secret of being content in any and every situation, whether well fed or hungry, whether living in plenty or in want.*

I can do everything through him who gives me strength.
. . . And my God will meet all your needs according to his
glorious riches in Christ Jesus.   (Philippians 4:12-13,19)

**6. Jesus Principle Churches remain strong and effective in
the midst of stress, pressure, disappointment, grief, frustration,
temptation, and fear.** Healthy people and healthy churches learn
to deal openly with pain and sorrow. When trouble comes, truth is
the best medicine. We must not live in denial nor hide facts. People
need clear and open information in order to understand and to
process troubling issues. Healing can come only when people are
allowed to grieve, to feel and express their hurt, and then move on
to overcome the setback.

God equips His people who are faithful to live an overcoming,
victorious Christian life. In the midst of sorrow, there is joy. In the
midst of pain, there is courage. In the midst of disappointment,
there is faith.

The church can count on being under attack by forces of evil.
Faithful Christian ministry often produces pressures, frustrations,
disappointments and fear. But a healthy church will not give in to
Satan's temptations or cave in to his attacks. We can be confident
in God's power and we can be sure of God's ultimate victory.

> **People are looking for those who
> know how to live successfully in the
> most difficult circumstances.**

Victorious living is the
Christian's greatest witness.
People are looking for those
who know how to live suc-
cessfully in the most difficult circumstances. As the Body of
Christ, the healthy church develops resiliency of spirit based on the
assurance that God has us in view and will equip us to withstand
times of testing. This is the truth that undergirds the church: God
cares for us and we know it.

Cast all your anxiety on him because he cares for you.
(1 Peter 5:7)

**7. Jesus Principle Churches understand that everything they
have is a gift from God.** Members of the Body faithfully seek to
use their time, energies, abilities and money so God's work is done
in the world. God's creation is respected through good stewardship

of resources. Healthy Christians rejoice to be partners with God in so great a work. Churches which attempt to determine their own destiny or strive to succeed out of their own creativity, cleverness and hard work do not understand that we can accomplish nothing except through God's presence and grace.

What do we actually own? Nothing really! God has given us everything we possess. We came into the world with nothing and we will take

> **What we hold in between birth and death is merely entrusted to our care.**

nothing with us when we die. What we hold in between birth and death is merely entrusted to our care. With that in mind, how well are we doing with the administration of the trust God has given us?

I heard a story about a young man who apparently was very serious about serving the Lord. He came to his pastor to discuss his recent new job and good income, and to ask for prayer that he would be faithful in tithing. They prayed together, and sure enough, the young man was blessed and prospered. Then, about ten years later, the man came back to tell his pastor about the success of the business he had started several years before.

He explained, "We prayed ten years ago about my commitment to a faithful tithe, and I have given a tithe all these years. But now my tithe has gotten to be so much! What I contribute to the church is more than I used to make in salary. I just can't afford to give that much."

At that, the pastor suggested, "If that's the case, why don't we get down on our knees as we did ten years ago and pray that God will get your income level down to the amount you are comfortable tithing."

Shocked, the young man said, "Oh, well I guess we should leave well enough alone!"

So many people go through life with a mentality of "scarcity." They live under the persistent fear that there might not be enough of what they need to be happy. Whatever they have, it never seems to be quite enough—not enough money, food, clothing, shelter, security, love. This can lead to a compulsive need to accumulate and selfishly protect what they have. They feel "robbed" not blessed when they give.

People characteristically grow in spiritual depth as they learn to freely share life's blessings with others. Learning how to share and to enjoy giving moves us past that fear of the unknown future and frees us to be confident that God is out there and that He will provide.

> **If we trust God to provide for our needs, we will show our trust in Him by faithfully giving back a tithe.**

If we trust God to provide for our needs, we will show our trust in Him by faithfully giving back a tithe . . . and then more . . . to be used in God's work. This is part of God's natural law of sowing and reaping.

Remember this: Whoever sows sparingly will also reap sparingly, and whoever sows generously will also reap generously. Each man should give whatever he has decided in his heart to give, not reluctantly or under compulsion, for God loves a cheerful giver. And God is able to make all grace abound to you, so that in all things at all times, having all that you need, you will abound in every good work.
(II Corinthians 9:6-8)

When we freely sow blessings into the lives of others, we will reap the blessing of God.

8. Jesus Principle Churches rejoice continually in their relationship with God and in their fellowship with other Christians. Praising God's greatness and being confident in His sustaining grace are the foundations of joyful worship. Sensitive and caring Christian fellowship nourishes our basic human needs to be loved and to feel significant. Fellowship does not exist just so we may enjoy each other, but to provide a source of support and nurture that will equip us to be effective in reaching out to the world.

Nothing is more important to spiritual growth than to be present and actively involved with fellow believers.

And let us consider how we may spur one another on toward love and good deeds. Let us not give up meeting together, as some are in the habit of doing, but let us encourage one another—and all the more as you see the Day approaching.
(Hebrews 10:24-25)

Fellowship is the skeletal structure of the Church—it holds the members of the body together. It provides the support system and the closeness needed for the body of Christ to function effectively. All of us need to be loved and to feel we are of value. These needs can be satisfied only in the context of healthy relationships.

Christian growth requires us to live in relationships with others. Relationships cannot be established or maintained without presence. Relation-

> **Relationships cannot be established or maintained without presence.**

ships require commitment to spend time with each other and to communicate openly and honestly. Many people attempt to make their faith into a private religion, withdrawing from fellowship rather than seeking it. Invariably, that results in isolation and spiritual poverty. The first rule of living in fellowship is simply to show up and to love one another. We are made one in Christ. We become a "family of faith."

> *Consequently, you are no longer foreigners and aliens, but fellow citizens with God's people and members of God's household, built on the foundation of the apostles and prophets, with Christ Jesus himself as the chief cornerstone.*
> *(Ephesians 2:19)*

It is an unceasing pleasure to see how church members, because of their love of God and relationship with Jesus Christ, reach out to each other both for fellowship and ministry. They learn to share on the deepest levels. They pray for and support each other in the rearing of children. They stay in touch as loving friends. They study together, worship together, eat together, and play together. When sorrow comes, they are there to comfort and share the grief. When joyous times come, they are there for each other to celebrate and give thanks.

9. Jesus Principle Churches seek to equip members for godly service in the world. Thoughtful Christians know how important it is to look beyond personal needs and desires and give themselves to a meaningful cause that will benefit oth-

> **There is true happiness in loving service.**

ers. So much of the world is composed of people who are takers rather than givers. Takers become self-centered and insensitive to the world around them. They rob themselves of the growth and the joy that comes through being there for others. There is true happiness in loving service.

A healthy church listens to the needs of people, challenges its members to respond in compassion, and equips them for service through training, material support, and prayer. A healthy church not only teaches its people to listen to God's call and to support ministry and missions, but it also provides opportunity for service and encourages its members to stretch their wings and fly.

The most effective Christian discipleship program is on-the-job training. As we learn to recognize needs and to respond in love, God equips us to handle whatever situation we are called to address. We learn by doing and our confidence grows, enabling us to become more and more effective as we minister to others. Ministry begins by being sensitive to the needs of others, by listening and being empathetic. Ministry suspends judgment and reaches out in love to heal and to restore in the name of Jesus. The quintessential text for ministry is Matthew 25:31-46.

> *Ministry suspends judgment and reaches out in love to heal and to restore in the name of Jesus.*

> *I tell you the truth, whatever you did for one of the least of these brothers of mine, you did for me.   (Matthew 25:40)*

10. Jesus Principle Churches naturally and openly share the good news of being disciples of Jesus Christ. Telling what's going on in our lives can become as natural as breathing. When the presence of God is real, we talk openly and naturally about what He is doing with us and let God use that testimony in the lives of all we meet. Discipleship is not complete until our decision to follow Jesus is joyously shared.

> *The first thing Andrew did was to find his brother Simon and tell him, "We have found the Messiah" (that is, the Christ). And he brought him to Jesus.   (John 1:41-42a)*

A healthy church is open to receive anyone whom Jesus would receive. There is no place for exclusiveness within the church. If a person comes to seek fellowship, to pray, to worship, and to study the Bible, members of the Body have a responsibility to open their arms and their hearts to that person and help him or her to grow.

> *A healthy church is open to receive anyone whom Jesus would receive.*

One of the most effective outreach ministries is simply to invite people to come to church with you. Give a friend or neighbor the opportunity to join you in Bible study, to enjoy a musical presentation, or to hear your pastor preach sermons that help people in daily life. I call it "invitation evangelism" and it works. Being confident that fellow church members will welcome any new person you could bring creates extra incentive to share the good you have found in the Christian life and in your church.

The health of a Jesus Principle church does not depend on its size but on the degree to which its members are becoming more like Jesus. Church growth is not just a question of "How many people have been added to the rolls?" More importantly, it is "How much have the people grown?" After five years of being part of the Body of Christ, are church members more like Jesus?

> *The health of a Jesus Principle church does not depend on its size but on the degree to which its members are becoming more like Jesus.*

God fully equips His people to handle anything He calls us to do. He makes the way known and He gives us strength for the journey. As we seek Him, He will help us to grow. Spiritual growth can come quickly, but maturity in Christ takes time. We learn through our experiences and we have our entire life to grow into the likeness of our Lord.

Just as the physical body needs a balance of good diet, physical exercise, intellectual stimulation, and spiritual nurture, the healthy church will keep all of its functional parts in balance to stay effective in building God's Kingdom in the hearts of His people. The church will joyfully worship, evangelize, disciple, minister, and create fellowship.

A healthy church will continually support and encourage its members to keep pressing on and not become discouraged. If one spiritual meal is missed, we must seek more nourishment at the next. If weariness sets in, then in the grace of God we need to take a rest to be restored. Exercise faith daily—if not at first in devoted service, at least in simple acts of kindness so the love of God shines through. God calls each of us to that journey—that Jesus Principle of love of God and love of others that transforms us into the likeness of Christ our Savior.

Hold on tight to what the apostle Paul was living for,

> . . . *I press on to take hold of that for which Christ Jesus took hold of me. Brothers, I do not consider myself yet to have taken hold of it. But one thing I do: Forgetting what is behind and straining toward what is ahead, I press on toward the goal to win the prize for which God has called me heavenward in Christ Jesus.* (Philippians 3:13-15)

⌘

⌘

WHAT HEALTHY CHURCHES DO
WHO LIVE JESUS PRINCIPLES

⌘ Depend on prayer as the greatest resource for discerning and accomplishing God's will.

⌘ Turn to the Bible and the character of Jesus as the basis for all guidance and decision-making.

⌘ Affirm that God notices and cares about everything that happens in the lives of individuals and within the Body of Christ.

⌘ Enthusiastically worship God and teach members to become knowledgeable and committed citizens of God's Kingdom.

⌘ Recognize that change is an inevitable and necessary part of life.

⌘ Remain strong, effective and faithful in the midst of stress, pressure, disappointment, grief, frustration, temptation and fear.

⌘ Understand and affirm that everything we have is a gift from God.

⌘ Rejoice continually in relationship with God and in fellowship with other Christians.

⌘ Seek to equip members for godly service.

⌘ Naturally and openly share the good news of being disciples of Jesus Christ.

GOD OF LIFE, MAKER OF HEAVEN AND EARTH, HOLY AND RIGHTEOUS FATHER:

WE PRAISE YOUR HOLY NAME. YOU ARE THE CREATOR AND REDEEMER, THE ONE TRUE GOD. YOU ARE KING OF HEAVEN AND EARTH AND ALL THAT EXISTS. WE HONOR YOUR RIGHTEOUS LAW. WE PRAISE YOU FOR YOUR LOVE AND MERCY. WE THANK YOU FOR YOUR SON, JESUS CHRIST OUR SAVIOR, THROUGH WHOM, AND IN WHOM WE HAVE EVERLASTING LIFE.

BOND US TOGETHER IN FELLOWSHIP AND SERVICE AS YOUR CHURCH. AS WE BECOME THE BODY OF CHRIST THROUGH FAITH AND OBEDIENCE TO OUR LORD JESUS, MAKE US ONE IN SPIRIT AND IN TRUTH. FILL US WITH YOUR PRESENCE SO WE WILL SHINE AS A LIGHT OF LOVE AND JUSTICE IN THIS DARK WORLD. GIVE US THE WISDOM TO DRINK NURTURE AS WE SEEK THE MIND OF CHRIST. AS CITIZENS OF YOUR KINGDOM, KEEP US PURE AND HEALTHY IN MIND, BODY AND SPIRIT. HELP US LIVE ACCORDING TO THE PRINCIPLES OF JESUS.

AMEN

Life Application

⌘

CHURCHES LIVING THE JESUS PRINCIPLE
Daily Seeking the Mind of Christ

1. Review the *Jesus Principles for Showing Our Love to God* at the end of Chapter 1. How can you and your church love God more like Jesus did?

2. Review the *Jesus Principles for Loving God and Loving Neighbor* at the end of Chapter 2. How can you and your church love people (inside your church family and outside in the community) more like Jesus did?

3. Consider the five functions of the church:
   - Worship
   - Evangelize
   - Disciple
   - Minister
   - Create Fellowship

   What areas of church health need attention in your church? What can be done to nurture and encourage better health and growth in these areas?

4. After reading this book, write down those things to which you need to give more attention in order to be more like Jesus and to live your life according to Jesus Principles.

THEN GET TO WORK! BE AND DO!

⌘ EPILOGUE

Healthy churches are a product of healthy believers who are
solidly grounded in the Word of God and are committed to
living out the example of Jesus Christ in their talk and
their walk. Making such a commitment is not easy. The world is
too close to us and too much with us to let go easily and let Christ
fully control our lives

LIVING THE JESUS PRINCIPLE

In this book we have challenged individual Christians and the
church as a corporate body to live THE JESUS PRINCIPLE. What
exactly does this mean? Jesus Christ, who is the incarnation of
God, came to earth to be the presence of God in our midst. He is
the imprint of what God wants each of us to be—the example of
true humanity.

In His character, Jesus provided the perfect example for us to
follow of God-inspired thought and behavior. He stayed in perfect
relationship with God through prayer and obedience.

In His ministry, Jesus gave the pattern for His church to follow
in doing His work in the world. He taught us how to worship, witness, disciple, minister and build unity in a loving fellowship.

In short, living out the Jesus Principle means to invest ourselves
in trusting obedience to Jesus Christ, to be transformed into the
likeness of Christ by the power of the Holy Spirit, and to take upon
ourselves the mantle of Christ's mission to redeem the world for
God through the ministry of His church.

FINDING WISDOM AND COURAGE

The task of living the Jesus Principle is a daunting one. It means
we may have to change some things and refine some others. We
must not sell ourselves short or settle for less than God's way. He
will equip us for the tasks to which we are called if we step forward and make ourselves fully available. It's a wonderful experience to be able to embrace personal challenges with inspiration,
confidence and enthusiasm, knowing we really are equipped,
ready, and capable of achieving the progress we desire.

If we are honest with ourselves, nearly every major life experience grows out of tension between an opportunity and our fear to
embrace it. As churches and as individuals, we are challenged with

an uncertain future. We are called to be like Jesus in our congregations and communities. We want to be wise, courageous and confident. However, we may feel burdened with doubt and apprehension. In the face of the challenge, we ask ourselves searching questions. Do we know enough? Do we have enough experience? Will we be adequate to the task? Our inside voice of fear cries, "Dear God, I'm not ready to handle this!" But with God's help, we can choose a different response.

Humility is the best starting point for any church or any Christian who faces a great opportunity or challenge. Certainly, we will encounter times of self-questioning and anxiety, but we do not have to suffer through our struggle alone. There is no shame in crying out to God our feelings of inadequacy or doubt. There is no weakness of character in seeking God's help as we apprehensively step out in faith. Only fools attempt to navigate life through their own wit and wrestle the world's demons in their own strength. God wants the best for us. He sent His Holy Spirit to equip us for life's mission and to guide us toward His will. We can respond, "Dear God, with You on my side, I can do what needs to be done!"

Two powerful Scripture passages have ministered to me in times of growth and challenge and uncertainty:

> *If you want to know what God wants you to do, ask him, and he will gladly tell you, for he is always ready to give a bountiful supply of wisdom to all who ask him.* *(James 1:5 Living Bible)*

> *Be bold and strong! Banish fear and doubt! Remember, the Lord your God is with you wherever you go.*
> *(Joshua 1:9 Living Bible)*

Courage without wisdom is dangerous. Wisdom without courage is useless. In Christ Jesus we have true wisdom and courage available to us. Healthy Christians and healthy churches will not shrink from the challenges that confront us. Jesus will provide wisdom to guide us on our way. He will supply courage to take the next step forward, and the next. As churches and as Christians, may wisdom and courage be ours as we commit to live in His Kingdom on earth according to the principles of Jesus.

⌘

BOOKS BY CLEAR STREAM PUBLISHING

The Jesus Principle,
Building Churches in the Image of Christ
by Charles Wade, Lee Bowman and Carol Bowman
$14.95   ISBN 0-9637741-3-1   346 pages
Dr. Charles Wade, Executive Director of the Baptist General Convention of Texas, shares from a wealth of wisdom gained from over forty years in Christian ministry. With great insight and spiritual maturity, he helps individual Christians, church leaders, and ministers focus on what it means to be the Body of Christ, courageously doing God's work in the world today. Valuable insights on understanding the church's mission, discovering a unique vision for each church in each community, and exercising leadership consistent with the character of Jesus Christ are the focus of this powerful book.

Los Principios de Jesus para Edificar su Iglesia
By Charles Wade, Lee Bowman y Carol Bowman
$14.95   ISBN 0-9637741-5-8   370 pages
El Dr. Charles Wade, Director Ejecutivo de la Convención Bautista General de Texas, nos presenta toda una riqueza de sabiduría respecto al discipulado cristiano y al liderazgo de la iglesia, adquirida en más de 45 años en el pastorado y como líder en su denominación y comunidad. Con profunda perspectiva y madurez espiritual, nos habla de sus experiencias al ayudar a pastores, otros colegas, líderes laicos y creyentes individuales a comprender la naturaleza de la iglesia, y lo que quiere decir funcionar como el cuerpo de Cristo haciendo la obra de Dios en el mundo.
Mediante centenares de referencias bíblicas, Wade nos da un cuadro claro de lo que la iglesia y los cristianos como individuos, son llamados a hacer en el mundo, basados en el ejemplo del mismo Jesús. Wade reta a los cristianos a buscar la visión distintiva de Cristo para la iglesia en sus comunidades ya cumplir la misión divina mediante la adoración Cristocéntrica, la evangelización, el discipulado, y el ministerio y la creación de comunión cristiana.
Los Principios de Jesús para Edificar su Iglesia, se ha usado ya eficazmente en universidades y seminarios como un programa de estudio para cursos sobre el ministerio cristiano, así como un recurso de estudio para la capacitación del líder de la iglesia, para las clases de la Escuela Dominical, y para un estudio personal, o en grupos pequeños.

Waking the Slumbering Spirit

by John Sandford, Paula Sandford and Lee Bowman
$12.00   ISBN 0-9637741-0-7   143 pages

Lack of loving nurture, extended periods of emotional stress, and patterns of sinful behavior can cause a person's God-given personal spirit to be dulled into what the authors call spiritual slumber. The slumbering spirit results in a dulling of the personal conscience, inability to learn from mistakes, difficulty in maintaining relationships, lack of spiritual focus and other debilitating problems. The authors reveal ways to discover the extent to which the personal spirit may be slumbering and what can be done to restore lost spiritual vitality

Choosing Forgiveness

by John Sandford, Paula Sandford and Lee Bowman
$12.95   ISBN 0-9637741-1-5   207 pages

Inability to forgive is the most common issue that destroys relationships and is among the most prevalent problem for which people seek help through counseling. This practical book explains the necessity for Christians to respond appropriately to personal woundings, how to keep bitterness from lodging in the heart, and how to receive healing and restore unity through the power of the Holy Spirit.

Wounded Warriors, Chosen Lives . . . Healing for Vietnam Veterans

by Howard J. Olsen
$12.95   ISBN 0-9637741-1-5   241 pages

An important book not only for Vietnam veterans, but for anyone who works with or is intimately connected with hurting people. It is an honest and confrontational look at the real issues we struggle with when faced with the pain of violence, loss of life, betrayal or unexpected tragedies. Olsen outlines a clear path to recovery from post-traumatic stress disorder while challenging the attitudes, beliefs and behaviors that keep deep emotional wounds from healing.

Poured Out, Preparing Vessels Fit for Kingdom Use

By Howard J. Olsen
$12.95   ISBN 0-96377416-6   184 pages

Never has there been a more critical time to call individual Christians and the church to radical discipleship. Howard Olsen has been listening to God and he speaks with prophetic passion about what he has heard. Olsen's call is first for repentance, then for moral integrity grounded in total commitment to Jesus Christ. He holds a mirror up to our lifestyle as Christians and challenges us to clean up, straighten up, and truly be vessels fit for Kingdom use.

ORDER DIRECT
FROM CLEAR STREAM PUBLISHING

\#
Copies   Title / Price   \$ Purchase Amount

____ *The Jesus Principle*   (\$14.95 ea.)   \$ _____

____ *Los Principios de Jesus para Edificar su Iglesia*   (\$14.95 ea.) \$ _____

____ *Waking the Slumbering Spirit*   (\$12.00 ea.)   \$ _____

____ *Choosing Forgiveness*   (\$12.95 ea.)   \$ _____

____ *Wounded Warriors Chosen Lives*   (\$12.95 ea.)   \$ _____

____ *Poured Out*   (\$12.00 ea.)   \$ _____

Subtotal \$ _____

Add 10% shipping and handling USPS   \$ _____

Total   \$ _____

Name: _____

Church/Organization _____

Address _____

City _____ State _____ Zip _____.

Phone _____Email _____.

➢Send to   **Clear Stream Publishing Inc.**
                  Box 122128
                  Arlington, TX 76012
➢Make check or money order payable to Clear Stream Publishing.

For more information or volume purchase discounts, email: info@clear-stream.com